MORAL
Dilemmas

BIBLICAL PERSPECTIVES ON CONTEMPORARY ETHICAL ISSUES

J. KERBY ANDERSON

CHARLES R. SWINDOLL, GENERAL EDITOR

WORD PUBLISHING
Nashville•London•Vancouver•Melbourne

MORAL DILEMMAS
Swindoll Leadership Library

Published by Word Publishing, a unit of Thomas Nelson, Inc.,
P. O. Box 14100, Nashville, Tennessee 37214. All rights reserved. No portion
of this book may be reproduced, stored in a retrieval system, or transmitted in
any form or by any means—electronic, mechanical, photocopy, recording, or
any other—except for brief quotations in printed reviews, without
the prior permission of the publisher.

Unless otherwise indicated, Scripture quotations used in this book are from
the Holy Bible, New International Version (NIV).
Copyright © 1973, 1978, 1984 International Bible Society.
Used by permission of Zondervan Bible Publishers.

Published in association with Dallas Theological Seminary (DTS):
General Editor: Charles Swindoll
Managing Editor: Roy B. Zuck
The theological opinions expressed by the author are not necessarily the
official position of Dallas Theological Seminary.

Library of Congress Cataloging-in-Publication Data

Anderson, J. Kerby
Moral dilemmas: biblical perspectives on contemporary ethical issues /
J. Kerby Anderson : Charles R. Swindoll, general editor.
p. cm.— (Swindoll leadership library)
Includes bibliographical references.

ISBN 0-8499-1446-9 (alk. paper)

1. Christian ethics. 2. Ethical problems. 3. Church and social problems.
4. Current events. 5. Moral conditions. I. Swindoll, Charles R. II. Title.
III. Series.

BJ1275.A46   1998   98-15087
241'.6–dc21   CIP

Printed in the United States of America

98 99 00 01 02 03 04 05 06 BVG 9 8 7 6 5 4 3 2 1

Contents

Foreword

SOME THREE DECADES after Jesus' death and resurrection, the apostle Peter penned a letter to a band of believers scattered throughout Asia Minor. This group of struggling saints found themselves increasingly at odds with a world that called evil good . . . wrong right . . . and perversion normalcy.

Peter reminded his readers of a different path—the path of righteousness—God had set before them. Yet this "holy walk" took them through a pagan landscape littered with twisted beliefs, fractured relationships, and wrecked lives. Their lives were to be different, which prompted the old fisherman-turned-apostle to write, "Live such good lives among the pagans that, though they accuse you of doing wrong, they may see your good deeds and glorify God on the day he visits us" (1 Pet. 2:12).

Peter was not only concerned with the believers' *walk*. He was also equally interested in their *talk*. These Christians were to be prepared with God's answers for the key questions of their faith, which led him to urge his readers, "But in your hearts set apart Christ as Lord. Always be prepared to give an answer to everyone who asks you to give the reason for the hope you have. But do this with gentleness and respect" (1 Pet. 3:15).

Fast-forward nineteen centuries. The styles have changed, the pace of life has quickened, and our high-tech society has become much more complex and sophisticated. Nevertheless the world around us is still at odds with God's standards, still questioning His authority, still opposing His plans. Not surprisingly, God's people are still called to "walk the walk and talk the talk" . . . to be men and women of integrity who, as authentic Christians, can clearly articulate God's answers to the questions being voiced by a society desperately seeking solutions.

All this explains why I'm excited about J. Kerby Anderson's penetrating volume, *Moral Dilemmas*. This seasoned author provides solid, practical answers to some of the most vexing issues facing our society today—issues that call for a Christian response. His insightful writing cuts to the heart of such issues as abortion, euthanasia, genetic engineering, drug abuse, divorce, pornography, and homosexuality. With surgeon-like skill Anderson lays open the entire debate and clearly explains what God's Word says on the subject. He does so in a way that anyone can understand. Best of all, his book equips believers with guidelines that enable us to maneuver our way through the ethical and moral land mines of our times.

Read slowly . . . underline freely. Take careful notes. You will return often to Kerby's refreshing, reliable answers to the contemporary questions that are making the front pages of today's newspapers.

—CHARLES R. SWINDOLL
General Editor

Acknowledgments

I T HAS BEEN SAID that the closest a man can come to childbirth is writing a book. The process of writing this book has been fulfilling and relatively free of pain. Perhaps after having so many published "children," I'm learning how to give birth. No doubt it is also due to a few helpful midwives that made the process so delightful.

Writing a book is always the work of more than one person. Although I have written every word, I do want to acknowledge those who critiqued and encouraged.

First and foremost I want to thank my colleagues at Probe Ministries and Dallas Theological Seminary. While this book took less than a year to write, it was the culmination of twenty-two years of ministry. The opportunity to speak, broadcast, and write on many of these topics over the years helped hone the final restuls.

Second, I would like to thank my co-host and friend, Penna Dexter. Even though we no longer work together on a daily basis, she was eager to read and critique many of these chapters. If I close my eyes, I can see many places in this manuscript where Penna's Flair Pen markings improved the final product.

Third, I would like to thank Kay Lyons. Years ago when I was editing and writing a book dealing with ethical issues, she gave critique and encouragement. When I was initially approached about this project, it was easy to say yes simply because I had Kay's earlier endorsement ringing in my ears.

Fourth, I would like to thank my editor Roy B. Zuck, who spotted every errant jot and tittle. Thank you for your tireless service and critical editorial work.

Finally I want to acknowledge the support of my entire family, who suffered through the birth pangs of this book and have been such a support to me. Although this book probably took less time away from family than any I have written, they were encouraging and supportive when necessary. Thank you Susanne, Amy, Jonathan, and Catherine for your love and loyalty.

1
Abortion

ABORTION IS ONE of the most controversial moral dilemmas of
our day. Women with an unplanned pregnancy often see abortion as their
only solution to the crisis in their lives. Abortion affects millions of
Americans. Social scientists estimate that abortion is the most frequently
performed surgery on adults in America.[1] In fact, one out of three babies
conceived in the United States is deliberately aborted.[2] Since about 40
percent of all pregnancies are unplanned,[3] this means that well over two
out of three unplanned pregnancies are terminated by abortion.[4] There
are 1.6 million abortions reported in this country every year, meaning
that over 40 million abortions have taken place since abortion was legalized in 1973.

A HISTORY OF ABORTION

Contrary to popular belief, debate and polarization over abortion is not a
recent phenomenon. The practice of abortion was common even in the
ancient world. Many cultures (Assyrian, Babylonian, Sumerian, Hittite)
considered abortion a serious crime. In this tradition was the portion of
the Hippocratic Oath that stated, "I will not give a woman a pessary to
produce an abortion." Other cultures, such as that of Hippocrates' own

1

classical Greece, condoned the practice of abortion. Plato wrote that ill-conceived embryos should not be brought to birth, and both Plato and Aristotle thought that deformed children should be exposed and left to die.

The Jewish historian Josephus wrote against abortion: "The Law has commanded to raise all children and prohibited women from aborting or destroying seed; a woman who does so shall be judged a murderess of children for she has caused a soul to be lost and the family of man to be diminished."[5]

The consensus of the early church was that abortion and infanticide were murder. The *Didache* (also known as the "Teaching of the Twelve Apostles") was a compilation of apostolic moral teachings from the end of the first century. It commanded, "Do not murder a child by abortion or kill a newborn infant."[6] The *Epistle of Barnabas*, an early second-century theological collection, also laid down a strong admonition against abortion and infanticide: "You shall love your neighbor more than your own life. You shall not slay a child by abortion. You shall not kill that which has already been generated."[7]

Athenagoras, a second-century apologist, wrote in a letter to Emperor Marcus Aurelius: "We say that women who induce abortions are murderers, and will have to give an account of it to God. . . . The fetus in the womb is a living being and therefore the object of God's care."[8]

Clement of Alexandria wrote that "our whole life can proceed according to God's perfect plan only if we gain dominion over our desires, practicing continence from the beginning instead of destroying through perverse and pernicious arts human offspring, who are given birth by Divine Providence. Those who use abortifacient medicines to hide their fornication cause not only the outright murder of the fetus, but of the whole human race as well."[9] Tertullian also wrote in his *Apology* that "murder is forbidden once and for all. We may not destroy even the fetus in the womb."[10]

Augustine condemned abortion and criticized married couples who attempted to avoid having children: "Sometimes this lustful cruelty or cruel lust comes to this, that they even procure poisons of sterility, and if these do not work, they extinguish and destroy the fetus in some way in the womb, preferring that their offspring die before it lives, or if it was already alive in the womb, to kill it before it was born."[11]

Modern laws against abortion came about in the nineteenth century with the discovery of the human ovum in the 1820s. This led to the realization that a distinct human life was created through the fertilization of the ovum so that the woman was "with child" from the moment of conception.

These laws against abortion were in effect until 1967, when a few states began to liberalize their abortion laws. By the end of 1970 eighteen states had passed statutes that allowed abortion in exceptional circumstances. Soon there was a backlash to the liberalization of these laws, and it appeared as if many of the laws would be overturned. However, on January 22, 1973, the Supreme Court handed down its *Roe v. Wade* decision, which went even further than the most permissive abortion laws passed by the various states.

ABORTION PROCEDURES

Although most people are aware of the existence of abortion, many do not know how abortions are performed. Here are at least seven ways abortions are carried out.

Dilation and Curettage is commonly called D & C. The physician dilates the cervix with a series of instruments to allow the insertion of a curette—a loop-shaped knife—into the womb. The instrument is used to scrape the placenta from the uterus and then cut the baby apart. The pieces are then pulled through the cervix. The tiny body must then be reassembled by an attending nurse to make sure no parts remain in the womb to cause infection.

Suction Aspiration is used in 80 percent of the abortions up to the twelfth week of pregnancy. The mouth of the cervix is dilated. A hollow tube with a knifelike-edged tip is inserted into the womb. A suction force twenty-eight times stronger than a vacuum cleaner literally tears the developing baby and the placenta to pieces. These pieces are sucked into a container.

Saline Injection is also known as salt poisoning. A strong salt solution is injected through the mother's abdominal wall into the amniotic fluid surrounding the baby. The baby then breathes and swallows the solution causing internal poisoning and burning. In a few hours the unborn child dies from salt poisoning, dehydration, and hemorrhaging. The mother goes into labor and delivers a dead (or dying) baby.

Prostaglandin involves the use of prostaglandin hormones, which are injected into the womb or released in a vaginal suppository. This causes the uterus to contract and deliver the child prematurely. A saline solution is sometimes injected first, killing the baby before birth, in order to make the procedure less distressful for the mother and the medical staff.

Dilation and Evacuation, commonly called a D & E, is used after the twelfth week of pregnancy. The doctor dilates the mother's cervix and uses forceps to reach into the uterus. He grasps the arms and legs, dismembers the body, and crushes the skull to remove it. The placenta and smaller pieces are removed by suction and sharp curetting.

Hysterotomy, similar to a Caesarean section, is performed in the last three months of pregnancy. This procedure involves opening the womb surgically and removing the baby. The purpose of this procedure, unlike that of a C-section, is to end the infant's life.

Dilation and Extraction is also known as "partial-birth abortion." The physician dilates the cervix and pulls the baby's body out, except for the head. Leaving the head inside, the doctor inserts scissors in the skull of the baby and sucks out the brains. The head collapses and the baby is brought out to die.

BIBLICAL ARGUMENTS AGAINST ABORTION

Any student of the Bible knows that the Scriptures say nothing directly about abortion. So why do most Christians oppose abortion? What biblical principles can be used to come to a pro-life perspective on the issues? Is an unborn baby of equal value to a child that is born? These questions must be addressed.

First, what about the silence of the Bible on abortion? The answer is simple. Abortion was so unthinkable to an Israelite woman that there was no need even to mention it in the criminal code. Why was abortion an unthinkable act? First, children were viewed as a gift or heritage from the

Lord (Ps. 127:3). Second, God opens and closes the womb and is sovereign over conception (Gen. 29:33; 30:22; 1 Sam. 1:19–20). Third, childlessness was seen as a curse (Deut. 25:6; Ruth 4:5). Barrenness would mean the extinction of the family name (see Jer. 11:19). Therefore abortion was so abhorrent to the Israelite mind that it was not necessary to have a specific prohibition in the Law to deal with it.

One of the key passages giving a biblical view of the sanctity of human life is Psalm 139, the inspired record of David's praise for God's sovereignty in his life. He began by acknowledging that God is omniscient and knew what David was doing (vv. 1–3). God was aware of David's thoughts before he expressed them (v. 4). Wherever David might go, he could not escape from God, whether he traveled to heaven (v. 8) or ventured into Sheol (v. 9). God is in the remotest part of the sea (v. 9) and even in the darkness (vv. 11–12). David contemplated the origin of his life and confessed that God was there forming him in the womb (vv. 13–16).

"For you created my inmost being; you knit me together in my mother's womb. I praise you because I am fearfully and wonderfully made; your works are wonderful, I know that full well. My frame was not hidden from you when I was made in the secret place. When I was woven together in the depths of the earth, your eyes saw my unformed body. All the days ordained for me were written in your book before one of them came to be." Here David wrote of God's relationship with him while he was growing and developing before birth. The Bible does not speak of fetal life as mere biochemistry. This was not a piece of protoplasm that became David. This was David already being cared for by God while in the womb.

Verse 13 of Psalm 139 speaks of God as the Master Craftsman fashioning David into a living person. In verses 14–15 David reflected on the fact that he was a product of God's creative work within his mother's womb, and he praised God for how wonderfully God had woven him together. David drew a parallel between his development in the womb and Adam's creation from the earth. Using figurative language in verse 15, he referred to his life before birth when "I was made in secret, and skillfully wrought in the depths of the earth." This poetic allusion hearkens back to Genesis 2:7, which says that Adam was made from the dust of the earth.

David also noted that "Your eyes saw my unformed body" (NASB). This shows that God knew David even before he was known to others. The term translated "unformed body" derives from the verb "to roll up." When David was forming as a fetus, God's care and compassion were already extended to him. The reference to God's "eyes" is an Old Testament figure of speech connoting divine oversight of God in the life of an individual or a group of people.

Other verses show divine involvement in the formation of the unborn baby. God is active in the event of conception (Gen. 29:31–35; 30:17–24; Ruth 4:13; 1 Sam. 1:19–20) and also in the formation of the human baby in the mother's womb. Jeremiah 1:5 says, "Before I formed you in the womb I knew you, before you were born I set you apart; I appointed you as a prophet to the nations." The word translated "formed" is used in Genesis 2:7–8 to describe God's special creation of Adam. It is also used of a potter fashioning clay into a vase or other piece of pottery. In essence God fashioned Jeremiah in the womb for his prophetic ministry.

Similar verses describe how God called out various servants of God while they were still in their mother's womb. God called Isaiah to serve: "Before I was born the LORD called me" (Isa. 49:1). God created Samson for his ministry and put his mother under the same dietary regimen that he would undergo: "But he said to me, 'You will conceive and give birth to a son. Now then, drink no wine or other fermented drink and do not eat anything unclean, because the boy will be a Nazirite of God before birth until the day of his death.' Then Manoah prayed to the LORD: 'O Lord, I beg you, let the man of God you sent to us come again to teach us how to bring up the boy who is to be born'" (Judg. 13:7–8).

Another significant passage is Psalm 51. It was written by David after his sin of adultery with Bathsheba and records his repentance. David confessed that his sinful act demonstrated the original sin that was within him. "Surely I was sinful at birth, sinful from the time my mother conceived me" (Ps. 51:5). David concluded that from his conception he had a sin nature. This would imply that he carried the image of God from the moment of conception, including the marred image scarred from sin.

Human beings are created in the image and likeness of God (Gen. 1:26–27; 5:1; 9:6). Bearing the image of God is the essence of humanness.

And though God's image in man was marred at the Fall, it was not erased (1 Cor. 11:7; James 3:9). Thus unborn babies are made in the image of God and therefore are fully human in God's sight.

This verse also provides support for what is called the *traducian* view of the origin of the soul. According to this perspective human beings were potentially in Adam (Rom. 5:12; Heb. 7:9–10) and thus participated in his original sin. The "soulish" part of humans is transferred through conception. Therefore an unborn baby is fully human.

A key passage that points to the humanness of the unborn child is Luke 1:41–44. "When Elizabeth heard Mary's greeting, the baby leaped in her womb, and Elizabeth was filled with the Holy Spirit. In a loud voice she exclaimed: 'Blessed are you among women, and blessed is the child you bear! But why am I so favored, that the mother of my Lord should come to me? As soon as the sound of your greeting reached my ears, the baby in my womb leaped for joy.'"

John the Baptist's prenatal ability to recognize Mary by leaping "for joy" illustrates his mental and spiritual capacity. Also of note is the fact that the term used to describe John in his prenatal state is "baby." The same Greek word is used for a baby inside the womb and outside the womb (cf. Luke 2:12, 16; 18:15; 2 Tim. 3:15).[12] Like Psalm 51:5, these verses also describe an unborn baby as a spiritual, rational, moral being (in essence a human being in the "image of God").

Another argument against abortion can be found in the Old Testament legal code, specifically Exodus 21:22–25. "If men who are fighting hit a pregnant woman and she gives birth prematurely but there is no serious injury, the offender must be fined whatever the woman's husband demands and the court allows. But if there is serious injury, you are to take life for life, eye for eye, tooth for tooth, hand for hand, foot for foot, burn for burn, wound for wound, bruise for bruise."

These verses seem to teach that if a woman gives birth prematurely but the baby is not injured then only a fine is appropriate. However, if the child dies then the law of retaliation (*lex talionis*) should be applied. In other words, killing an unborn baby carried the same penalty as killing a born baby. A baby inside the womb had the same legal status as a baby outside the womb.

Some commentators have come to a different conclusion because they believe Exodus 21:22–23 refers to a case of accidental miscarriage in which the baby dies. Since only a fine is levied, they argue that an unborn baby is merely potential life and does not carry the same legal status as a baby that has been born. This interpretation has at least two problems. First, the normal Hebrew word for "miscarry" is not used in this passage (see Gen. 31:38; Exod. 23:26; Job 2:10; Hos. 9:14). Most commentators now believe that the action described in Exodus 21:22 is a premature birth, not a miscarriage. Second, even if verses 22–25 do describe a miscarriage, the passage cannot be used to justify abortion. The injury was accidental, not intentional (as abortion would be). Also the action was a criminal offense and punishable by law.

OTHER ARGUMENTS AGAINST ABORTION

In addition to various biblical arguments against abortion, a number of other arguments speak against abortion. The medical arguments against abortion are compelling. For example, at conception the embryo is genetically distinct from the mother. To say that the developing baby is no different from the mother's appendix is scientifically inaccurate. A developing embryo is genetically different from the mother. A developing embryo is also genetically different from the sperm and egg that created it. A human being has forty-six chromosomes (sometimes forty-seven chromosomes). A sperm and an egg each have twenty-three chromosomes. A trained geneticist can distinguish between the DNA of an embryo and the DNA of a sperm and egg. But that same geneticist cannot distinguish between the DNA of a developing embryo and the DNA of a full-grown human being.

Another set of medical arguments against abortion surrounds the definition of life and death. If one set of criteria has been used to define death, could those criteria also be used to define life? Death used to be defined by the cessation of heartbeat. A stopped heart was a clear sign of death. If the cessation of heartbeat could define death, could the onset of a heartbeat define life? The heart is formed by the eighteenth day in the womb. If heartbeat were used to define life, then nearly all abortions would be outlawed.

Physicians now use a more rigorous criterion for death: brain-wave activity. A flat EEG (electroencephalograph) is one of the most important criteria used to determine death. If the cessation of brain-wave activity can define death, could the onset of brain-wave activity define life? Individual brain waves are detected in the fetus in about forty to forty-three days. Using brain-wave activity to define life would outlaw at least a majority of abortions.

Opponents to abortion also raise the controversial issue of fetal pain. Does the fetus feel pain during abortion? The evidence seems fairly clear and consistent. Consider this statement made in a British medical journal: "Try sticking an infant with a pin and you know what happens. She opens her mouth to cry and also pulls away. Try sticking an eight-week-old human fetus in the palm of his hand. He opens his mouth and pulls his hand away. A more technical description would add that changes in heart rate and fetal movement also suggest that intrauterine manipulations are painful to the fetus."[13]

Obviously other medical criteria could be used. The point is simple. Medical science leads to a pro-life perspective rather than a pro-choice perspective. If medical science can be used at all to draw a line, the clearest line is at the moment of conception.

In addition to medical arguments, there are legal arguments against abortion. The case of *Roe v. Wade* violated standard legal reasoning. The Supreme Court decided not to decide when life begins and then turned around and overturned antiabortion laws of many states.

Most of the Supreme Court's verdict rested on two sentences: "We need not resolve the difficult question of when life begins. When those trained in the respective disciplines of medicine, philosophy, and theology are unable to arrive at any consensus, the judiciary, at this point in the development of man's knowledge, is not in a position to speculate as to an answer."

Although the sentences sounded both innocuous and unpretentious, they were neither. The Supreme Court's nondecision was not innocuous. It overturned state laws that protected the unborn and has resulted in over 40 million abortions (more than the population of Canada) in the United States.

The decision also seemed unpretentious by acknowledging that it did not know when life begins. But if the Court did not know, then it should have acted "as if" life is in the womb. A crucial role of government is to protect life. Government cannot remove a segment of the human population from its protection without adequate justification.

The burden of proof should lie with the life-taker, and the benefit of the doubt should be with the lifesaver. Put another way, "When in doubt, don't." A hunter who hears rustling in the bushes should not fire until he knows what is in the bushes. Likewise, a Court which does not know when life begins should not declare open season on the unborn.

The burden of proof in law is on the prosecution. The benefit of doubt is with the defense. This is also known as a presumption of innocence. The defendant is assumed to be innocent unless proven guilty. Again the burden of proof is on the entity that would take away life or liberty. The benefit of the doubt lies with the defense.

The Supreme Court clearly stated that it does not know when life begins and then violated the very spirit of that legal principle by acting as if it had just proved that no life existed in the womb. Even more curious was the fact that to do so, it had to ignore the vast majority of the religious community and international community on the subject of the unborn.

Had the religious community really failed to reach a consensus? Although there were some intramural disagreements, certainly the weight of evidence indicated that a Western culture founded on Judeo-Christian values held abortion to be morally wrong. People with widely divergent theological perspectives (Jewish, Catholic, evangelical and fundamental Protestants) shared a common agreement about the humanity of the unborn.

The same could be said about the international legal community. Physicians around the world subscribed to the Hippocratic Oath (which states in part, "I will not give a woman a pessary to produce abortion"). The unborn children were protected by various international documents like the Declaration of Geneva ("I will maintain the utmost respect for human life, from the moment of conception") and the U.N. Declaration of the Rights of the Child ("The child, by reason of his physical and mental immaturity, needs special safeguards and care, including appropriate legal protection, before as well as after birth").

One of the strongest legal arguments against abortion was that the Supreme Court decided not to decide when life begins. Then it violated the standard legal principles that the burden of proof should lie with the life-taker. The Court did not prove its case and should not have over-turned the laws of states governing abortion.

Philosophic arguments are a third set of arguments against abortion. A key philosophic question is: Where do you draw the line? Put another way: When does a human being become a person?

The Supreme Court's decision in *Roe v. Wade* separated personhood from humanity. In other words, the justices argued that a developing fetus was a human (i.e., a member of the species *Homo sapiens*) but not a person. Since only persons are given Fourteenth Amendment protection under the Constitution, the Court argued that abortion could be legal at certain times. This left to doctors, parents, or even other courts the responsibility of arbitrarily deciding when personhood should be awarded to human beings.

The Supreme Court's cleavage of personhood and humanity made inevitable the ethical slide down society's slippery slope. Once the Court allowed people to start drawing lines, some drew them in unexpected ways and effectively opened the door for infanticide and euthanasia.

The Court, in the tradition of previous line-drawers, opted for biological criteria in their definition of a "person" in *Roe v. Wade.* In the past, such criteria as implantation or quickening had been suggested. The Court chose the idea of viability and allowed for the possibility that states could outlaw abortions performed after a child was viable. But viability was an arbitrary criterion, and there was no biological reason why the line had to be drawn near the early stages of development. The line, for example, could be drawn much later.

Ethicist Paul Ramsey frequently warned that any argument for abortion could logically be also used as an argument for infanticide. As if to illustrate this, Dr. Francis Crick demonstrated that he was less concerned about the ethics of such logical extensions and proposed a more radical definition of personhood. He suggested in the British journal *Nature* that if "a child were considered to be legally born when two days old, it could be examined to see whether it was an 'acceptable member of human society.'"[14]

Obviously this is not an argument for abortion; it is an argument for infanticide.

Other line-drawers have suggested a cultural criterion for personhood. Ashley Montagu, for example, argued that "a newborn baby is not truly human until he or she is molded by cultural influences later."[15] Again, this is more than just an argument for abortion. It is also an argument for infanticide.

More recently some line-drawers have focused on a mental criterion for personhood. Joseph Fletcher argued in his book *Humanhood* that "humans without some minimum of intelligence or mental capacity are not persons, no matter how many of these organs are active, no matter how spontaneous their living processes are."[16] This is not only an argument for abortion and infanticide; it is also adequate justification for euthanasia and the potential elimination of those who do not possess a certain IQ. In other writings Fletcher suggested that an "individual" was not truly a "person" unless he or she had an IQ of at least 40.[17]

By separating personhood from humanhood, the Supreme Court opened the door for such bizarre line-drawing. The biblical perspective is clear that human beings are also persons created in the image of God. Those who promote abortion try to separate these two issues and thus open the door to dangerous line-drawing and such issues as infanticide and euthanasia.

ANSWERS TO PRO-ABORTION RHETORIC

The abortion debate has been full of rhetoric on both sides, but those supporting the right to abortion have been especially good at throwing out clichés in this debate. The pro-life movement needs to be able to respond to pro-abortion rhetoric in an effective way.

One of the most frequent clichés is this: "Every woman has a right to control her own body." Let's consider the four elements of this slogan. First are the words "every woman." Half of the aborted fetuses are female, so abortion isn't exactly pro-woman. So the cliché only applies to grown women seeking abortions, not to females in the womb who would grow up to be women if they were not aborted. Second is the statement "has a right." Our legal system does not recognize an absolute right over one's body. We do not allow someone the "right" to get drunk and then drive a car. We do not give people an absolute right to use dangerous drugs, to commit suicide, to walk around without clothes. Third is the verb "to control." If a woman wanted to control her own body, she could have prevented the pregnancy before it happened. Abstinence is 100 percent effective. The final words are "her own body." As already discussed, pregnancy means there are *two* bodies. In a sense the baby controls the mother's body through various hormonal cues. The fetus would be rejected as foreign tissue if it were not for the placenta, which creates an effective barrier between mother and child. The argument that a woman has a right to control her own body may sound good, but flaws emerge as we begin to analyze it.

Another cliché is: "Abortion should be every woman's legal right." As already noted, a woman does not have an absolute legal right over her own body. This is especially true when it comes to abortion, which ends the life of the one in the womb. The Bible clearly shows that abortion is taking another human life. Even an injury to an unborn baby resulted in exacting a penalty (Exod. 21:22–25), just as if the child were already born. A woman may have many legal rights, but these must be tempered by the right to life of the one in the womb.

A third cliché is "The fetus is mere tissue and not a person." This slogan ignores the previous biblical arguments about the humanity of the fetus (Ps. 139) and the arguments that the unborn already possesses the image of God corrupted by sin (51:5). God's care as stated in the Psalms extended not merely to tissue that would become David, but to him (personal pronoun). Many Old Testament prophets were called to their ministry while yet in their mother's womb (Samson, Isaiah, Jeremiah). These were more than just pieces of protoplasm; these were prophets God called to ministry.

Pro-abortion advocates often argue, "Abortion is the best solution to a crisis pregnancy." Often an unplanned pregnancy seems like a crisis, but on further reflection it can become a wonderful blessing. But even if the child was conceived under stress or duress, two wrongs do not make a right. The Bible teaches that it is wrong to add sin to sin (Isa. 30:1–2). If a mother cannot care for the child, she can give it to those who will care for him or her (Ps. 27:10). Adoption is a better option than abortion. The proliferation of crisis-pregnancy centers around the country (there are now more crisis-pregnancy centers in the United States than there are abortion clinics), provides an effective means for a woman to deal with her crisis pregnancy.

A corollary cliché is that "abortion is necessary because sometimes there is no other way out." A woman facing a crisis pregnancy often feels the only solution to her problem is abortion, and so she fails to consider the potential implications, including infertility and emotional scars. In the Bible God says He will make a way when there seems to be no way out (Jer. 32:17; 1 Cor. 10:13; Heb. 4:15–16). We have the firm promise that if we call on Him, He will answer us (Jer. 33:3; James 1:5–7).

HOW CAN THE CHURCH BECOME INVOLVED?

The church can be involved in the battle for life in many practical ways. First, individual Christians can become involved in the pro-life movement. Some may choose to join a pro-life organization and work to overturn abortion at the state or national level. Involvement can range from working full-time on the issue to lobbying legislators to writing an occasional letter about the issue of abortion. Although it seems unlikely that abortion will be outlawed in the near future, individual Christians can do a number of things at state and local levels to limit the number of abortions that take place (e.g., legislation requiring parental consent or a specified waiting period).

Another way the church can be involved is through prayer. The Bible admonishes Christians to be in prayer for their leaders (1 Tim. 2:1–2). The church and individual Christians should also be in prayer for various pro-life organizations (national, state, local). They should also pray for women facing abortion, as well as those who have been exploited by abortion.

A third area of involvement is financial. This can include financial gifts (one-time or monthly) to organizations fighting abortion. Also, gifts in kind (maternity clothes, baby clothes, baby items) given to crisis-pregnancy centers are helpful. And when we give of our time and talents (as volunteers for pro-life groups or crisis-pregnancy centers), we help reduce the financial needs of pro-life organizations.

Fourth, churches should also be centers of information. Christians should become informed through Christian media (TV, radio, news magazines) and organizational newsletters. They should attend local rallies, debates, marches, pickets. And pastors and others should disseminate information to their congregations and encourage action by them.

Social action is a fifth area of involvement. Christians should find out if their local doctors and hospitals perform abortions and take necessary action. In some cases pro-life advocates may want to picket a local abortion clinic or hospital. Social action also includes voting intelligently about political candidates and knowing where they stand on the issue of abortion.

Involvement in crisis pregnancy ministry is another important action step. Christians should support or start a crisis-pregnancy center in their community if needed. They should also inform local churches of its existence and the extent of its services. Churches should consider funding a center as part of their local missions outreach and even provide counselor training for members of their congregations. Some churches have even developed a shepherding home within their congregation. This provides temporary housing and care for unwed mothers with crisis pregnancies.

Sixth, pastors and Christian counselors need to be informed about how to help women with crisis pregnancies. They should be willing to listen and have compassion. Pastors should be sensitive to the pressures on such women from family, friends, and others. Male pastors and counselors should involve another woman in the counseling or else refer the pregnant woman to a local center. In addition, pastors should be informed about how to minister to those exploited by abortion in their congregation.

2
Euthanasia

T HE ETHICS OF DEATH and dying have always been troubling, but pastors and physicians today agonize even more as controversy intensifies over the ethics of euthanasia. Is it moral to withhold medical treatment from a terminally ill patient? Is it ever right to "pull the plug" on a patient? When this is done, is it mercy or murder? These are just a few of the difficult questions surrounding the issue of euthanasia.

The term *euthanasia* is derived from the Greek prefix *eu*, meaning "good" or "easy," and the Greek noun *thanatos*, meaning "death." Critics, however, have said that euthanasia is anything but easy and anything but good. Euthanasia means different things to different people: It can imply anything from keeping terminally ill patients free from pain to ending a life not considered worthy of living. Most laypeople once assumed the focus was merely on what can properly be called "palliative care," which includes attempts by doctors and nurses to ease pain in terminal patients. Today, however, euthanasia means much more.

A HISTORY OF EUTHANASIA

Debate over euthanasia is not a modern phenomenon. The Greeks carried on a robust debate on the subject. The Pythagoreans opposed euthanasia, while the Stoics favored it in the case of incurable disease. Plato approved of it in cases of terminal illness.[1] But his influence lost out to Christian principles and to the Hippocratic Oath, which includes the statement, "I will neither give a deadly drug to anybody if asked for it, nor will I make a suggestion to that effect."

In 1935 the Euthanasia Society of England was formed to promote the option of a painless death for patients with incurable diseases. A few years later the Euthanasia Society of America was formed with essentially the same goals. In the last few years debate about euthanasia has been advanced by two individuals: Derek Humphry and Dr. Jack Kevorkian.

Derek Humphry has used his prominence as head of the Hemlock Society to promote euthanasia in this country. His book *Final Exit: The Practicalities of Self-Deliverance and Assisted Suicide for the Dying* (Denver: Hemlock Society, 1991) became a best-seller and further influenced public opinion. A Gallup poll in 1975 found that 41 percent of the respondents believed that someone in great pain, with "no hope of improvement," had the moral right to commit suicide. By 1990 that figure had risen to 66 percent.[2]

Another influential figure is Jack Kevorkian, who has been instrumental in helping people commit suicide. His book *Prescription—Medicide: The Goodness of Planned Death* (Amherst, N.Y.: Prometheus, 1991) promotes his views of euthanasia and describes his patented suicide machine, which he calls "the Mercitron." He first gained national attention by enabling Janet Adkins, of Portland, Oregon, to kill herself in 1990. They met for dinner and then drove to a Volkswagen van, where the machine waited. He placed an intravenous tube into her arm and dripped a saline solution in until she pushed a button that first sent a drug causing unconsciousness and then a drug into her veins that killed her. Since then Kevorkian has helped dozens of other people commit suicide.

Over the years public opinion has also been influenced by the tragic cases of a number of persons described as being in a "persistent vegetative state." The first was Karen Ann Quinlan. Her parents, wanting to turn her respirator off, won approval in court. However, when it was turned off in 1976, Karen continued breathing and lived for another ten years. Another case was Nancy Cruzan, who was injured in an automobile accident in 1983.

Her parents went to court in 1987 to receive approval to remove her feeding tube. Various court cases ensued in Missouri, and even the U.S. Supreme Court heard her parents' appeal in 1990. Eventually they won the right to pull the feeding tube, and Nancy Cruzan died shortly thereafter.

Seven years after the Cruzan case, the Supreme Court had occasion to rule again on the issue of euthanasia. On June 26, 1997, the Supreme Court rejected euthanasia by stating that state laws banning physician-assisted suicide were constitutional. Some feared that these cases (*Glucksburg v. Washington* and *Vacco v. Quill*) would become for euthanasia what *Roe v. Wade* became for abortion. Instead the justices rejected the concept of finding a constitutional "right to die" and chose not to interrupt the political debate (as *Roe v. Wade* had), instead urging that the debate on euthanasia continue "as it should in a democratic society."

Crucial to any further debate on this issue is a proper definition of the various forms of euthanasia. Some forms of what is called euthanasia can be justified from a biblical perspective, while many others are clearly immoral and even criminal in nature.

FORMS OF EUTHANASIA

Ethical and medical discussions of euthanasia frequently include various forms of treatment or lack of treatment that fall under the general term *euthanasia*. Four categories of euthanasia are frequently discussed in medical literature.

Voluntary, passive euthanasia. This form of euthanasia assumes that medical personnel, at the patient's request, will merely allow nature to take its course. In the past, passive euthanasia meant that the physician did nothing to hasten death but did provide care, comfort, and counsel to dying patients.[3]

Voluntary, active euthanasia. This means that the physician, by request, hastens death by taking some active means (e.g., lethal injection). This raises the controversial issue of whether nonmedical personnel such as a spouse or friend would be permitted to end the suffering of another.

Involuntary, passive euthanasia. This assumes that the patient has not expressed a willingness to die or cannot do so. The medical personnel do not go to any extraordinary measures to save the patient and often with-hold food (by removing nasogastric tubes), antibiotics, or life-support systems (respirators).

Involuntary, active euthanasia. This category begins to blur into homicide. In this case the physician does something active to hasten death, regardless of the patient's wishes, for humanitarian reasons, economic considerations, or genetic justifications.

In recent years these categories have been blurred by discussions of the right to die, death with dignity, patient autonomy, death selection, physician-assisted suicide, living wills, and a durable power of attorney. Nevertheless, these four categories provide the basis for an extended discussion of the various concepts surrounding the issue of euthanasia.

Voluntary, Passive Euthanasia

This is not truly euthanasia in the modern sense. In these situations it is assumed that death is imminent and inevitable. At this point the medical personnel's attention turns from curing the disease to making the patient as comfortable as possible. Further medical treatment to prolong life becomes pointless and an entirely different medical strategy is implemented. This medical strategy is frequently referred to as "palliative care." The prime focus is on alleviating pain rather than curing the patient.

One of the great fears of patients is the prospect of intractable pain in the dying process. But medical science has made great strides in treating pain. New ways of administering morphine, for example, can effectively manage pain and also lower the risk of respiratory complications. David Cundiff, practicing oncologist and hospice care physician, says, "It is a disgrace that the majority of our health care providers lack the knowledge and the skills to treat pain and other symptoms of terminal disease properly. The absence of palliative care training for the medical professional results in sub-optimal care for almost all terminally ill patients and elicits the wish to hasten their own deaths in a few."[4]

Fear of pain is often unwarranted. Physicians can administer medications that deaden pain but do not dim consciousness, thus allowing patients to converse with their family and friends even in their last days.

Some patients can be released to hospices, where they can spend their last days with family and friends rather than in a clinical hospital setting. The hospice program provides a coordinated program of doctors, nurses, and special consultants, who help the dying patient and his or her family through their time of struggle.

But even this form of euthanasia is not without its controversy. Many physicians are reluctant to discontinue medical efforts to cure terminal patients. Their reluctance is not so much driven by a belief that they will be successful as it is by their concern about possible malpractice suits from the family. Patients who are ready "to go to be with the Lord" may find themselves at odds with doctors who are fearful they may have to prove in a court of law that they did "all they could" for the patient.

Sometimes attempts to prolong life are futile and certainly not warranted from a biblical perspective. According to Job 14:5, "Man's days are determined; you have decreed the number of his months and have set limits he cannot exceed." Modern medicine sometimes tries to exceed those natural limits. Christians are not required to use extraordinary measures to keep a comatose person with an incurable disease alive by artificial means. In a sense, using this kind of technology would actually be working against God's appointed limits described in Job 14:5.

In certain medical situations there are times when giving food or water can be futile and burdensome. Rita Marker, of the Anti-Euthanasia Task Force, wrote, "A patient who is very close to death may be in such a condition that fluids would cause a great deal of discomfort or may not be assimilated by his body. Food may not be digested as the body begins "shutting down" during the dying process. There comes a time when a person is truly, imminently dying."[5]

In 1981 the President's Commission for the Study of Ethical Problems in Medicine provided guidelines for patients and also drafted a Uniform Determination of Death (to be discussed later). The commission came to the following conclusions concerning terminally ill patients:

1. A terminally ill patient generally should have the right to choose to die without interference from lawyers, legislators, or bureaucrats.

2. Patients suffering loss of consciousness should have the type of care that is dictated largely by their families' wishes.

3. Resuscitation need not always be attempted on a hospitalized patient whose heart stops. Patients likely to suffer cardiac arrest should be informed before the operation and allowed to decide in advance for or against resuscitation.

4. Patients should have greater rights to give instructions in advance of becoming incapacitated. They should have the right to appoint a proxy to carry out their wishes.

These conclusions of the President's Commission have provided the basis for revision of state laws governing medical care of the terminally ill. In general they provide doctors with greater latitude in making decisions concerning dying patients. But they do raise significant questions for Christians.

First, is there such a thing as a "right to die"? From a Christian perspective this is certainly questionable (as discussed later in the section "Biblical Perspectives"). But it also raises important legal questions never addressed by the founders of this country or by modern courts. While the Declaration of Independence does recognize a "right to life," it does not recognize (or even assume) a "right to die."

Second, the conclusions suggest that a patient's decisions about life and death can be made by proxy. In most cases this has been done through what are known as advanced directives. These usually are found in one of three forms: (1) A living will outlines what medical treatment a patient might desire. The patient can specify what he or she wants and does not want. The legal limits vary from state to state. (2) Healthcare proxy designates an agent (friend, family member) to act for the patient in healthcare matters. It is often included within a living will and may have limited powers. (3) A durable power of attorney is the most inclusive and comprehensive arrangement. It permits the patient's agent to act for him or her in most healthcare matters.

Most states allow individuals to draw up an advanced directive like a living will or a durable power of attorney (DPOA), in which they specify their desires regarding medical treatment if they become terminally ill and incompetent. A DPOA, in particular, gives a third party, or proxy, power to make decisions on behalf of the patient. In the past these covered only financial decisions, but court precedents have extended DPOAs to cover healthcare decisions as well.

In 1991 the Patient Self-Determination Act became law. It requires medical facilities receiving federal reimbursements such as Medicaid and Medicare to inform patients of the right to some form of advance directives. Therefore more and more patients are being confronted with questions and choices about their healthcare.

One problem with these directives is that they are often ignored. A study done by University of North Carolina at Chapel Hill researchers on the use of advanced directives found that treatment received was not in accord with the patients' instructions in 25 percent of the cases.[6] Similar findings have been reported in the *New England Journal of Medicine* and the AMA's *Archives of Internal Medicine*.

Critics of living wills say it is like signing a blank check because they are broad documents and cannot cover every contingency. The attending physician therefore must interpret a patient's wishes. A patient not wanting any heroic measures carried out may envision a heart/lung machine, whereas the attending physician may interpret this to mean something quite different.

Another problem with these proxy arrangements is that they are usually based on some "quality of life" standard and delegate the interpretation of those standards to someone else. A Christian perspective on human life sees all life as sacred and given by God. Decisions about life and death should be governed by a "sanctity of life" standard rather than by a "quality of life" standard.

Voluntary, Active Euthanasia

This implies that something is done to hasten death. This raises both moral and legal questions. Does active euthanasia constitute an act of murder or assisted suicide? Or is it merely a compassionate act of mercy killing?

It is helpful to distinguish between mercy killing and what could be called mercy dying. Taking a human life is not the same as allowing nature to take its course by allowing a terminally ill patient to die. The former is immoral (and perhaps even criminal), while the latter is not.

However, drawing a sharp line between these two categories is not as easy as it used to be. Modern medical technology has significantly blurred the line between hastening death and allowing nature to take its course.

Certain analgesics, for example, ease pain, but they can also shorten a patient's life by affecting respiration. An artificial heart will continue to beat even after the patient has died and therefore must be turned off by the doctor. So the distinction between actively promoting death and passively allowing nature to take its course is sometimes difficult to determine. But this fundamental distinction between life-taking and death-permitting is still an important philosophical distinction.

Another concern with active euthanasia is that it eliminates the possibility of recovery. While this should be obvious, somehow this problem is frequently ignored in the euthanasia debate. Terminating a human life eliminates all possibility of recovery, while passively ceasing extraordinary means may not. Miraculous recovery from a bleak prognosis sometimes occurs. A doctor who prescribes active euthanasia for a patient may unwittingly prevent a possible recovery he or she did not anticipate.

A further concern with this so-called voluntary, active euthanasia is that these decisions might not always be freely made. The possibility for coercion is always present. Richard D. Lamm, former governor of Colorado, said that elderly, terminally ill patients have "a duty to die and get out of the way." Though those words were reported somewhat out of context, they nonetheless illustrate the pressure many elderly feel from hospital personnel.

The Dutch experience is instructive. A survey of Dutch physicians was made in 1990 by the Remmelink Committee. They found that 1,030 patients were killed without their consent. Of these, 140 were fully mentally competent and 110 were only slightly mentally impaired. The report also found that another 14,175 patients (1,701 of whom were mentally competent) were denied medical treatment without their consent and died.[7]

A more recent survey of the Dutch experience is even less encouraging. Studies of doctors in the Netherlands have found that though euthanasia was originally intended for exceptional cases, it has become an accepted way of dealing with serious or terminal illnesses. The original guidelines (that patients with a terminal illness make a voluntary, persistent request that their lives be ended) have been expanded to include chronic ailments and psychological distress. It was also found that 60 percent of Dutch physicians do not report their cases of assisted suicide (even though reporting is required by law) and about 25 percent of the physicians admit to ending patients' lives without their consent.[8]

Former Surgeon General C. Everett Koop has said that proponents of active euthanasia "have gotten across to a whole segment of the elderly population that somehow because they are living, they are depriving someone else of a prior right to resources. That is a most reprehensible thing." He added, "When I was doing research for *Whatever Happened to the Human Race?*, I went to nursing homes and talked to people who felt that pressure. Old people were apologizing to me for using a bed, for being alive, for taking medication, because they knew somebody else deserved it more. I think that's pitiful."[9]

Involuntary, Passive Euthanasia

In this form of euthanasia, which is an act of omission, medical personnel do not go to any extraordinary measures to save the patient. This can be a morally acceptable omission when dealing with terminal patients.

Unfortunately this omission often includes actions that are more accurately described as active euthanasia. Withholding food (by removing nasogastric tubes), antibiotics, or life-support procedures (respirator) is much more than passive euthanasia. As already mentioned, candidates for euthanasia have been known to make miraculous recoveries, but such a possibility is eliminated when a patient is starved to death.

Sometimes, however, decisions must be made about "pulling the plug." A comatose patient without any brain-wave activity, as indicated by a flat electroencephalogram, should be removed from life-support systems. But in other situations a comatose patient might recover. These difficult decisions should be left to the neurophysiologist, who can evaluate a patient's prognosis. But in general one may assume that the patient will recover and therefore life-support systems should be continued, thus placing the burden of proof on those who wish to "pull the plug."

Key to this discussion is an accurate definition of death. Prior to the 1960s a terminally ill patient who stopped breathing and continued in that state was pronounced dead. With the advent of CPR and artificial respirators, that respiratory criterion for death had to be changed. In 1968 the Harvard Medical School developed more specific criteria for death: (1) lack of response to external stimuli, (2) absence of spontaneous muscular movements and spontaneous respiration, (3) no elicitable reflexes, and (4) a flat electroencephalogram (EEG).

In 1981 the President's Commission drafted a Uniform Determination of Death Act, which has been universally adopted. It defines death as irreversible cessation of circulatory and respiratory functions and irreversible cessation of all functions of the entire brain, including the brain stem. In other words brain death (a flat EEG) has become the established criterion for death and decisions about when to remove life-support systems.

Another concern about involuntary euthanasia is motive. Motives are frequently mixed. Are the medical personnel recommending euthanasia because of bed shortages or depleted medical facilities? Or are they suggesting euthanasia out of a compassionate concern for the patient? Is a son, for example, agreeing to euthanasia out of concern for his mother's well-being or out of a desire to gain his inheritance?

C. Everett Koop said this: "The whole thing about euthanasia comes down to one word: motive. If your motive is to alleviate suffering while a patient is going through the throes of dying, and you are using medication that alleviates suffering, even though it might shorten his life by a few hours, that is not euthanasia. But if you are giving him a drug intended to shorten his life, then your motivation is for euthanasia."[10]

The mixed motives behind these decisions are not easy to sort out, and they add further moral and legal questions to the medical landscape. Motives are clearer when nature is allowed to take its course and agonizing decisions are not thrust on the patient or family about when to terminate a patient's life.

Involuntary, Active Euthanasia

In this form of euthanasia a second party makes decisions about whether active measures should be taken to end a life. Ever since the Supreme Court ruled in *Roe v. Wade* that the life of unborn babies could be terminated for reasons of convenience, there has been an erosion of the doctrine of the sanctity of life, even though the Supreme Court has been reluctant to legalize euthanasia.

This progression was inevitable. Once society begins to devalue the life of an unborn child, it is but a small step to begin to do the same with a child who has been born. Abortion slides naturally into infanticide and eventually into euthanasia. In the past few years doctors have allowed a number of so-called Baby Does to die (either by failing to perform life-saving operations or else by not feeding the infants).

The progression from this toward euthanasia is inevitable. Once society becomes accustomed to using a "quality of life" standard for infants, it will more willingly accept the same standard for the elderly. As C. Everett Koop has said, "Nothing surprises me anymore. My great concern is that there will be 10,000 Grandma Does for every Baby Doe."[11]

Again the Dutch experience is instructive. In the Netherlands, physicians have at times performed involuntary euthanasia because they thought the family had suffered too much or were tired of taking care of patients. American surgeon Robin Bernhoft relates an incident in which a Dutch doctor euthanized a twenty-six-year-old ballerina with arthritis in her toes. Since she could no longer pursue her career as a dancer, she was depressed and requested to be put to death. The doctor complied with her request and merely noted that "one doesn't enjoy such things, but it was her choice."[12]

PHYSICIAN-ASSISTED SUICIDE

In recent years media and political attention has been given to the idea of physician-assisted suicide. Some states have even attempted to pass legislation that would allow physicians in this country the legal right to put terminally ill patients to death. While the Dutch experience should be enough to demonstrate the danger of granting such rights, there are other good reasons to reject this idea.

First, physician-assisted suicide would change the nature of the medical profession itself. Physicians would be cast in the role of killers rather than healers. The Hippocratic Oath was written to place the medical profession on the foundation of healing, not killing. For twenty-four hundred years patients have had the assurance that doctors have taken an oath to heal them, not kill them. This would change with legalized euthanasia.

Second, medical care would be affected. Physicians would begin to ration healthcare so that elderly and severely disabled patients would not be receiving the same quality of care as everyone else. Legalizing euthanasia would result in less care for the dying, rather than better care.

Third, legalizing euthanasia through physician-assisted suicide would effectively establish a right to die. The Constitution affirms that fundamental rights cannot be limited to one group (e.g., the terminally ill). They must apply to all. Legalizing physician-assisted suicide would open the door to anyone wanting the "right" to kill themselves. Soon this would apply not only to voluntary euthanasia but also to involuntary euthanasia as various court precedents began to broaden the application of the right to die to other groups in society, like the disabled or the clinically depressed.

BIBLICAL PERSPECTIVES

Foundational to a biblical perspective on euthanasia is a proper understanding of the sanctity of human life. For centuries Western culture in general and Christians in particular have believed in the sanctity of human life. Unfortunately this view is beginning to erode into a "quality of life" standard. The disabled, retarded, and infirm were once seen as having a special place in God's world, but today some medical personnel judge a person's fitness for life on the basis of a perceived quality of life or lack of such quality.

No longer is life seen as sacred and worthy of being saved. Now patients may be evaluated, and life-saving treatment frequently denied, based on a subjective and arbitrary standard for the supposed quality of life. If a life is not judged worthy to be lived any longer, people may feel obliged to end that life.

The Bible teaches that human beings are created in the image of God (Gen. 1:26) and therefore have dignity and value. Human life is sacred and should not be terminated merely because life is difficult or inconvenient.

Psalm 139 teaches that humans are fearfully and wonderfully made. Society must not place an arbitrary standard of quality above God's absolute standard of human value and worth. This does not mean that people will no longer need to make difficult decisions about treatment and care, but it does mean that these decisions will be guided by an objective, absolute standard of human worth.

The Bible also teaches that God is sovereign over life and death. Christians can agree with Job when he said, "The LORD gave and the LORD has taken away. Blessed be the name of the LORD" (Job 1:21, NKJV). The Lord said, "See now that I myself am He! There is no god besides me. I put to death and I bring to life, I have wounded and I will heal, and no one can deliver out of my hand" (Deut. 32:39). God has ordained our days (Ps. 139:16) and is in control of our lives.

Another foundational principle involves a biblical view of life-taking. The Bible specifically condemns murder (Exod. 20:13), and this would include active forms of euthanasia in which another person (doctor, nurse, or friend) hastens death in a patient. While there are situations described in Scripture in which life-taking may be permitted (e.g., self-defense or a just war), euthanasia should not be included with any of these established biblical categories. Active euthanasia, like murder, involves premeditated intent and therefore should be condemned as immoral and even criminal.

Although the Bible does not specifically speak to the issue of euthanasia, the story of the death of King Saul (2 Sam. 1:9–16) is instructive. Saul asked that a soldier put him to death as he lay dying on the battlefield. When David heard of this act, he ordered the soldier put to death for "destroying the LORD's anointed." Though the context is not euthanasia per se, it does show the respect we must show for a human life even in such tragic circumstances.

Christians should also reject the attempt by the modern euthanasia movement to promote a so-called "right to die." Secular society's attempt to establish this "right" is wrong for two reasons. First, giving a person a right to die is tantamount to promoting suicide, and suicide is condemned in the Bible. Man is forbidden to murder, and that includes murder of oneself. Moreover, Christians are commanded to love others as they love themselves (Matt. 22:39; Eph. 5:29). Implicit in the command is an assumption of self-love as well as love for others. Suicide, however, is hardly an example of self-love. It is perhaps the clearest example of self-hate. Suicide is also usually a selfish act. People kill themselves to get away from pain and problems, often leaving those problems to friends and family members who must pick up the pieces when the one who committed suicide is gone.

Second, this so-called "right to die" denies God the opportunity to work sovereignly within a shattered life and bring glory to Himself. When Joni Eareckson Tada realized that she would be spending the rest of her life as a quadriplegic, she asked in despair, "Why can't they just let me die?" When her friend Diana, trying to provide comfort, said to her, "The past is dead, Joni; you're alive," Joni responded, "Am I? This isn't living."[13] But through God's grace Joni's despair gave way to her firm conviction that even her accident was within God's plan for her life. Now she shares with the world her firm conviction that "suffering gets us ready for heaven."[14]

The Bible teaches that God's purposes are beyond our understanding. Job's reply to the Lord shows his acknowledgment of God's purposes: "I know that you can do all things; no plan of yours can be thwarted. You asked, 'Who is this that obscures my counsel without knowledge?' Surely I spoke of things I did not understand, things too wonderful for me to know" (Job 42:2–3). Isaiah 55:8–9 teaches, "For my thoughts are not your thoughts, neither are your ways my ways, declares the LORD. As the heavens are higher than the earth, so are my ways higher than your ways and my thoughts than your thoughts."

Another foundational principle is a biblical view of death. Death is both unnatural and inevitable. It is an unnatural intrusion into our lives as a consequence of the Fall (Gen. 2:17). It is the last enemy to be destroyed (1 Cor. 15:26, 56). Therefore Christians can reject humanistic ideas that assume death is nothing more than a natural process. But the Bible also teaches that death (under the present conditions) is inevitable. There is "a time to be born and a time to die" (Eccles. 3:2). Death is a part of life and the doorway to another, better life.

When does death occur? Modern medicine defines death primarily as a biological event; yet Scripture defines death as a spiritual event that has biological consequences. Death, according to the Bible, occurs when the spirit leaves the body (12:7; James 2:26).

Unfortunately this does not offer much by way of clinical diagnosis for medical personnel. But it does suggest that a rigorous medical definition for death should be used. A comatose patient may not be conscious, but from both a medical and biblical perspective he is very much alive, so treatment should be continued unless crucial vital signs and brain activity have ceased.

On the other hand, Christians must also reject the notion that everything must be done to save life at all costs. Believers, knowing that to be at home in the body is to be away from the Lord (2 Cor. 5:6), long for the time when they will be absent from the body and at home with the Lord (5:8). Death is gain for Christians (Phil. 1:21). Therefore they need not be so tied to this earth that they perform futile operations just to extend life a few more hours or days.

In a patient's last days everything possible should be done to alleviate physical and emotional pain. Giving drugs to a patient to relieve pain is morally justifiable. Proverbs 31:6 says, "Give strong drink to him who is perishing, and wine to him whose life is bitter (NASB)." As previously mentioned, some analgesics have the secondary effect of shortening life. But these should be permitted since the primary purpose is to relieve pain, even though they may secondarily shorten life.

Moreover, believers should provide counsel and spiritual care to dying patients (Gal. 6:2). Frequently emotional needs can be met both in the patient and in the family. Such times of grief also provide opportunities for witnessing. People are often more open to the gospel when suffering loss than at any other time.

Difficult philosophical and biblical questions are certain to continue swirling around the issue of euthanasia. But in the midst of these confusing issues should be the objective, absolute standards of Scripture, which provide guidance for the hard choices of providing care to terminally ill patients.

3
Genetic Engineering

THE AGE OF GENETICS has arrived. Society is in the midst of a genetic revolution that some futurists predict will have a greater impact on the culture than the industrial revolution. Knowledge in genetics is doubling every few years. Genetic engineering is no longer science fiction; it is now science fact.

The future of genetics, like that of any other technology, offers great promise but also great peril. Nuclear technology has provided nuclear medicine, nuclear energy, and nuclear weapons. Genetic technology offers the promise of a diverse array of good, questionable, and bad technological applications. Christians therefore must help shape the ethical foundations of this technology and its future applications.

How powerful a technology is genetic engineering? For the first time in human history it is possible to redesign existing organisms completely, including humans, and to direct the genetic and reproductive constitution of every living thing. Scientists are no longer limited to breeding and cross-pollination. Powerful genetic tools allow us to change genetic structure at the microscopic level and bypass the normal processes of reproduction.

For the first time in human history it is also possible to make multiple copies of any existing organism or of certain sections of its genetic structure. This ability to clone existing organisms or their genes gives scientists a powerful tool to reproduce helpful and useful genetic material within a population.

Scientists are also developing techniques to treat and cure genetic diseases through genetic surgery and genetic therapy. They can already identify genetic sequences that are defective, and soon scientists will be able to replace these defects with properly functioning genes.

GENETIC DISEASES

Genetic diseases arise from a number of causes. The first are single-gene defects. Some of these single-gene diseases are dominant and therefore cannot be masked by a second normal gene on the homologous chromosome (the other strand of a chromosome pair). An example is Huntington's chorea, a fatal disease that strikes in mid-life and leads to progressive physical and mental deterioration. Many other single-gene diseases are recessive and are expressed only when both chromosomes have a defect. Examples of these diseases are sickle-cell anemia, which leads to the production of malformed red blood cells, and cystic fibrosis, which leads to a malfunction of the respiratory and digestive systems.

Another group of single-gene diseases includes the sex-linked diseases. Because the Y chromosome in men is much shorter than the X chromosome it pairs with, many genes on the X chromosome are absent on the homologous Y chromosome. Therefore men will show a higher incidence of genetic diseases such as hemophilia or color blindness. Even though these are recessive, males do not have a homologous gene on their Y chromosome that could contain a normal gene to mask it.

Another major cause of genetic disease is chromosomal abnormalities. Some diseases result from an additional chromosome. Down's syndrome is caused by "trisomy-21" (three chromosomes at chromosome twenty-one). Klinefelter's syndrome results from the addition of an extra X chromosome (these men have a chromosome pattern that is XXY). Other genetic defects result from the duplication, deletion, or rearrangement (called translocation) of a gene sequence.

GENETIC COUNSELING

As scientists have learned more about the genetic structure of human beings, they have been able to predict with greater certainty the likelihood of a couple bearing a child with a genetic disease. Each human being carries approximately three to eight genetic defects that might be passed on to their children. By checking family medical histories and taking blood samples (for chromosome counts and tests for recessive traits), a genetic counselor can make a fairly accurate prediction about the possibility of a couple having a child with a genetic disease.

Most couples, however, do not seek genetic counsel in order to decide if they should have a child, but rather to decide if they should abort a child that is already conceived. In these cases where the mother is already pregnant, the focus is not whether to prevent a pregnancy but whether to abort the unborn child. These circumstances raise some of the same ethical concerns already discussed in the chapter on abortion.

Physicians also have powerful tools to discover major deformities as well as genetic defects within the womb. As recently as the 1950s the genetic makeup of a child born in a delivery room was pretty much a surprise to both the doctor and the parents. A standard prenatal exam involved placing a stethoscope on the mother's stomach and listening for signs of life. This began to change in the following decades.

Major deformities can now be discovered through many advanced new techniques. One is ultrasound, which uses a type of sonar to determine the size, shape, and sex of the fetus. An ultrasound transducer is placed on the mother's abdomen and sound waves are sent through the amniotic sac. The sonar waves are then picked up and transmitted to a video screen that provides important information about the characteristics of the fetus.

Another important tool is laparoscopy. A flexible fiber-optic scope is inserted by the doctor through a small incision in the mother's abdomen. This tool allows the doctor to probe into the abdominal cavity. This procedure can also be used for microsurgery (e.g., to repair the fallopian tubes) or to take a blood sample from the fetus.

Genetic defects can be detected in the womb through various prenatal tests. These tests can detect approximately two hundred genetic disorders.[1] In the mid-1960s physicians began to use amniocentesis. A doctor inserts a four-inch needle into a pregnant woman's anesthetized abdomen in order to withdraw up to an ounce of amniotic fluid. As the fetus grows, cells are shed from the skin of the fetus, and these can be collected from the fluid and used to discover the sex and genetic makeup of the fetus.

For years, doctors used this procedure to identify congenital defects by the twentieth week of pregnancy. Now more doctors use another technique called chorionic villus sampling (CVS), which can produce the same information at ten weeks. Doctors also use a blood test known as maternal serum alfa-fetoprotein (MSAFP). This test, usually done between the fifteenth and twentieth week, can detect a neural tube defect of the spinal cord or brain, such as spina bifida or Down's syndrome.

The newest procedure is called BABI (blastomere analysis before implantation). Using reproductive technologies (discussed in chapter 4), a couple can conceive several embryos in test tubes and discard those exhibiting known defects. A doctor gives a woman a drug to stimulate ovulation, then extracts eggs from her ovaries and mixes them with her partner's sperm. So far, the procedure has been used to test embryos for such hereditary diseases as Tay-Sachs and Duchenne muscular dystrophy.[2]

Using these techniques to give genetic information to couples is not wrong. But since most of these genetic diseases cannot be cured, the tacit assumption is that abortion will be used if any defects are found. Many doctors and clinics will not do genetic tests unless a couple gives prior consent to abortion. Thus genetic counseling can often raise ethical questions, especially when abortion is involved.

In the future, genetic counseling will change because of advances in technology. Genetic engineering will allow doctors to treat genetic diseases as well as diagnose them. Genetic surgery and genetic therapy may be used to replace or recondition existing genes. This is the great promise of gene splicing, also known as recombinant DNA technology (rDNA).

RECOMBINANT DNA TECHNOLOGY

Recombinant DNA research (rDNA) began in the 1970s with new genetic techniques that allowed scientists to cut small pieces of DNA (known as plasmids) into small segments that could be inserted into host DNA. The new creatures that were designed have been called DNA chimeras because they are conceptually similar to the mythological Chimera (a creature with the head of a lion, the body of a goat, and the tail of a serpent).

Recombinant DNA technology is fundamentally different from other forms of genetic breeding used in the past. Earlier breeding programs worked on existing arrays of genetic variability in a species, isolating specific genetic traits through selective breeding. Now scientists using rDNA technology can essentially "stack" the deck or even produce an entirely new deck of genetic "cards."

But this powerful ability to change the genetic deck of cards also raises substantial scientific concerns that some "sleight-of-hand" could produce dangerous consequences. Ethan Singer said, "Those who are powerful in society will do the shuffling; their genes will be shuffled in one direction, while the genes of the rest of us will get shuffled in another."[3] Also there is the concern that a reshuffled deck of genes might create an "Andromeda strain" similar to the one envisioned by Michael Crichton in his book by the same title.[4] A microorganism might inadvertently be given the genetic structure for some pathogen for which there is no antidote or vaccine.

In the early days of this research, scientists called for a moratorium until the risks of this new technology could be assessed. Even after the National Institute of Health issued guidelines, public fear was considerable. When Harvard University planned to construct a genetic facility for rDNA research, the mayor of Cambridge, Massachusetts, expressed his concern that "something could crawl out of the laboratory, such as a Frankenstein."[5]

The potential benefits of rDNA technology are significant. First, the technology can be used to produce medically important substances. The list of these substances is quite long and would include insulin, interferon, and human growth hormone. The technology also has great application in the field of immunology. In order to protect organisms from viral disease, doctors must inject a killed or attenuated virus. Scientists can use the new technology to disable a toxin gene, thus producing a viral substance that triggers production of antibodies without the possibility of producing the disease in the organism.

A second benefit is in the field of agriculture. This technology can improve the genetic fitness of various plant species. Basic research using this technology could increase the efficiency of photosynthesis, increase plant resistance (to salinity, to drought, to viruses), and reduce a plant's demand for nitrogen fertilizer.

Third, rDNA research can aid industrial and environmental processes. Industries that manufacture drugs, plastics, industrial chemicals, vitamins, and cheese will benefit from this technology. Also scientists have begun to develop organisms that can clean up oil spills or toxic wastes.

This last benefit, however, also raises one of the greatest scientific concerns over rDNA technology. The escape (or even intentional release) of a genetically engineered organism might wreak havoc on the environment. Scientists have created microorganisms that dissolve oil spills or reduce frost on plants. Critics of rDNA technology fear that radically altered organisms could occupy new ecological niches, destroy existing ecosystems, or drive certain species to extinction.

Legal concerns also surround this technology. The Supreme Court ruled that genetically engineered organisms as well as the genetic processes that created them can be patented. The original case involved an oil-slick eating microorganism patented by General Electric. Since 1981 the U.S. Patent and Trademark Office has approved nearly twelve thousand patents for genetic products and processes.[6] Scientists have been concerned that the prospects of profit have decreased the relatively free flow of scientific information. Often scientists-turned-entrepreneurs refuse to share their findings for fear of commercial loss.

Even more significant is the question of whether life should even be "patented" at all. Most religious leaders say no. A 1995 gathering of 187 religious leaders representing virtually every major religious tradition spoke out against the patenting of genetically engineered substances. They argued that life is the creation of God, not humans, and should not be patented as human inventions.[7]

The broader theological question is *whether* genetic engineering should be used and, if permitted, *how* it should be used. The natural reaction for many in society is to reject new forms of technology because they are dangerous. Christians, however, should take into account God's command to humankind in the cultural mandate (Gen. 1:28). Christians should avoid the reflex reaction that scientists should not tinker with life; instead Christians should consider how this technology should be used responsibly.

One key issue is the worldview behind most scientific research. Modern science rests on an evolutionary assumption. Many scientists assume that life on this planet is the result of millions of years of a chance evolutionary process. Therefore they conclude that intelligent scientists can do a better job of directing the evolutionary process than nature can do by chance. Yet even evolutionary scientists warn of this potential danger. Ethan Singer believes that scientists will "verify a few predictions, and then gradually forget that knowing something isn't the same as knowing everything. . . . At each stage we will get a little cockier, a little surer we know all the possibilities."[8]

In essence, rDNA technology gives scientists the tools they have always wanted to drive the evolutionary spiral higher and higher. Julian Huxley looked forward to the day in which scientists could fill the "position of business manager for the cosmic process of evolution."[9] Certainly this technology enables scientists to create new forms of life and alter existing forms in ways that have been impossible until now.

How should Christians respond? They should humbly acknowledge that God is the sovereign Creator and that man has finite knowledge. Genetic engineering gives scientists the technological ability to be gods, but they lack the wisdom, knowledge, and moral capacity to act like God.

Even evolutionary scientists who deny the existence of God and believe that all life is the result of an impersonal evolutionary process express concern about the potential dangers of this technology. Erwin Chargaff asked, "Have we the right to counteract, irreversibly, the evolutionary wisdom of millions of years, in order to satisfy the ambition and curiosity of a few scientists?"[10] His answer is no. The Christian's answer should also be the same when we realize that God is the Creator of life. We do not have the right to "rewrite the fifth day of creation."[11]

What is the place for genetic engineering within a biblical framework? The answer to that question can be found by distinguishing between two types of research. The first could be called genetic repair. This research attempts to remove genetic defects and develop techniques that will provide treatments for existing diseases. Applications would include various forms of genetic therapy and genetic surgery as well as modifications of existing microorganisms to produce beneficial results.

The Human Genome Project has been able to pinpoint the location and sequence of the approximately one hundred thousand human genes.[12] Further advances in rDNA technology will allow scientists to repair these defective sequences and eventually remove these genetic diseases from our population.

Genetic disease is not part of God's original plan for the world. It is the result of the Fall (Gen. 3). Christians can apply technology to fight these evils without being accused of fighting against God's will.[13] Genetic engineering can and should be used to treat and cure genetic diseases.

A second type of research is the creation of new forms of life. While minor modifications of existing organisms may be permissible, Christians should be concerned about the large-scale production of novel life forms. The potential impact on the environment and on mankind could be considerable. Science is replete with examples of what can happen when an existing organism is introduced into a new environment (e.g., the rabbit into Australia, the rat into Hawaii, or the gypsy moth into the United States). One can only imagine the potential devastation that could occur when a newly created organism is introduced into our environment.

God created plants and animals as "kinds" (Gen. 1:24). While there is minor variability within these created kinds, there are built-in barriers between these created kinds. Redesigning creatures of any kind cannot be predicted the same way new elements on the periodic chart can be predicted for properties even before they are discovered. Recombinant DNA technology offers great promise in treating genetic disease, but Christians should also be vigilant. While this technology should be used to repair genetic defects, it should not be used to confer the role of creator on scientists.

CLONING

In 1970 Paul Ramsey devoted an entire chapter to human cloning in his book *Fabricated Man.*[14] And during much of the 1970s ethicists debated the pros and cons of human cloning until scientists were able to convince nearly everyone that cloning a mammal (much less a human being) would be difficult to impossible.

All that changed when scientists in Scotland announced in 1997 that they had successfully cloned an adult sheep. Commentators were predicting that a "brave new world" was just around the corner, and ethicists began to dust off arguments that had been mothballed in the 1970s. The cloning of the sheep named Dolly implied that it might eventually be possible to clone a human being.

A few years earlier, in 1993, two scientists from George Washington University announced the first artificial twinning of human embryos. The press erroneously announced that humans had been cloned. Actually this was not the case. What the scientists did was to begin with seventeen human embryos and multiply them like the Bible's loaves and fishes into forty-eight different embryos.

When an embryo grows, the cells begin to differentiate. Only a certain part of the genetic structure is utilized to form a skin cell or an eye cell. In a sense DNA is like a CD album that will play only a single track. The genetic melody for a skin cell is the only track of the DNA that is actually played in a skin cell. The scientists in Scotland found a way to get adult cells to once again play each and every genetic note. They did this by putting them in a state of "quiescence." When the cell became dormant, all the genes once again had the potential of being played.

The scientists took normal mammary cells from an adult ewe and starved them in order to allow the cells to reach a dormant stage that apparently allowed these cells to be deprogrammed. These were then fused with an egg cell that had its nucleus removed. The cell was then electrically stimulated so that it would begin cell division.

The successful cloning of a lamb raises the question: "Wherever the lamb went, was Mary sure to follow? In other words, how soon will scientists clone humans?"[15] Scientists point out that the procedure used to clone a sheep may not work for other mammals. Human beings use nuclear DNA differently from the way sheep embryos use DNA. And similar experiments, for example, have not worked in mice. Therefore quite possibly humans may not be able to be cloned by this procedure. Nevertheless ethicists are once again considering the possibility that humans could be cloned.

The scientific concerns are significant. The procedure used to produce Dolly was very inefficient. Out of 277 cell fusions, researchers eventually produced only twenty-nine embryos that survived longer than six days. All twenty-nine embryos were implanted in ewes; thirteen became pregnant; and only one lamb was born as a result. This alone should raise pro-life concerns, considering the significant loss of human embryos that would be needed to produce one human clone.

Proponents of human cloning argue that it would be a worthwhile scientific endeavor for at least three reasons. First, cloning could be used to produce spare parts. The clone would be genetically identical to the original person, so that a donated organ would not be rejected by the immune system. Second, they argue that cloning might be a way to replace a lost child. A dying infant or child could be cloned so that a couple would replace the child with a genetically identical child. Third, cloning could produce biological immortality. One woman approached scientists to ask them to clone her deceased father and offered to carry the cloned baby to term herself.[16]

While cloning of various organisms may be ethically permissible, cloning a human being raises significant questions, beginning with the issue of the sanctity of life. Human beings are created in the image of God (Gen. 1:27) and therefore differ from animals. Human cloning would certainly threaten the sanctity of human life at a number of levels. First, cloning is an inefficient process of procreation, as shown in the cloning of a sheep. Second, cloning would no doubt produce genetic accidents. Previous experiments with frogs produced numerous embryos that did not survive, and many of those that did survive developed into grotesque monsters. Third, researchers often clone human embryos for various experiments. Although the National Bioethics Advisory Commission did ban cloning of human beings, it permitted the cloning of human embryos for research.

Since these embryos are ultimately destroyed, this research raises the same pro-life concerns discussed in the chapter on abortion.

Cloning (like artificial reproduction considered in the next chapter) represents a tampering with the reproductive process at the most basic level. Cloning a human being certainly strays substantially from God's intended procedure of a man and woman producing children within the bonds of matrimony (Gen. 2:24). All sorts of bizarre scenarios can be envisioned. Some homosexual advocates argue that cloning would be an ideal way for homosexual men to reproduce themselves.

Although this would be an alternative form of reproduction, it is reasonable to believe that human clones would still be fully human. For example, some people wonder if a clone would have a soul, since this would be such a diversion from God's intended process of procreation. A traducian view of the origin of the soul (discussed in chapter 1) would imply that a cloned human being would have a soul. In a sense a clone would be no different from an identical twin.

Human cloning, like other forms of genetic engineering, could be used to usher in a "brave new world." James Bonner says "there is nothing to prevent us from taking a thousand [cells]. We could grow any desired number of genetically identical people from individuals who have desirable characteristics."[17] Such a vision conjures up images of Alphas, Betas, Gammas, and Deltas from Aldous Huxley's book *Brave New World* (1932; reprint, New York: Time, 1963) and provides a dismal contrast to God's creation of each individual as unique.

Each person contributes to both the unity and diversity of humanity. This is perhaps best expressed by the Jewish Midrash: "For a man stamps many coins in one mold and they are all alike; but the King who is king over all kings, the Holy One blessed be he, stamped every man in the mold of the first man, yet not one of them resembles his fellow."[18] Christians should reject future research plans to clone a human being and should reject using cloning as an alternative means of reproduction.

4
Reproductive Technologies

INFERTILITY HAS ALWAYS been a devastating blow to any couple. In the past, very little could be done. But recent advances in reproductive biology now provide millions of couples with the possibility of starting a family. While some reproductive technologies raise few moral concerns, many others are fraught with substantial ethical issues.

The demand for artificial reproduction has increased for two reasons: declining levels of fertility and legalized abortion. Male infertility has increased to a level estimated to be about one in ten. Various reasons have been suggested, including environmental factors such as pesticides, chemicals in food, and heightened levels of stress.[1] Female infertility may be due to congenital, environmental, and/or behavioral factors. The latter factor has become most significant because of increased sexual activity by young women, who then sustain low-level gynecological infections that may damage their reproductive system when left untreated.[2] Approximately one in every six couples of childbearing age has an infertility problem.[3]

Legalized abortion has also been a factor in the increased interest in artificial reproduction. Ready access to abortion has significantly reduced the number of children available for adoption. Couples wanting a child began to seek medical solutions to infertility that were being developed in the 1970s and 1980s, solutions that have fueled the revolution in reproductive technologies.

Artificial insemination is used as an alternative means of reproduction when male infertility is present. It was first done with humans in 1785 in London by a doctor named John Hunter. Today there are two types of artificial insemination: using the sperm of the husband (AIH: artificial insemination by the husband) and using sperm of a donor (AID: artificial insemination by a donor). More recently artificial insemination has also been used for female infertility. Women who are fertile are impregnated with donor sperm from a husband or an outside donor so that couples can adopt children born to these surrogate mothers, who carry the baby to term essentially "for" the infertile mothers.

In vitro fertilization is also used for female infertility. Conception takes place outside the womb (which accounts for the popular term "test-tube babies"). The woman is treated with hormones to stimulate the maturation of her eggs. The eggs are removed by means of laparoscopy and placed in a dish and fertilized with sperm. After a period of time the developing embryos are surgically placed in the uterus.

Other forms of artificial reproduction include artificial sex selection, embryo transfer, and frozen embryos. Surrogate parenting is possible by using artificial insemination, in which the husband's sperm is used to impregnate a donor mother.

ARTIFICIAL INSEMINATION BY THE HUSBAND

Artificial insemination by the husband (AIH) consists of collecting the husband's sperm and injecting it into his wife. Couples often seek this procedure either because the husband is fertile but unable to participate in normal sexual relations or because the husband's sperm count is low. Periodically collecting sperm can increase the probability of pregnancy.

AIH is much less controversial than artificial insemination by a donor (AID) because it involves the husband's own sperm. Although conception is not by means of the natural sexual act, AIH does not destroy the personal and sexual aspects of the marriage bond and thus is open to less criticism. Few legal concerns surround this method, since the child is genetically related to the parents. Questions of paternity and legal status are not a problem for a child conceived by AIH.

AIH raises few theological concerns as well. The only theological issue is the question of masturbation to procure sperm. The Roman Catholic Church has objected to AIH because it separates sex from the conjugal marital relationship. According to natural law theory, procreation through means other than those natural to the conjugal act is illicit and immoral.

But to claim that masturbation in this case is sin is to remove it from its context. Although a couple does not experience the sex act together (though they can if they wish), the purpose is to provide a pregnancy and birth they will experience together. And if this poses an ethical problem for the couple, the sperm can be collected from the vagina or a condom. Thus AIH does not seem to inhibit sexual expression in the couple or to damage the marriage bond and is therefore an acceptable method of artificial reproduction.

ARTIFICIAL INSEMINATION BY A DONOR

Artificial insemination by a donor (AID) is similar to AIH except that sperm from a donor is used instead of sperm from the husband. This singular exception leads to most of the questions surrounding this reproductive procedure. Most of those concerns are legal or ethical, but others are relevant as well.

More than twenty thousand children are born each year through AID. Sperm samples are usually obtained from undergraduate students or medical students, who have their genetic history checked thoroughly. Most doctors try to match the physical characteristics of the husband with those of the sperm donor.

Couples may seek AID for one of three reasons. First, the husband may be carrying a genetic disease he does not want to pass on to his child. Second, he may be sterile as a result of a disease or accident. Third, AID might be prescribed because of a concern over an antibody reaction from the mother (the husband may be Rh positive while she is Rh negative).

However, in most cases injections of anti-Rh antibodies into the mother are sufficient to prevent damage to future Rh positive children.

The only major scientific concern with AID is the possibility of accidental incest. When the same sperm donor is used in lots of pregnancies, the potential for inbreeding increases. This is less of a concern in cities or larger communities, but looms larger in small communities, especially when the same sperm donor is used extensively. For example, researchers at the University of Wisconsin found that an average sperm donor is used for up to six pregnancies and some for as many as fifty pregnancies.[4]

Although AID has been practiced for many years, legal concerns can still surface. Most state laws concerning parent-child relations were not written with artificial insemination in mind. For that reason, sometimes the legal status of the child produced by AID can be uncertain. The major focus usually is on the legitimacy of the child. Since the child is not genetically related to the father, there is the potential that a court could declare the child illegitimate.[5]

The social concerns surrounding AID are significant. First, AID has increased the number of single-parent homes. Each year many single women use artificial insemination to bear children. A survey of physicians that appeared in the *Journal of the American Medical Association* estimated that approximately 10 percent of the AID cases involved single women. Approximately half were heterosexuals without partners; the other half were lesbians using the procedure to produce a child for their "relationship."[6]

A second problem is that AID can adversely affect the marriage relationship. The psychological impact of AID can be quite profound in many marriages. Having to resort to AID is often a blow to the husband's masculinity.[7] His inability to produce children can develop into a deep feeling of failure or inferiority within a marriage relationship.

The psychological trauma is often heightened by the fact that much of the procedure is kept secret. The couple rarely know the identity of the donor and often do not make public the fact that they have used AID. The secret gives the procedure an illicit aura and can reinforce feelings of guilt.

A couple with an AID child may have difficulty explaining "who the child looks like," since they often want to keep the procedure secret. By contrast, a couple with an adopted child has less difficulty with these problems than a couple with an AID child. One psychotherapist found that AID mothers often struggled with guilt and fear that took on "undue proportion and power within the family."[8]

The major ethical and theological concern with AID is that it introduces a third party into the pregnancy and thereby weakens the marriage bond. This is especially true when artificial insemination is used to produce children through surrogate mothers. Surrogates are usually arranged through business associations that link women solicited through newspaper ads with couples who choose them according to their physical and mental characteristics as well as ethnic and religious backgrounds.

Whether donor sperm is used (normal AID) or a donor egg and a donor womb (surrogate mother) are used, a third party is introduced into the pregnancy. God's ideal for parenthood was for a man and woman to give birth to a child who is genetically related to them. While there are obvious exceptions to that ideal (e.g., adoptions), the divine ideal should be the standard used to judge AID.

Two Old Testament examples are often cited to support AID. The first is the story of Abraham and Sarah. When Sarah could not bear a child for Abraham, she said to him, "Go, sleep with my maidservant; perhaps I can build a family through her" (Gen. 16:2). The second is the provision of the levirate marriage of the kinsman-redeemer, who was to impregnate his deceased brother's wife if there was no heir (Deut. 25:5–10).

Neither of these examples gives much support for AID. There is no indication of God's approval of the act by Abraham and Sarah. If anything, Sarah's suggestion clouded God's lesson for them. Moreover, the application of either event to today is questionable. Abraham and Sarah's example took place within a polygamous relationship and the levirate marriage law was applicable only within the Old Testament theocracy. And in both examples the unitive and procreative aspects of marriage remained intact; this is not true when AID is used.

Another theological question is whether AID is an act of adultery. Some similarities exist between the two. In normal AID, the wife becomes pregnant from someone else's sperm. In the case of surrogate parenting, the surrogate mother becomes pregnant from the husband's sperm.

But this is the only real similarity with adultery. Adultery involves sexual infidelity through a sexual relationship that exists between a married person and someone who is not his or her spouse. AID involves the transfer of gametes between consenting adults. There is no sexual contact, and there is mutual consent of the husband and wife.

The New Testament identifies two factors that constitute adultery: attitude and action. Jesus taught that "anyone who looks at a woman lustfully has already committed adultery with her in his heart" (Matt. 5:28). This attitude is not present in AID. Paul taught that a man becomes "one body" with a prostitute (1 Cor. 6:12–16). No such action is found in AID. Therefore it is inappropriate to call AID a form of adultery.

Nevertheless AID cannot be endorsed by Christians as a form of artificial reproduction. AID violates a biblical view of parenthood by introducing a third party into the pregnancy.

ARTIFICIAL SEX SELECTION

Artificial insemination has spawned a separate question: Should parents select the gender of their child? Using new sperm-separation techniques, couples can improve the probability of obtaining a child of the desired sex.

Until recently this was nothing more than science fiction. Folklore was full of stories of how to predetermine the sex of a child. Both Aristotle and the Talmud recommended placing the bed on a north-south axis for those wanting boys. Anaxagoras believed that lying on the right side (considered the superior side) would produce a boy (considered the superior sex). One folk myth said a man should hang his pants on the right bedpost in order to have a son and on the left for a daughter. One German folk tradition recommended that a man take an ax along to bed in order to produce a son and leave the ax in the woodshed to produce a daughter.

In 1970 David Rorvick wrote a book entitled *Your Baby's Sex: Now You Can Choose.*[9] It focused on certain physical indications, such as those used in the rhythm method of birth control, to increase the likelihood of having a child of a particular gender. While somewhat more effective than chance, the techniques only slightly improved the odds over the 50:50 ratio.

New techniques have now been developed based on reproductive physiology. The gender of a child is determined by the sperm of the male. Sperm with Y chromosomes will produce boys, while sperm with X chromosomes will produce girls. Researchers have found at least five methods by which to separate the two types of sperm, using such differences as sperm weight, sperm "swimming" speed, and electrical charge.

The most commonly used means is the Ericsson method developed by reproductive physiologist Ronald Ericsson more than twenty years ago. Since Y sperm tend to swim faster and stronger under certain conditions, physicians can separate them from X sperm by having them swim through a series of viscous layers. Though not totally foolproof, the method has a published success rate of 75 percent for boys and 69 percent for girls.[10]

Future advances in the technology will no doubt improve the success rate. Scientists have, for example, observed slightly different charges on the two types of sperm. By using electrical charges, they can further separate Y sperm from X sperm and thereby make the procedure even more effective.

While sex selection may be very beneficial in agriculture and animal husbandry, its application to humans is more questionable. Some couples have used it to prevent a genetic disease that might be sex-linked, but most use it simply to produce a child of the desired sex.

The social implications are significant. Research has shown that couples would choose the sex of their child if the procedure was relatively simple and inexpensive.[11] Of the couples who expressed a preference, about 90 percent wanted the firstborn to be a boy. If they could have only one child, 72 percent wanted a boy.

The actual impact on society is difficult to determine. Surveys give only a rough guideline of actual preference. Sex selection may well be influenced by social pressure and personal taste. Also, only a fraction of couples are choosing to use artificial sex selection, and the technology is not 100 percent effective. But as more couples choose this procedure and as its effectiveness increases, the impact on society could be significant.

Widespread use of sex selection could dramatically increase the number of boys. And even if the procedure did not increase the number of boys, it could certainly transform society into a nation of older brothers and younger sisters, at least subtly implying that women are second-class citizens.

An important ethical question is whether parents even have the right to determine the sex of their child. And a broader question is whether society at large has a right to decide the sex of children born into it.

At a time when more and more rights are being claimed, more parents will likely demand the right to determine the sex of their children. But will that right lead to demands for other rights? Is it not possible that the right of sex selection will eventually lead to the right of genetic specification? Selecting the gender of one's child is considered the most fundamental aspect of that child. Choosing hair color, eye color, stature, and other characteristics would be a logical next step.

Moreover, shouldn't we be concerned about sexual stereotyping? The present chauvinistic condition in the world is troubling. Selecting the sex of a child is more than just picking out blue or pink baby outfits. And preferring boys over girls has led to disastrous consequences in other countries. Selective abortion and infanticide are routinely practiced in countries like India and China, on the assumption that boys have more value than girls.

The Bible teaches that all children are a gift from God (Ps. 127:3) and are entrusted to parents for care and nurture. Parents who want control over the gender of their child should evaluate their motives and consider the possible implications of their decision, both for their family and for society.

IN VITRO FERTILIZATION

When Aldous Huxley wrote *Brave New World* in 1932, few thought that what he predicted would take place in their lifetimes. When Louise Brown, the first test-tube baby, was born on July 25, 1978, many believed a new era had arrived. While in some ways the new reproductive technologies are a fulfillment of that vision, but in most ways they are not.

In vitro fertilization (known as IVF) is a procedure that allows an egg to be fertilized and grown outside the womb for a short period of time before being implanted in the mother. With the future development of an artificial placenta, this period could be extended to perhaps the entire gestational period.

Since the initial pioneering work on IVF, many other methods have been developed in an effort to treat millions of infertile couples in the U.S.[12] These include Gamete Intrafallopian Transfer (GIFT), in which a physician using a laparoscope inserts eggs and sperm directly into a woman's fallopian tube so that fertilization can take place; Intrauterine Insemination (IUI), in which frozen sperm of the husband or a donor is inserted by a catheter into the uterus, bypassing the cervix and upper vagina; Zygote Intrafallopian Transfer (ZIFT), a two-step procedure whereby eggs are fertilized in the laboratory and any resulting zygotes are transferred to a fallopian tube; and Intracytoplasmic Sperm Injection (ICSI), in which a physician using a microscopic pipette injects a single sperm into an egg and the zygote is placed in the uterus.

Costs for these procedures vary dramatically since treatments can vary from fertility drugs to microsurgery to fairly exotic, high-tech methods. The cost of an IVF treatment can range from $6,000 to more than $50,000 per live birth.[13] A national survey of all high-tech infertility treatments found an average cost of $7,000, with a range of prices from $4,000 to $11,000 per try.[14] Usually only the rich or the well-insured can afford these reproductive technologies.

How effective are these technologies? In 1993 the 267 clinics reporting to the American Society for Reproductive Medicine initiated 41,209 assisted-reproduction procedures and 8,741 resulted in live births. That is a "success rate" of 21.2 percent.[15]

The major scientific concern with IVF has been the limited amount of prior experimentation. Critics charge that experimentation should have been done before the technique was applied to human subjects. A moratorium had been proposed on IVF in 1972 in order to have time to determine the potential risk of abnormalities. One prominent scientist said, "It is my feeling that we must be very sure we are able to produce normal young by this method in monkeys before we have the temerity to move ahead in the human."[16] Nevertheless concerns about potential abnormalities were quickly pushed aside as more and more test-tube babies were born.

A number of legal concerns have arisen from these reproductive procedures. The 1981 case of Mario and Elsa Rios demonstrates the legal tangle that can develop. The Rioses wanted children and went to a clinic in Australia. Three of Mrs. Rios's eggs were fertilized in vitro with sperm from an anonymous sperm donor. One was implanted and the other two were frozen. Ten days later the implanted embryo spontaneously aborted. But before the clinic could implant the other two, the Rioses were killed in a plane crash in South America.

Two kinds of questions surfaced. First, did these frozen embryos have a right to inheritance, and do they have a right to life? Mr. and Mrs. Rios were multimillionaires. Were those embryos potential millionaires? Did they have a right to inherit the Rioses fortune? Second, did those frozen embryos even have a right to life? Are IVF clinics obliged to protect embryos produced there? Should the Australian clinic implant those embryos in a surrogate mother who would carry them to term?

Other questions surfaced as well. For example, who would be the legal father and mother? Here are Mr. Rios, Mrs. Rios, an anonymous sperm donor, a surrogate mother, and possibly an adoptive father and mother. The child that would be born could have as many as six "potential parents."

Questions of paternity especially loom large with surrogate parenting. The most famous case was the battle of custody over "Baby M." William and Elizabeth Stern entered into a contract with Mary Beth Whitehead to carry their child. As her pregnancy progressed, Mrs. Whitehead began to have doubts and developed the inevitable maternal feelings a mother would expect to have for a child she is carrying. She decided to keep the child and forced a judge in New Jersey to resolve this modern-day "Solomon dilemma."

The reverse of the "Solomon dilemma" also occurred. This was a case in which neither the couple nor the surrogate mother wanted the child. Alexander Malahoff contracted with Judy Stiver to be a surrogate mother for his child. Unfortunately young Christopher was born with an infection and microcephaly. Malahoff disavowed the child and threatened to sue. The issue was uncertain, and the child remained in a foster-care facility. Then, during the airing of the *Phil Donahue Show,* blood and tissue tests were brought forward revealing that the child was Judy Stiver's and her husband's. They were required to raise the child.

The various legal issues surrounding IVF and related procedures merely underscore the proliferating nature of the technology. Reproductive endocrinologist Martin Quigley distinguishes "old fashioned IVF" from these newer forms. "The modern way," he notes, "mixes and matches donors and recipients."[17] A woman's egg could be fertilized by a donor's sperm or a donor's egg might be fertilized by the husband's sperm. Any of these matches could then be placed in the wife or in a surrogate mother. The reproductive possibilities are staggering.

The surrogate mother could actually be a surrogate grandmother. In 1988 Pat Anthony, a forty-nine-year-old grandmother in South Africa, was able to give birth to her own grandchildren. She was implanted with her daughter's eggs, which had been fertilized in the laboratory, and subsequently gave birth to triplets.[18]

As this example shows, age may no longer be a limitation for women wanting to become pregnant. Physicians have been able to take an egg from a younger woman and implant it in an older woman (one woman in her sixties gave birth in this way), even if she has been through menopause. Egg donation is also becoming more widely available and accepted as egg brokerage houses match recipients with donors.[19]

Some reproductive technologies open up the possibility of female reproduction without male involvement. Initial research on egg fusion at Vanderbilt University demonstrated the future possibility of taking an egg from one woman and fusing it with the egg of another woman.[20] The procedure has attracted the attention of lesbian groups because the procedure would produce a girl who is genetically related to both of the women who donated an egg.

A major ethical concern with IVF and other forms of reproductive technology is the status and loss of embryos. The low success rate of some of the procedures and the willingness of some clinics to fertilize many eggs and then choose a likely candidate for implantation raise moral questions about the status of the unborn who are being produced by artificial reproduction. Proponents argue that the loss is not excessive. Opponents argue that any loss of embryos is unacceptable, or they call for at least defining an acceptable level of success.

Another ethical concern is with the proliferating technologies. While IVF may be less ethically problematic, it has spawned a whole array of technologies that allow for mixing and matching genetic material and implanting in different women. The possible arrangements are nearly limitless, but the ethical consequences of many of these arrangements are questionable.

BIBLICAL PERSPECTIVES

Providing a comprehensive answer to IVF and the associated reproductive technologies is becoming more difficult because of the rapid proliferation of such technologies. A better way to discern the ethics of these procedures is to consider each of them in light of the following biblical principles.

The first principle is the sanctity of all human life. Human beings are created in the image of God (Gen. 1:27) and therefore have dignity and value. God's special care and protection extend even to unborn children (Ps. 139:13–16). Reproductive technologies that threaten the sanctity of human life come under the same criticism as abortion.

The sanctity of life may be threatened in at least three ways. First, there is the potential loss of fetal life. Some reproductive technologies are very inefficient and therefore result in an unacceptable loss of life. Second, there is the practice of destroying fertilized ova if they appear abnormal. Third, there is the practice of hyperfertilization, in which many eggs are fertilized simultaneously, one is selected for implantation, and the others are thrown away.

This is a concern not only for the clinical use of embryos; it also concerns the research use of embryos. In the past a moratorium was placed on research by means of embryo and fetal experimentation. The Clinton administration has lifted the ban and federal funding has been recommended for research on human embryos up to fourteen days after fertilization.[21] This research also violates the biblical principle of the sanctity of human life.

A second principle is a biblical view of sexual relations (Gen. 2:24). Many reproductive technologies separate the unitive from the procreative aspects of human reproduction. Sexual intimacy, the communication of love, and the desire for children are supposed to be unified within the bounds of matrimony. Artificial reproduction frequently separates these functions and thus poses a potential threat to the completeness God intended for marriage. While some ethicists believe that such an intervention is sufficient reason to reject all reproductive technologies, most others accept such an intervention as permissible if other ethical problems are not present.

A third principle is a biblical view of parenthood (Gen. 1:28). God ordained marriage as the union of a man and a woman who would give birth to a child that is genetically related to them. While there are exceptions to this ideal, this standard should be used to judge reproductive technologies. As stated earlier, procedures such as surrogate parenting and embryo transfer clearly introduce a third party into the pregnancy and affect the marriage bond.

Motherhood may also be affected. Childbearing would no longer be a natural outcome of procreation if these technologies were widely used. The proliferation of surrogate mothers blurs the true relationship between procreation and parenthood. God intends that the family thrive (Eph. 6:1–4; Col. 3:18–21), and some of these procedures pose a threat to the stability of the family.

By contrast, a family can survive without children. God determines birth (Gen. 4:1; 17:16; Ruth 4:13) and is in control over even barren wombs (Deut. 7:14). Childless women are not displeasing to God, as the testimonies of Sarah (Gen. 18), Rachel (Gen. 29–30), Hannah (1 Sam. 1), and Anna (Luke 2:36–38) attest. God is in control and can bring great blessing out of the heartbreak of infertility.

Couples considering artificial reproduction should also consider other less ethically questionable options. These include medical options such as reconstructive surgery (tuboplasty) and drug treatments, adoption, foster care, or remaining childless and having more time for a church or community ministry.

Fundamental to all this should be an attitude of seeking the Lord's will. Abraham and Sarah asked the Lord for a child (Gen. 18). When He did not meet their timetable, they took matters into their own hands, with disastrous results. By contrast Hannah (1 Sam. 1) sought the Lord and was patient for His provision. Before a couple seeks medical counsel, they should first seek the Lord's will and then count the costs and consider the ethical issues involved.

5
Sexual Promiscuity

Eᴀᴄʜ ᴅᴀʏ approximately seventy-seven hundred teenagers relinquish their virginity. In the process many will become pregnant and many more will contract a sexually transmitted disease (STD). Already one in four Americans have an STD, and this percentage is increasing each year.

The reason for the increase in sexual promiscuity is both philosophical and cultural. In the last few decades society has shifted from a Judeo-Christian foundation to a secular one. This philosophical shift has been accelerated by two cultural forces. The first is the entertainment media (television, movies, rock music, MTV)—a topic that will be discussed further in chapter 16. The second is the area of sex education (sex education classes, school-based clinics). These two forces have transformed the social landscape of America and made promiscuity a virtue and virginity a "problem" to be solved.

TEENAGE SEXUALITY

America faces a teenage sexuality crisis. Consider these alarming statistics of children having children. A *New York Times* article reported, "Some studies indicate three-fourths of all girls have had sex during their teenage years and 15 percent have had four or more partners."[1] A Louis Harris poll commissioned by Planned Parenthood discovered that 46 percent of sixteen-year-olds and 57 percent of seventeen-year-olds have had sexual intercourse.[2]

Moreover, these numbers are not skewed by impoverished, inner-city youths from broken homes. One New York polling firm posed questions to thirteen hundred students in sixteen high schools in suburban areas in order to get a reading of "mainstream" adolescent attitudes. They discovered that 57 percent lost virginity in high school and 79 percent lost virginity by the end of college. The average age when the respondents first had sex was 16.9. Thirty-three percent of the high school students said they had sex once a month to once a week, and 52 percent of college students had sex once a month to once a week.[3]

Former Secretary of Education William Bennett, in speaking to the National School Board Association, warned that "the statistics by which we measure how our children—how our boys and girls—are treating one another sexually are little short of staggering."[4] Here are just a few of the heartbreaking statistics from his message:

- More than one-half of America's young people have had sexual intercourse by the time they are seventeen.

- More than one million teenage girls in the U.S. become pregnant each year. Of those who give birth, nearly half are not yet eighteen.

- Teen pregnancy rates are at an all-time high. A 25 percent decline in birth rates between 1970 and 1984 is due to a doubling of the abortion rate during that period. More than four hundred thousand teenage girls now have abortions each year.

- Unwed teenage births rose 200 percent between 1960 and 1980.

- Forty percent of today's fourteen-year-old girls will become pregnant by the time they are nineteen.

"These numbers," Bennett concluded, "are an irrefutable indictment of sex education's effectiveness in reducing teenage sexual activity and pregnancies."

Kids are trying sex at an earlier age than ever before. More than a third of fifteen-year-old boys have had sexual intercourse, as have 27 percent of the fifteen-year-old girls. Among sexually active teenage girls, 61 percent have had multiple partners.[5] The reasons for such early sexual experimentation are many.

Biology is one reason. Teenagers are maturing faster sexually because of better health and nutrition. Since the turn of the century, for example, the onset of menstruation in girls has dropped three months each decade. Consequently, urges that used to arise in the mid-teens now explode in the early teens. Meanwhile the typical age of first marriage has increased more than four years since the 1950s.

A sex-saturated society is another reason. Sex is used to sell everything from cars to toothpaste. Sexual innuendo clutters almost every TV program and movie. The explicit nudity and sensuality that used to be reserved for R-rated movies has found its way into homes through broadcast and cable television. Media researchers calculate that teenagers see approximately five hours of television each day. This means they have seen nearly fourteen thousand sexual encounters within a year just on television.

Lack of parental supervision and direction is a third reason. Working parents and reductions in after-school programs have left teenagers with less supervision and a looser after-school life. In the inner city, the scarcity of jobs and parents coupled with a cynical view of the future invites teenage promiscuity and its inevitable consequences. Adolescent boys in the suburbs trying to prove their masculinity herd into groups like the infamous score-keeping Spur Posse gang in California.

Even when teenagers want to sit out the sexual revolution, they often get little help from parents, who may be too embarrassed or intimidated to talk to their children. Parents, in fact, often lag behind their kids in sexual information. At one sex-education workshop held by Girls Inc. (formerly Girls Club of America), nearly half of the mothers had never seen a condom. Other mothers did not want to talk about sex because they were molested as children and were fearful of talking about sex with their daughters.[6]

Teenagers are also getting mixed messages. In any given week they are likely to hear contradictory messages. "No sex until you're married." "No sex unless you're older." "No sex unless you're protected." "No sex unless you're in love." No wonder adolescents are confused.

SEX EDUCATION

For more than thirty years proponents of comprehensive sex education have argued that giving sexual information to young children and adolescents would reduce the number of unplanned pregnancies and sexually transmitted diseases. In that effort nearly three billion dollars have been spent on federal Title X family planning services; yet teenage pregnancies and abortions keep rising.

Perhaps one of the most devastating popular critiques of comprehensive sex education came from Barbara Dafoe Whitehead. The journalist who said that Dan Quayle was right also was willing to say that sex education was wrong. Her article "The Failure of Sex Education" in the October 1994 issue of *Atlantic Monthly* demonstrated that sex education neither reduced pregnancy nor slowed the spread of STDs.[7]

Comprehensive sex-education is mandated in at least seventeen states, so Whitehead chose one of those states and focused her analysis on the sex education experiment in New Jersey. Like other curricula the New Jersey sex-education program rested on certain questionable assumptions.

The first is that children are "sexual from birth." Sex educators reject the classic notion of a latency period until approximately age twelve. They argue that you are "being sexual when you throw your arms around your grandpa and give him a hug."

Second, children are sexually miseducated. Parents, to put it simply, have not done their job, so we need "professionals" to do it right. Parents try to protect their children, fail to affirm their sexuality, and even discuss sexuality in a context of moralizing. The media, they say, is also guilty of providing sexual misinformation.

Third, if miseducation is the problem, then sex education in the schools is the solution. Parents are failing miserably at the task, so "it is time to turn the job over to the schools. Schools occupy a safe middle ground between Mom and MTV."[8]

Learning about Family Life is the curriculum used in New Jersey. While it discusses such things as sexual desire, AIDS, divorce, condoms, and masturbation, it nearly ignores such issues as abstinence, marriage, self-control, and virginity. One technique promoted to prevent pregnancy and STDs is noncoital sex, or what some sex educators call "outercourse." Yet there is good evidence to suggest that teaching teenagers to explore their sexuality through noncoital techniques will lead to coitus. Ultimately, outercourse will lead to intercourse.

Whitehead concluded that comprehensive sex education has been a failure. For example, the percent of teenage births to unwed mothers was 67 percent in 1980 and rose to 84 percent in 1991. In the place of this failed curriculum, Whitehead described a better program. She found that "sex education works best when it combines clear messages about behavior with strong moral and logistical support for the behavior sought."[9] One example she cited is the Postponing Sexual Involvement program at Grady Memorial Hospital in Atlanta, Georgia, which offers more than a "Just say no" message. It reinforces the message by having adolescents practice the desired behavior and enlists the aid of older teenagers to teach younger teenagers how to resist sexual advances. Whitehead also found that "religiously observant teens" are less likely to experiment sexually, thus providing an opportunity for church-related programs to help stem the tide of teenage pregnancy.

Contrast this, however, with what has been derisively called "the condom gospel." Sex educators today promote the dissemination of sex-education information and the distribution of condoms to deal with the problems of teen pregnancy and STDs.

THE CASE AGAINST CONDOMS

At the 1987 World Congress of Sexologists, Theresa Crenshaw asked the audience, "If you had the available partner of your dreams and knew that person carried HIV, how many of you would have sex, depending on a condom for your protection?" None of the eight hundred members of the audience raised their hand.[10] If condoms do not eliminate the fear of HIV-infection for sexologists and sex educators, why encourage the children of America to play STD Russian roulette?

Are condoms a safe and effective way to reduce pregnancy and STDs? Sex educators seem to think so. Every day sex-education classes throughout this country promote condoms as a means of safe sex or at least safer sex. But the research on condoms provides no such guarantee.

For example, Texas researcher Susan Weller, writing in the 1993 issue of *Social Science Medicine*, evaluated all research published prior to July 1990 on condom effectiveness. She reported that condoms are only 87 percent effective in preventing pregnancy and 69 percent effective in reducing the risk of HIV infection.[11] This 69 percent effectiveness rate is the same as a 31 percent failure rate in preventing AIDS transmission. And according to a study in the 1992 *Family Planning Perspectives*, 15 percent of married couples who use only condoms for birth control end up with an unplanned pregnancy within the first year.[12]

So why has condom distribution become the centerpiece of the U.S. AIDS policy and the most frequently promoted aspect of comprehensive sex education? For many years the answer to that question was a prior commitment to condoms and a safe-sex message over an abstinence message. But in recent years sex educators and public health officials have been pointing to one study that seemed to vindicate the condom policy.

The study was presented at the Ninth International Conference on AIDS held in Berlin on June 9, 1993. The study involved 304 couples with one partner who was HIV positive. Of the 123 couples who used condoms with each act of sexual intercourse, not a single negative HIV partner became positive.[13] So proponents of condom distribution thought they had scientific vindication for their views.

Unfortunately that is not the whole story. Condoms do appear to be effective in stopping the spread of AIDS when used "correctly and consistently." Most individuals, however, do not use them "correctly and consistently." What happens to them? Well, it turns out that part of the study received much less attention. Of 122 couples who could not be taught to use condoms properly, 12 became HIV positive in both partners. Undoubtedly, over time even more partners would contract AIDS.

And how well does this study apply to the general population? Not very well. This study group was quite dissimilar from the general population. For example, they knew the HIV status of their spouse and therefore had a vested interest in protecting themselves. They were responsible partners and in a committed monogamous relationship. In essence their actions and attitudes differed dramatically from teenagers and single adults who do not know the HIV status of their partners, are often reckless, and have multiple sexual partners.

The study does show that condoms will reduce the risk of STDs if they are used correctly and consistently. But what percentage of the population will use condoms in that way, especially when they begin to understand the strict requirements that must be met? Dr. Nicholas Fiumara, director of the Massachusetts Department of Public Health, explains the conditions necessary for condoms to work. For condoms to be effective, "there is no preliminary sex play, the condom is intact before use, the condom is put on correctly and taken off correctly. However, the male population has never been able to fulfill the very first requirement."[14]

Indeed, how many will fulfill that requirement each and every time? Contrary to claims by sex educators, condom education does not significantly change sexual behavior. The April 1988 *American Journal of Public Health* stated that a yearlong effort at condom education in San Francisco schools resulted in only 8 percent of the boys and 2 percent of the girls using condoms every time they had sex.[15]

And even when sexual partners use condoms, sometimes condoms fail. Most consumers do not know that the FDA quality-control standards allow for a maximum failure rate of four per one thousand using a water fill test. Electron micrographs reveal voids five microns in size (about fifty times larger than the HIV virus), with some inherent flaws as large as fifty, microns.

The Department of Health and Human Services reports that "one of every five batches of condoms tested in a government inspection program over the last four months failed to meet the minimum standards for leaks."[16] Present FDA standards allow up to four condoms per thousand to leak water in batches deemed acceptable for sale to the public.[17] Many health professionals question the relevance of pouring ten ounces of water in a condom, especially when some data show that leakage in condoms is higher in biological situations.

And even if condoms are used correctly, do not break, and do not leak, they are still far from 100 percent effective. The Medical Institute for Sexual Health reported that "medical studies confirm that condoms do not offer much, if any, protection in the transmission of chlamydia and human papillomavirus, two serious STDs with prevalence as high as 40 percent among sexually active teenagers."[18]

Nevertheless condoms have become the centerpiece of U.S. AIDS policy and the major recommendation of most sex-education classes in America. Many sex educators have stopped calling their curricula "safe sex" and have renamed them "safer sex"—focusing instead on various risk reduction methods. But is this false sense of security and protection actually increasing the risks young people face? Victor Cline, professor of psychology at the University of Utah, thinks so. He believes the condoms-equal-safe-sex message is offering kids a deadly false sense of security:

> If kids buy the notion that if they just use condoms they will be safe from AIDS or any other sexually transmitted disease whenever they have sex, they are being seriously misled. They should be correctly informed that having sex with any partner having the AIDS virus is life-threatening, condoms or no condoms. It would be analogous to playing Russian roulette with two bullets in your six chambers. Using condoms removes only one of the bullets. The gun still remains deadly with the potential of lethal outcome.[19]

School-Based Health Clinics

As comprehensive sex education curricula have been promoted in the schools, clinics have been established to provide teens greater access to birth-control information and devices. Proponents cite studies that supposedly demonstrate the effectiveness of these clinics on teen sexual behavior. Yet a more careful evaluation of the statistics involved suggests that school-based health clinics do not lower the teen pregnancy rate.

The first major study to receive nationwide attention was DuSable High School. School administrators were rightly alarmed that before the establishment of a school-based health clinic, three hundred of their one thousand female students became pregnant. After the clinic was opened, the media widely reported that the number of pregnant students dropped to thirty-five.

As more facts came to light, it appeared clear that the claims had seemed to have been embellished. School officials admitted that they kept no records of the number of pregnancies before the operation of the clinic and that three hundred was merely an estimate. Moreover, school officials could not produce statistics for the number of abortions the girls received as a result of the clinic.

The most often cited study involved the experience of a clinic at Mechanics Arts High School in St. Paul, Minnesota. Researchers found that a drop in the number of teen births during the late 1970s coincided with an increase in female participation at the school-based clinics. But at least three important issues undermine the validity of this study.

First, some of the statistics are anecdotal rather than statistical. School officials admitted that the schools could not document the decrease in pregnancies. Douglas Kirby acknowledged that "most of the evidence for the success of that program [school-based clinics] is based upon the clinic's own records and the staff's knowledge of births among students. Thus, the data undoubtedly do not include all births."[20]

Second, an analysis of the data done by Michael Schwartz of the Free Congress Foundation found that the total female enrollment of the two schools included in the study dropped from 1268 in 1977 to 948 in 1979.[21] Therefore the reduction in reported births could have been merely attributable to an overall decline in the female population at the school.

Third, the study actually shows a drop in the teen birthrate rather than the teen pregnancy rate. The reduction in the fertility rate listed in the study was likely due to more teenagers obtaining an abortion.

Today, more and more advocates of school-based health clinics are citing a three-year study headed by Laurie Zabin at Johns Hopkins University, which evaluated the effect of sex education on teenagers. The study of two school-based clinics in Baltimore, Maryland, showed there was a 30 percent reduction in teen pregnancies.[22]

But even this study leaves many unanswered questions. The size of the sample was small to begin with, and over 30 percent of the female sample dropped out between the first and last measurement periods. Since the study did not control for student mobility, critics point out that some of the girls who dropped out of the study may have dropped out of school because they were pregnant. Others were not accounted for with follow-up questionnaires. Other researchers point out that the word *abortion* is never mentioned in the brief report, leading them to conclude that only live births were counted.

On the other hand, an extensive, national study done by the Institute for Research and Evaluation shows that community-based clinics used by teenagers actually increase teen pregnancy. A two-year study by Joseph Olsen and Stan Weed found that teenage participation in these clinics lowered teen birthrates. But when pregnancies ending in miscarriage or abortion were factored in, the total teen pregnancy rates increased by as much as 120 pregnancies per 1,000 clients.[23] When their research was challenged because of their use of weighting techniques and reliance on statewide data, Olsen and Weed reworked the data to answer these objections for a second report and found that their conclusion stood.

Douglas Kirby, former director of the Center for Population Options, released the results of their study of school-based health clinics. Even though committed to comprehensive sex education and school-based clinics, he had to admit the following: "We have been engaged in a research project for several years on the impact of school-based clinics. . . . We find basically that there is no measurable impact upon the use of birth control, not upon pregnancy rates or birthrates."[24]

SEX EDUCATION DOES NOT WORK

The problem is simple: Education is not the answer. Teaching comprehensive sex education, distributing condoms, and establishing school-based clinics is not effective. When the audience is made up of impressionable teens entering puberty, explicit sex education does more to entice than educate. Teaching them the "facts" about sex without providing any moral framework merely breaks down mental barriers of shame and innocence and encourages teens to experiment sexually.

A Louis Harris poll conducted for Planned Parenthood found that the highest rates of teen sexual activity were among those who had comprehensive sex education, as opposed to those who had less.[25] In the 1980s a congressional study found that a decade and a half of comprehensive "safe-sex" education resulted in a doubling in the number of sexually active teenage women.[26]

Perhaps the most disturbing statistic comes from Deborah Anne Dawson, a survey research consultant. Writing in Planned Parenthood's *Family Planning Perspectives*, she concluded that "prior contraceptive education increases the odds of starting intercourse [at the age of 14] by a factor of 1.5."[27] While a factor of 1.5 might not seem like much, it is in actuality a 50 percent increase. In other words comprehensive sex education increases a teenager's likelihood of sexual activity (thus increasing a girl's chances of pregnancy and STDs) by 50 percent.

Sex-education programs do not prevent pregnancy; they promote it. Education does not reduce the likelihood of getting pregnant and contracting disease; it increases it. Students' heads may be full of facts about preventing pregnancy, but that does not necessarily change their behavior. A *New York Times* writer vividly illustrated this as she began her story about teenage pregnancy by relating a personal experience: "I was sitting at a table with half a dozen 16-year-old girls, listening with some amazement as they showed off their knowledge of human sexuality. They knew how long sperm lived inside the body and how many women out of 100 using a diaphragm were statistically likely to get pregnant. One girl recited the steps of the ovulation cycle from day one to day twenty-eight. There was just one problem with this performance. Every one of the girls was pregnant."[28]

Our society today is filled with teenagers and young adults who know a lot about human sexuality. It is probably fair to say that they know more about sex than any generation that has preceded them, but education is not enough. Sex education can increase the knowledge students have about sexuality, but it does not necessarily affect their values or behavior. Since 1970 the federal government has spent nearly three billion dollars on Title X sex-education programs. During that period of time nonmarital teen births have increased 61 percent and the nonmarital pregnancy rate of the fifteen-to-nineteen-year-old girls has increased 87 percent.[29]

Douglas Kirby wrote these disturbing observations in the *Journal of School Health*:

> Past studies of sex education suggest several conclusions. They indicate that sex education programs can increase knowledge, but they also

indicate that most programs have relatively little impact on values, particularly values regarding one's personal behavior. They also indicate that programs do not affect the incidence of sexual activity. According to one study, sex education programs may increase the use of birth control among some groups, but not among others. Results from another study indicate they have no measurable impact on the use of birth control. According to one study, they are associated with lower pregnancy rates, while another study indicates they are not. Programs certainly do not appear to have as dramatic an impact on behavior as professionals once had hoped.[30]

ABSTINENCE IS THE ANSWER

Less than a decade ago an abstinence-only program was rare in public schools. Today directive abstinence programs can be found in many school districts, while battles are fought in other school districts for their inclusion or removal. While proponents of abstinence programs run for school board membership or seek to influence existing school board members, groups like Planned Parenthood bring lawsuits against districts that use abstinence-based curricula, arguing that they are inaccurate or incomplete. At least a dozen abstinence-based curricula are on the market, with the largest being *Sex Respect* (Bradley, Ill.) and *Teen-Aid* (Spokane, Wash.).

The emergence of abstinence-only programs as an alternative to comprehensive sex-education programs was due to both popularity and politics. Parents concerned about the ineffectiveness of the safe-sex message eagerly embraced the message of abstinence, and political funding helped spread the message and legitimize its educational value. The Adolescent Family Life Act enacted in 1981 by the Reagan Administration created Title XX and set aside $2 million a year for the development and implementation of abstinence-based programs. Although the Clinton administration later cut funding for abstinence programs, the earlier funding in the 1980s helped groups like Sex Respect and Teen-Aid launch abstinence programs in the schools.

Parents and children have embraced the abstinence message in significant numbers. One national poll by the University of Chicago found that 68 percent of adults surveyed said premarital sex among teenagers is "always wrong."[31] A 1994 poll for *USA Weekend* asked more than twelve hundred teens and adults what they thought of "several high profile athletes [who] are saying in public that they have abstained from sex before marriage and are telling teens to do the same." Seventy-two percent of the teens and 78 percent of the adults said they agreed with the pro-abstinence message.[32]

Their enthusiasm for abstinence-only education is well-founded. Even though the abstinence message has been criticized by some as naive or inadequate, there are good reasons to promote abstinence in schools and society.

First, teenagers want to learn about abstinence. Contrary to the often-repeated teenage claim, not "everyone is doing it." A 1992 study by the Centers for Disease Control found that 43 percent of teenagers from ages fourteen to seventeen had engaged in sexual intercourse at least once.[33] Put another way, the latest surveys suggest that a majority of teenagers are *not* "doing it." A majority of teenagers are abstaining from sex; also more want help in staying sexually pure in a sex-saturated society. Emory University surveyed one thousand sexually experienced teen girls by asking them what they would like to learn to reduce teen pregnancy. Nearly 85 percent said, "How to say no without hurting the other person's feelings."[34]

While serving as Secretary of Education, William Bennett delivered a speech to the National School Board Association and commented about this study. "A teen service program at Atlanta Grady Memorial Hospital, for example, found that of the girls under age sixteen surveyed, nine out of ten wanted to learn how to say "no." Let me underline this. This is not just Reagan and Bennett talking—it's girls under sixteen talking. Well, one way to help them to say "no" is for adults who care to teach them the reasons to say "no" and to give them the necessary moral support and encouragement to keep on saying it."[35]

Second, abstinence prevents pregnancy. Proponents of abstinence-only programs argue that abstinence will significantly lower the teenage pregnancy rate, and they cite numerous anecdotes and statistics to make their case. Consider the following examples.

- After the San Marcos Junior High in San Marcos, California, adopted the Teen-Aid abstinence-only program, the school's pregnancy rate dropped from 147 to 20 in a two-year period.[36]

- An abstinence-only program for girls in Washington, D.C., has seen only one of four hundred girls become pregnant. Elayne Bennett, director of "Best Friends," says that between twenty and seventy pregnancies are common for this age group in the District of Columbia.[37]

- Nathan Hale Middle School near Chicago adopted the abstinence-only program Project Taking Charge to combat its pregnancy rate among eighth-graders. Although adults were skeptical, the school graduated three pregnancy-free classes in a row.[38]

- Evaluations of the Sex Respect programs reveal a pregnancy rate of only 5 percent—far lower than that of a typical safe-sex program.[39]

Critics of abstinence programs believe it is not realistic to teach abstinence when young people are sexually active; these critics often question the statistics cited by proponents of abstinence. They question the methodology of the studies and note they are not subjected to peer-review journals. The *San Diego Union* looked into the success story from San Marcos, California, where the pregnancy rate supposedly went from 147, to only 20. The reporter was not able to document the 20 figure.[40]

Sex Respect notes that Stan Weed is working on articles concerning the effectiveness of the Sex Respect program that will be submitted to peer-review journals.[41] Teen-Aid's response to the *San Diego Union* story is that the reporter did not talk to the right people and that the 147 figure and the 20 figure are the school district's figures. Nevertheless, abstinence proponents need more respectable studies if they are to effectively build their case for abstinence-only programs.

Third, abstinence prevents sexually transmitted diseases (STDs). After more than three decades the sexual revolution has taken lots of prisoners. Before 1960, doctors were concerned about only two STDs: syphilis and gonorrhea. Today there are more than twenty significant STDs, ranging from the relatively harmless to the fatal. Twelve million Americans are newly infected each year, and 63 percent of these new infections are in people under twenty-five years of age. Eighty percent of those infected with an STD have absolutely no symptoms.[42]

Many Americans have not even heard of some of the newest STDs. Chlamydia first appeared in increasing numbers in the 1970s and is now the most common bacterial STD in the country. The human papilloma virus (HPV) increased dramatically in the 1980s; it can result in venereal warts and can lead to deadly cancers. By the early 1990s pelvic inflammatory disease (PIV) was affecting one million new women each year. The inevitable scarred fallopian tubes contributed to infertility and the shocking rise in tubal pregnancies. And of course there are the better known STDs such as AIDS, herpes, and resistant forms of venereal diseases, which have brought so much fear and concern into our society.

Even less known to most Americans is the fact that teenagers face a greater risk from STDs than do the general population. For example, a teenage girl's cervix has a lining that produces mucus that provides a growth medium for viruses and bacteria. As a girl reaches her twenties or has a baby, this lining is replaced with a tougher, more resistant lining. This biological difference puts teenage women at greater risk for contracting an STD. A sexually active fifteen-year-old girl has a one in eight chance of developing PIV, while a twenty-four-year-old girl has a one in eighty chance under the same circumstances.

Doctors warn that if a person has sexual intercourse with another sexually active individual, he or she is not only having sexual intercourse with that person but also with every person with whom that individual might have had intercourse for the last ten years, as well as all the people with whom *they* had intercourse. If that is true, then consider the case of one sixteen-year-old girl who was responsible for 218 cases of gonorrhea and more than 300 cases of syphilis. According to the reporter, this illustrates the rampant transmission of STDs through multiple sex partners. "The girl had sex with sixteen men. Those men had sex with other people who had sex with other people. The number of contacts finally added up to 1,660." As one person interviewed in the story asked, "What if the girl had had AIDS instead of gonorrhea or syphilis? You probably would have had 1,000 dead people by now."[43]

Abstinence prevents the spread of STDs, while safe-sex programs do not. Condoms are not always effective even when they are used correctly and consistently, and most sexually active people do not use them correctly and consistently. Sex-education programs have begun to promote "outercourse" instead of intercourse, but many STDs can be spread even through this method, and, as stated, outercourse almost always leads to intercourse. Abstinence is the only way to prevent the spread of a sexually transmitted disease.

Fourth, abstinence prevents emotional scars. Abstinence speakers relate dozens and dozens of stories of young people who wish they had postponed sex until marriage. Sex is the most intimate form of bonding known to the human race, and it is a special gift to be given to one's spouse. Unfortunately too many throw it away and are filled with feelings of regret.

Surveys of young adults show that most of those who have engaged in sexual activity regret their earlier promiscuity and wish they had been virgins on their wedding night. Even secular agencies that promote a safe-sex approach acknowledge that sex brings regrets. A Roper poll of high schoolers conducted in association with SIECUS (Sexuality Information and Education Council of the United States) found that 62 percent of the sexually experienced girls said they "should have waited."[44]

Fifth, abstinence builds strong marriages. Saving sex for marriage not only prevents pregnancy, STDs, and emotional scars; it also contributes to a strong marriage. Premarital sex and cohabitation do not provide a strong foundation for marriage. One study published in the *Journal of Marriage and the Family* found that "cohabiting unions are much less stable than [unions] that begin as marriages." Specifically, 40 percent of cohabiting unions disrupt before marriage, and marriages that began as cohabiting unions have a 50 percent higher disruption rate than those that did not.[45]

Abstinence before marriage seems to lead to better sex within marriage. A 1992 University of Chicago survey of Americans between the ages of eighteen and fifty-nine found that monogamous married couples register the highest levels of sexual satisfaction. According to the survey 87 percent of all monogamous marrieds report that they are "extremely" or "very" physically satisfied by their sexual relationship, and 85 percent report that they are "extremely" or "very" emotionally satisfied. Those who were least satisfied sexually (both physically and emotionally) are those singles and marrieds who had multiple partners.[46]

Religious commitment also seems to be an important ingredient in a good marriage and a good sex life. A 1975 study of more than one hundred thousand women by *Redbook* magazine found that strongly-religious women are less likely to engage in sexual behavior before marriage and are more likely to describe their current sex lives as "good" or "very good" than moderately religious or nonreligious women. The study also found that strongly religious women are "more responsive" sexually than other women.[47]

Society is ready for the abstinence message, and it needs to be promoted widely. Anyone walking on the Washington Mall in July 1993 could not miss the acres of "True Love Waits" pledge cards signed by over two hundred thousand teenagers. The campaign, begun by the Southern Baptist Convention, provided a brief but vivid display of the desire by teenagers to stand for purity and promote abstinence. For every teenager who signed a card pledging abstinence, there are no doubt dozens of others who plan to do the same.

Teenagers want and need to hear the message of abstinence. They want to promote the message of abstinence. Their health, and even their lives, are at stake.

6
Crime and Punishment

AMERICANS ARE AFRAID. The scary orgy of violent crime has made many citizens afraid to walk the streets in front of their homes. And this fear has fueled a public cry to end the killing fields in America. Americans have had enough, and they want to know why known criminals are let back out on the streets so they can kill thousands of innocent Americans.

Bombings in Oklahoma City and at the World Trade Tower, serial killers stalking playgrounds and train cars, and drive-by shootings in supposedly safe neighborhoods all conspire to strike fear in the hearts of law-abiding citizens. Each new headline or news story serves as a profound reminder of how our world has changed. No longer can we take safety and security for granted.

How bad has crime become? Listen to the ticks of the crime clock: one murder every twenty-two minutes, one rape every five minutes, one robbery every forty-nine seconds, and one burglary every ten seconds.[1] And the cost of crime continues to mount: $78 billion for the criminal justice system, $64 billion for private protection, $202 billion in loss of life and work, $120 billion in crimes against business, $60 billion in stolen goods and fraud, $40 billion from drug abuse, and $110 billion from drunk driving. When all the costs are totaled, crime costs Americans a stunning $675 billion each year.[2]

In addition to the financial cost is the psychological cost of devastated lives and loss of security. Even apathetic Americans have been shaken from their false sense of security as they have seen criminals invade nearly every sanctuary where they felt they were safe: their cars (the killing of James Jordan); their workplace (World Trade Tower bombing); their public transit (the Long Island Railroad murders by Colin Ferguson); and even their bedrooms (the abduction of Polly Klaas).

The increase in crime in our society has created a moral dilemma. How should we respond to crime in the streets? What punishments are appropriate? Past solutions seem ineffective. Massive spending on social programs, massive spending on prisons, and sweeping changes in judicial sentences seem to have little effect. No wonder there is such anger and a clamor for change.

THE TRUE FACTS ABOUT CRIME

The amount of information and misinformation about crime is staggering. Hardly any other issue is more fraught with myths, lies, and distortions than the issue of crime. Moreover, most citizens have become almost numb to the impact of crime.

In his famous 1992 essay, "Defining Deviancy Down," Daniel Patrick Moynihan described how society was willing to redefine deviant behavior as normal. He noted, "In 1929 in Chicago during Prohibition, four gangsters killed seven gangsters on February 14. The nation was shocked. The event became legend. It merits not one but two entries in the *World Book Encyclopedia*. I leave it to others to judge, but it would appear that the society in the 1920s was simply not willing to put up with this degree of deviancy."[3]

By contrast, Americans today have "normalized" street crime. They avoid bad neighborhoods and public parks. They lock their doors and windows, install burglar alarms, and live in gated communities. And they try not to think of crime, accepting assurances from politicians that the problem is getting better. In essence people are willing to "define deviancy down."

Christians who want to make their faith relevant to the public arena—especially the criminal justice system—must overcome both ignorance and apathy. It is essential that Christians learn to navigate the maze of misinformation and get to the facts about crime. To make our homes and neighborhoods safe Christians should first understand why crime has become such a problem. Here are a few key facts and statistics about crime.

First, the crime rate has been increasing for decades. The recent string of heinous crimes does not represent a sudden wave of crime in America. Nor does the gradual drop in crimes necessarily signal an end to the long-term crime wave in this country.

Since the 1960s the crime rate has risen steadily. While the population has increased only 41 percent since 1960, crime has increased over 300 percent. Moreover, the violent crime rate has increased more than 550 percent.[4] In fact, the rate of violent crime in the United States is worse than in any other industrialized country. Eight out of every ten Americans will be a victim of violent crime at least once in their lives.[5]

President Lyndon Johnson's Crime Commission in 1967 stated that "there is much crime in America . . . far too much for the health of the nation." The commission especially singled out the crime of robbery. But nearly thirty years later there were *five times* as many robberies per capita.[6]

In addition to the steady increase of crime has been the changing nature of these crimes. In the past the criminal usually knew the victim. Now there has been a pronounced increase in the prevalence of stranger-on-stranger robberies and drive-by shootings. This can be seen by noting statistics on the relationship of victims to their murderers. Approximately 12 percent are family members, and another 35 percent are acquaintances. The rest are strangers (13 percent) or have an unknown relationship (39 percent) to the victim.[7]

Second, teenagers are responsible for a disproportionate share of violent crime. The violent crime rate seems to rise and fall in tandem with the number of teens in the population. But recently teen violence has exploded. Teen arrests for all violent crimes have doubled within the last ten years, and murder arrests of teens have also doubled even though the teen population count remained relatively steady during that period. Also disturbing has been the fact that as the arrest rate for white teen males has doubled, the arrest rate for blacks has multiplied three and a-half times.[8]

Third, the median age of criminals is dropping. The perception that criminals are getting younger and younger is backed up by statistics. Kids barely entering puberty are just as likely as twenty-year-old thugs to pull a gun and use it. In 1982, 390 teens between the ages of thirteen and fifteen were arrested for murder. A decade later this total jumped to 740.[9]

Fourth, violent juvenile crime will continue to increase. Even though the crime rate has dropped within the last few years, many are bracing for a new surge of youth violence. While the total population will increase about 12 percent in the next ten years, the teen population will balloon by 21 percent to nearly 21 million. The population of young black and Hispanic men (who have the highest violent crime rates in the population) will increase 24 percent and 47 percent, respectively.[10]

But population increase is only part of the problem. Not only are there more teenagers on the streets; each teen is committing more crimes. Since the mid-1980s juvenile violence has grown faster than the juvenile population, and teen arrests for nearly every category of violent crimes have doubled in less than ten years.

Why the increase? Hopelessness is one reason. More than one in five American children already live below the poverty line, and the percentage of illegitimate births is increasing. Single-parent families are another reason. Teen boys without a strong male role model often pick up the values of the street. Kids from broken and dysfunctional homes find acceptance in gangs and relief from their emotional pain in drugs and alcohol. Already more than 30 percent of all births are out of wedlock, and some social commentators predict that the percentage could swell to 40 percent by the year 2000.

Drugs and the growing "gun culture" among urban youth are another reason for increasing juvenile violence. Battles between gangs over turf and drugs are dangerous enough. But the proliferation of automatic weapons and other lethal firearms in the hands of young criminals further fuels the fire of violent juvenile crime.

Fourth, a majority of the crimes are committed by habitual criminals. Criminologist Marvin Wolfgang compiled arrest records for males born and raised in Philadelphia (in 1945 and in 1958). He found that just 7 percent in each age group committed two-thirds of all violent crime. This included three-fourths of the rapes and robberies, and nearly all of the murders. This 7 percent had five or more arrests before the age of eighteen (and this did not include getting away with dozens of additional crimes). One article using the Wolfgang studies concluded that about seventy-five thousand new, young, habitual criminal predators are added to our population each year.[11]

Later studies found that a minority of this minority is extremely violent and persistent in committing crimes. A Rand study of these so-called "super predators" found that even among the prison population of criminals, they were responsible for a disproportionate number of burglaries and drug deals.[12]

Fifth, crime does not strike all members of society evenly. The media publicity surrounding the deaths of ordinary citizens through bombings and random shootings masks the harsh reality that some members of society are much more likely to become victims of violence. For example, half the victims of rape, robbery, or assault are between twelve and twenty-five years old, even though teenagers and young adults are less than a quarter (22 percent) of the population aged twelve and older. More African Americans are murdered than Caucasians, even though Caucasians outnumber African Americans nearly seven to one. And the overall rate of violent crime in central cities is one and a half times higher than in the suburbs.[13]

Sixth, unfortunately crime does pay. Most criminals are not caught or convicted. Recent statistics show that nearly three of every four convicted criminals are not incarcerated and fewer than one in ten serious crimes results in imprisonment.[14]

Contrary to popular belief, crime is not an irrational act. Some crimes may be deemed irrational, such as crimes of passion and drug-induced crimes, but not all. Many crimes are actually calculated decisions based on cost and benefit. If the expected punishment is low, potential criminals commit a crime. If the expected punishment is high, many potential criminals are deterred. Expected punishment can be calculated by multiplying four probabilities: the probability of being arrested for a crime, the probability of being prosecuted, the probability of being convicted, and the probability of going to prison.

Morgan Reynolds of Texas A&M University compiled interesting facts regarding the expected punishment for burglary. Each month 500,000 burglaries take place; 250,000 of these are reported to the police; 35,000 arrests are made; 30,450 prosecutions take place; 24,060 are convicted; and 6,010 are sent to prison (the rest are paroled). Thus of the 500,000 burglaries each month, only 6,000 burglars went to jail. Stated another way, essentially 98 percent of all burglaries never result in a prison sentence! And if this 2 percent effectiveness ratio is not disturbing enough, Reynolds found that the average time served was only thirteen months.[15]

Since more than 98 percent of burglaries never result in a prison sentence, and since the average burglary sentence is thirteen months, we multiply 98 percent times 13 months and have an expected punishment for burglary of 4.8 days.[16] Put another way, stealing is profitable as long as the object stolen is worth more than five days behind bars. No wonder crime has increased in this country.

Seventh, prison rehabilitation programs do not reduce crime. The United States has one of the highest incarceration rates in the world. Putting violent criminals behind bars may make the world a safer place by keeping them from committing crimes. But when these criminals return to society, usually their attitude and behavior have not changed. They are likely to end up in jail again. Currently the recidivism rate—the percentage of released criminals who commit crimes again—hovers at about 70 percent.

HOW CRIME IS CHANGING SOCIETY

Crime is changing American society in ways that are almost imperceptible unless viewed over several decades. For example, the rise in crime has led to greater fear and subsequent feelings of loneliness and isolation. Citizens afraid of crime are barricading streets, fortifying office buildings, and walling off neighborhoods. Communities are gated, windows are barred, and lights bathe secluded corners.

Just a few years ago, architects designed neighborhoods to withstand natural disasters such as fires, earthquakes, and tornadoes. Now architects and city planners design neighborhoods and buildings to withstand social disasters, including crime, riots, and terrorism. From office buildings to parking garages, from suburban neighborhoods to shopping malls, architects are creating a fortress mentality in America. Already three million Americans live in gated communities.[17]

The social landscape of America is changing. Citizens weary of violence are surrounding themselves with concrete and wrought iron, effectively cutting themselves off from their neighbors and the world. Neighborhoods and communities lose their social cohesion not only because people are apathetic, but because they are scared. Ultimately the nation suffers. How can you have a social contract without social contact? A nation of lonely strangers does not provide a positive social context in which to raise the next generation.

How did this happen? At first the change was imperceptible. What started with bars on the windows and metal detectors at airports led to architectural designs that have transformed the cultural landscape of society. Soon the values of citizens changed. Fiercely independent people who cherished their privacy jettisoned those values and welcomed surveillance cameras and security guards at every turn. They convinced themselves that stopping at security checkpoints was necessary and allowed themselves to be stopped and questioned in order to "feel safe."

Over time, many of these changes have been self-reinforcing. Additional crime-prevention procedures and designs have fed the fear of more crime and encouraged a fortress mentality. While some of the anticrime changes may actually bring communities together (such as front porches and crime-watch programs), the most natural inclination has been to wall and barricade. Like a medieval moat and drawbridge, most designs separate and isolate.

Today concrete barriers block Pennsylvania Avenue in front of the White House. The World Trade Tower is surrounded by hundreds of concrete planters, and entrances are blocked by anti-ram barricades. And concrete barricades turn neighborhood grid-pattern streets into cul-de-sacs that block criminals' escape routes.

Clerks at gas stations take our money from behind bulletproof glass. Customers entering convenience stores see hash marks set on doorjambs, and signs state that cashiers cannot open safes. Signs on delivery trucks explain that the drivers never carry more than twenty dollars. Surveillance cameras, antitheft devices on cars, concrete barricades, electronically coded hotel-room keys, and protective seals on food and drugs are just a few of the daily reminders that we live in a world of chaos and anarchy.

Crime has also changed the inner city. Hospitals have been turned into MASH units where emergency-room doctors and nurses work in war-zone conditions to save the lives of those assaulted on the streets. Children wander streets where bullet shells and pools of blood are frequent sights. Families watch their dreams for a better future shattered when parents and children are cut down in gangland crossfire. And even the criminals themselves become hardened to life and feel little if any remorse for their victims.

Faced with the real prospect of violence, many citizens have armed themselves. Americans own 70 million pistols and 130 million rifles and shotguns. More and more citizens are looking to themselves for protection rather than to law enforcement.

Others are hiring security forces to protect themselves, their homes, and their businesses. Almost three times as many people work for private security companies than for public law enforcement. The Justice Department estimates that spending on private security will soon exceed one hundred billion dollars per year.[18]

But can't something else be done to fight crime? Aren't there special action steps we can take to make a difference in our communities? Let's look at some concrete steps by which government and private citizens can help end the crime wave in America.

HOW TO FIGHT CRIME

First, place more police on the streets. The statistics from Morgan Reynolds cited earlier illustrate why America has a problem with burglary. Less than 2 percent of all burglaries result in a prison sentence. Similar statistics exist for other major crimes, including murder. Twenty-five years ago there were three police officers for every crime committed. Today 3.3 times as many violent crimes are committed as there are police officers.[19] It is not surprising that we have an epidemic of crime in this country when the chances of being caught, prosecuted, and convicted are so low. The average criminal has little reason to fear law enforcement. The obvious solution is to increase the deterrent through more police and through swift and sure punishments.

Second, put violent criminals in prison. The premise is simple: A criminal in prison cannot shoot your family. While the idea of incarceration is not new, some of the recent findings are. A 1992 publication by the Justice Department entitled "The Case for More Incarceration" stated the following:

- Although the crime rate is high, the rate of increase has been going down since we started putting more people in prison.

- Blacks and whites are treated equally and the vast majority of law-abiding African Americans would gain most from more incarceration of criminals because African Americans are more likely to be victims of violent crime.

- Putting criminals behind bars keeps them off the streets and is less expensive to society than letting them back out on the streets.[20]

But is it really less expensive to keep criminals in prison? What about the expense of building new prisons? While the cost of building prisons is high, a study by the National Institute of Justice suggests that the cost of *not* building prisons is even higher. Their study demonstrates that a typical career offender turned loose in society will engage in a personal crime wave that is seventeen times more costly than incarceration.[21]

The cost of sending someone to prison for one year is about $25,000. A Rand Corporation survey of professional criminals estimates that an average criminal commits 187 to 287 crimes a year, costing society an average of $2,300. Therefore releasing a career criminal would cost $430,000 a year—compared to $25,000 for the cost of imprisonment.

Third, focus on habitual criminals. One publication by the Justice Department stated that most violent crimes are committed by people who have already been in the criminal justice system. This includes those who have been arrested, convicted, or imprisoned, or who are on probation or parole. The chronic offender has had five or more arrests by the age of eighteen and has gotten away with dozens of other crimes.

Police departments that target "serious habitual offenders" and put them behind bars have found the number of violent crimes as well as property crimes drop significantly. In the early 1980s the Justice Department funded projects in twenty cities, where police, prosecutors, schools, and welfare and probation workers pooled information to focus on "serious habitual offenders." They found violent crimes sometimes dropped by as much as 38 percent. Arresting, prosecuting, convicting, and incarcerating this small percentage of criminals will make communities safer.[22]

Some criminologists recommend that courts release juvenile crime records at the first adult felony conviction so that longtime juvenile offenders can be quickly identified. While obviously controversial, this would greatly enhance the efforts of targeting and prosecuting "serious habitual offenders" who will continue to threaten members of society.

Arresting, prosecuting, convicting, and incarcerating this small percentage of criminals will make communities safer.

Fourth, keep violent criminals in prison longer. Contrary to the popular assumption that judges "lock 'em up and throw away the keys," most criminals serve much less time than their sentences specify. Most citizens are shocked to learn that violent criminals serve only five and a-half years for murder, three years for rape, two and a-quarter years for robbery, and one and a-quarter years for assault. Government statistics (for thirty-six states and the District of Columbia) show that although violent offenders received an average sentence of seven years and eleven months imprisonment, they actually served an average of only two years and eleven months in prison—or only 37 percent of their imposed sentences. The statistics also show that, typically, 51 percent of violent criminals were discharged from prison in two years or less, and 76 percent were back on the streets in four years or less.[23] Those are the sobering facts wrought from lenient early-release practices and prison overcrowding.

Clearly the current parole and probation procedures need revision. Criminals who know how to work the system can be set free on bond, on their own recognizance, for rehabilitation, or for supervision. Three out of four people serving a criminal sentence are currently on probation or parole.[24] In other words, they are out on the streets ready to commit another crime!

Many states have been enacting "truth-in-sentencing" laws, which stipulate that a violent criminal will be required to serve at least 85 percent of his prison sentence before becoming eligible for parole or other early-release possibilities. Other states and the federal government are considering proposals like "three strikes and you're out." If a criminal is convicted of three violent crimes, he or she will be put in jail for life.

But such proposals are not without controversy. Mandatory life sentences for three-time violent offenders may eventually fill prisons with elderly men who pose less danger to society as they grow older. Fewer than 1 percent of those arrested for violent crimes are aged sixty-five or older, according to the Federal Bureau of Investigation.[25]

Incarceration incapacitates violent criminals and keeps them off the streets. If the criminals who killed Polly Klaas and James Jordan had merely served out their previous sentences, their victims would be alive today.

Incarceration also deters would-be criminals. Criminologists have shown that an increase in arrest rates reduces the crime rate, and they have also demonstrated that an increase in sentence length also decreases crime rates. Catching more criminals, convicting more criminals, and keeping more criminals behind bars will reduce the crime rate.

Fifth, focus national and state resources on criminals, not weapons. Many politicians seem to think that crime can be fought through gun control rather than criminal control. No matter where a person stands on the issue of gun control, consider the following statistics. Only 1 percent of all guns purchased in America are ever used in committing a crime. And of that 1 percent, five out of six guns were obtained illegally.[26] At its best, any gun-control measures will affect only a minute portion of the criminal element.

Sixth, provide alternative sentencing for nonviolent offenders. Criminals who are not a physical threat to society should not be locked up with violent criminals but instead should be sentenced to projects that will pay back the community. Check forgers and petty thieves should not be thrown in prison alongside murderers and rapists. This involves paying the cost of incarcerating someone who can work off his or her debt to society and provide restitution for their victims. All criminals should pay restitution to their victims, but nonviolent criminals can do so without being sent to prison.

Two key biblical principles concerning crime and punishment are retribution and restitution. Retribution is the act of punishing a criminal. This concept can be seen in the *lex talionis* principle (a life for a life, an eye for an eye) found in such passages as Exodus 21:23–25 and Leviticus 24:17–21, and in other regulations in the Mosaic Law (Deut. 19:16–21; 22:24; 25:5–12). Another key principle is restitution, repaying to the victim what was lost or stolen. The numerous fines described in Exodus 21:18–22:17 were not paid to the government; they were paid to the victim by the offender.

Locking up violent criminals makes sense; locking up nonviolent criminals does not. Currently it costs more to warehouse a criminal for one year than it does to send the brightest student to Harvard University. Alternative sentencing for nonviolent offenders will reduce taxpayer costs and generate funds that can provide restitution for the crimes committed.

Most crimes are not committed against the state; they are committed against people. Victims will benefit more if the offender is paying them restitution, and taxpayers will benefit by not having to warehouse criminals who pose little danger to society.

Seventh, transform the lives of criminals. The crime problem will not go away by merely locking up criminals. They will eventually return to society and commit more crimes if they do not change their attitudes and behaviors. Texas, for example, has one of the largest prison systems in the world, with more than 145,000 inmates behind bars in 1995. But these prisoners will not stay behind bars indefinitely. Penologists estimate that 95 percent of these inmates will be returned to society within five years. They also estimate that 43 percent of those released will be back in prison within three years of their release date.[27]

Government prison rehabilitation programs are for the most part a dismal failure. More than 70 percent of all prisoners will return to prison. Prison does not transform lives. Often it perpetuates criminal behavior.

However, Christian ministries like Chuck Colson's Prison Fellowship or the Bill Glass Crusades can and do make a difference. Convicts involved with these and other Christian organizations that minister to prisoners have a recidivism rate in the single digits.[28] Churches should encourage their members to work with these ministries and consider developing their own outreach to those in prison or who have have been released from prison.

Certain government programs can also make a difference. Boot camps for young offenders and drug treatment for drug offenders can change behavior. The criminal justice system should also require inmates to attend school, undergo drug testing and treatment, and work in prison-based industries. The importance of work, education, and drug-free living will greatly increase a released prisoner's chance to return to a productive life when he or she returns to society.

Eighth, develop community programs that deter crime. Many cities have introduced curfews prohibiting minors from being on the streets from 10 P.M. to 6 A.M. Exceptions are made for those passing through town or on their way to or from a political or religious event.

Other neighborhoods have erected roadblocks. Drug dealing drops dramatically when police check drivers' licenses and when local citizens write down license plate numbers or film suspicious activities with hand-held video cameras. Setting up a neighborhood crime-watch program has been a major deterrent to crime in many communities as well.

Citizens and legislators need to take back the streets. Implementing these common-sense measures in the legislature and in our communities will help make our streets safe again. But crime is also fed by the explosion of the drug culture. The problem of drugs in our society must also be addressed and will be discussed in chapter 8.

Christians need to see our responsibility in this area of social service. Most citizens only think about crime when they have been affected by it. But all Christians should be salt and light in society, and should encourage the government to reduce crime. Also the church should seek to be a positive influence on those whose lives are caught up in criminal activity.

7
Capital Punishment

Sʜᴏᴜʟᴅ ᴄʜʀɪsᴛɪᴀɴs sᴜᴘᴘᴏʀᴛ the death penalty? The answer to that question is controversial, and Christians are somewhat divided on the issue. Many feel that the Bible has clearly mandated this, but others believe that the New Testament ethic of love replaces the Old Testament law.

OLD TESTAMENT EXAMPLES

The Old Testament records a number of cases in which God commanded the use of capital punishment. The Old Testament is replete with references and examples of God taking life. In a sense, God used capital punishment to deal with Israel's sins and the sins of nations surrounding Israel.

One example was the flood in Noah's day (Gen. 6–8). God destroyed all human life and animal life except for those in the ark. Another example of God's destruction is Sodom and Gomorrah (Gen. 18–19), destroyed because of their heinous sin. In the time of Moses, God took the lives of the Egyptian firstborn (Exod. 11) and destroyed the Egyptian army in the Red Sea (Exod. 14). When the Israelites were wandering in the wilderness, God punished the people at Kadesh Barnea (Num. 13–14) and caused 14,700 to die of a plague because of Korah's sin (Num. 16:49).

The Old Testament also teaches that God instituted capital punishment

91

in the Mosaic Law, though the principle of capital punishment preceded the Old Testament code of law. According to Genesis 9:6, capital punishment is based on the sanctity of life. "Whoever sheds man's blood, by man his blood shall be shed, for in the image of God, He made man"(NKJV). This verse clearly establishes the principle of capital punishment: Murder is to be punished by death because of the sanctity of human life. Humans are created in the image of God, and murder is an offense against man and an outrage against God.

Some scholars have pointed to the style in which that pronouncement is given. The verse displays chiastic parallelism, in that every word of the first section is repeated in reverse order in the second section. Apparently this reflects the principle of measure for measure in God's system of justice.[1]

The Mosaic Law set forth numerous offenses punishable by death. The first is murder. In Exodus 21 God commanded capital punishment for murderers. Premeditated murder (or what the King James Version refers to as "lying in wait") was punishable by death. A second offense punishable by death was involvement in the occult (Exod. 22; Lev. 20; Deut. 18–19). This included sorcery, divination, or being a medium. Third, capital punishment was also to be used against perpetrators of certain sexual sins such as rape, incest, or homosexuality (Lev. 20:11–13).

Within the Old Testament theocracy capital punishment was extended to various offenses beyond murder. While the death penalty for these offenses was limited to that particular dispensation of revelation, the principle in Genesis 9:6, as noted, preceded the theocracy. The principle of *lex talionis* (a life for a life, an eye for an eye) is tied to the creation order. Capital punishment in the Old Testament was implemented because of the sanctity of life.

NEW TESTAMENT PRINCIPLES

Some Christians believe that capital punishment does not apply to the New Testament and the church age. However, as already discussed, capital punishment was established long before the New Testament era.

Even so, some Christians argue that in the Sermon on the Mount, Jesus seems to have been arguing against capital punishment. However,

He was speaking against the personal desire for vengeance. He was not denying the power and responsibility of the government; instead, He was telling believers they should not try to replace government. They should love their enemies and turn the other cheek.

Some have said that Jesus was setting aside capital punishment in John 8, since He did not call for the woman caught in adultery to be stoned. But the Pharisees were trying to catch Jesus in a trap between the Roman law and the Mosaic Law. If He said they should stone her, they would break the Roman law. If He refused to allow them to stone her, He would break the Mosaic Law (Lev. 20:10; Deut. 22:22). Jesus' answer avoided the conflict: He said that the one without sin should cast the first stone. Since He did suggest that a stone be thrown (John 8:7), He was not abolishing the death penalty.

The New Testament includes other examples of the principle of capital punishment being reinforced. Romans 13:1–7, for example, teaches that human government is ordained by God and that the civil magistrate is a servant of God. People are to obey the government because it does not bear the sword in vain. The fact that the apostle Paul used the image of the sword (v. 4) further supports the idea that capital punishment was to be used by government in the New Testament age as well. Rather than abolish the idea of the death penalty, Paul used the emblem of the Roman sword to reinforce the idea of capital punishment. The Greek word for "sword" refers not to the weapon the emperor carried as a symbol of the authority of his office but to the one worn in Roman provinces by the magistrates who had authority to execute criminals.

Paul taught in Romans 13 that government has the right and responsibility to take the life of a criminal under certain circumstances; this continues the principle of capital punishment first stated in Genesis 9:6. Paul's attitude toward capital punishment is seen in Acts 25:11. While standing before Festus, he stated that if "I am guilty of doing anything deserving death, I do not refuse to die." Paul acknowledged that if he had indeed committed a capital crime, then he would not seek to escape capital punishment. Therefore one can conclude that the New Testament does not abolish the death penalty; instead it reinforces the principle of capital punishment found in the Old Testament.

CAPITAL PUNISHMENT AND DETERRENCE

Is capital punishment a deterrent to crime? At the outset it should be acknowledged that the answer to this question should not change one's perspective on this issue. Although it is an important question, it should not be the basis for one's view on this issue. A Christian's belief about capital punishment should be based on what the Bible teaches, not on a pragmatic assessment of whether capital punishment works.

If anything, the Bible does seem to teach that capital punishment deters crime. When justice is done, "all the people will hear and be afraid, and will not be contemptuous again" (Deut. 17:13). If nothing else, capital punishment will deter the criminal who is executed from repeating another crime.

Opponents of capital punishment argue that it is not a deterrent because in some states where capital punishment is allowed the crime rate goes up. Does this mean then that capital punishment is not a deterrent?

First, it should be recognized that crime rates have been increasing for some time. The United States has become a more violent society as the social and moral fabric of society has been breaking down. So the increase in the crime rate is most likely due to many other factors and cannot be correlated with a death penalty that has been implemented sparingly and sporadically.

Second, some evidence exists that capital punishment *is* a deterrent. And even if we cannot be absolutely sure of its deterrence value, it should be implemented. If it is a deterrent, then implementing capital punishment certainly will save lives. If it is not, then we still will have followed biblical injunctions and put convicted murderers to death.

In a sense opponents of capital punishment, who argue that it is not a deterrent, are willing to give the benefit of the doubt to the criminal rather than to the victims. The poet Hyman Barsham put it this way: "The death penalty is a warning—just like a lighthouse throwing its beam out on the water. We hear about shipwrecks but we do not hear about the ships the lighthouse guides safely on its way. We do not have proof of the number of ships it saves, but we do not tear the lighthouse down."[2] If capital punishment is a potential deterrent, that is significant social reason enough to implement it.

Statistical analysis by Isaac Ehrlich of the University of Chicago suggests that capital punishment is a deterrent.[3] Further cross-sectional analysis has confirmed these original conclusions.[4] His research has shown that if the death penalty were used in a consistent way, it might deter as many as eight murders for every execution carried out. If these numbers are indeed accurate, it demonstrates that capital punishment could be a significant deterrent to crime in American society.

Certainly capital punishment will not deter all crime. Psychotic and deranged killers, members of organized crime, and street gangs will no doubt kill whether capital punishment is implemented or not. A person who is irrational or wants to commit a murder will do so regardless of capital punishment. But social statistics as well as logic suggest that rational people will be deterred from murder because capital punishment is part of the criminal code.

CAPITAL PUNISHMENT AND DISCRIMINATION

Many people oppose capital punishment because they feel it is discriminatory. This charge is somewhat curious since most of the criminals who have been executed in the last decade are white rather than black. Nevertheless a higher percentage of ethnic minorities (African American, Hispanic) are on death row. So is this a significant argument against capital punishment?

First, much of the evidence for discrimination is circumstantial. The fact that there is a higher percentage of a particular ethnic group on death row does not constitute discrimination. A high percentage of whites playing professional ice hockey or a high percentage of blacks playing professional basketball does not necessarily mean that discrimination has taken place. We need to look beneath the allegation and see if true discrimination is taking place.

Second, some discrimination does take place in the criminal justice system. Discrimination occurs not only on the basis of race but also on the basis of wealth. Wealthy criminals can hire a battery of lawyers and legal experts to defend themselves, whereas poor criminals must depend on court-appointed public defenders.

Still even if there is some evidence of discrimination in the criminal justice system, does this mean there is discrimination with regard to capital punishment? The U.S. Solicitor General in his amicus brief for the case *Gregg v. Georgia* argued that sophisticated sociological studies show no evidence of racial discrimination in carrying out capital punishment.[5] These studies found consistent percentages when the actual crimes committed were compared to the actual number who went to trial and to the number in which a guilty verdict was rendered.

Even if evidence for discrimination does exist in the criminal justice system, that is not really an argument against capital punishment. Rather it is a compelling argument for reform of the criminal justice system and for more carefully implementing capital punishment.

In fact the Bible teaches that capital punishment must be correctly administered. For example, even though the Mosaic code in the Old Testament provided an extensive list of capital crimes, it also required a strict standard of proof for conviction. Two or three witnesses were required for conviction (Deut. 19:15). Circumstantial evidence alone was not sufficient to convict an individual. So the death penalty should be used only in a limited number of cases where certainty exists (through eyewitness accounts and videotape evidence).

Most of the social and philosophical arguments against capital punishment are actually not arguments against it at all. If discrimination is taking place and guilty people are escaping penalty, then that is an argument for extending the penalty, not doing away with it. Furthermore, opponents of capital punishment candidly admit they would still oppose the death penalty even if one could conclusively prove it is an effective deterrent.[6] So while these are important social and political issues to consider, they are not sufficient justification for abolishing the death penalty.

OBJECTIONS TO CAPITAL PUNISHMENT

One objection is that in carrying out capital punishment the government is committing murder. Put theologically, does the death penalty violate the sixth commandment, which teaches "You shall not murder" (Exod. 20:13)?

First, the context of this verse must be noted. The verb used in Exodus

20:13, though sometimes translated "to kill", should best be translated "to murder." It is used forty-nine times in the Old Testament and always describes premeditated murder. It is never used of the killing of animals or of enemies in battle. So the commandment does not teach that all killing is wrong; it teaches that murder is wrong.

Second, the penalty for breaking this commandment was the death penalty (Exod. 21:12; Num. 35:16–21). Therefore when the government took the life of a murderer, the government was not itself guilty of murder. Opponents of capital punishment who accuse the government of committing murder when implementing the death penalty fail to see the irony of using Exodus 20 to define murder while ignoring Exodus 21, which specifically teaches that government is to punish murderers.

A second objection to capital punishment questions the validity of applying the Old Testament Law to today's society. After all, was not the Mosaic Law only for the Old Testament theocracy? There are a number of ways to answer this objection.

First, the premise is questionable. There is and should be a relation between Old Testament laws and modern laws. Christians are not subject to the Old Testament Law, but that does not invalidate God's moral principles set down in the Old Testament. Murder is still wrong. Thus since murder is wrong, the penalty for murder must still be implemented.

Second, while the Mosaic Law was given specifically and uniquely for the Old Testament theocracy, this does not mean the death penalty should be abolished. As stated, Genesis 9:6 precedes the Old Testament theocracy and its principle is tied to the creation order. Capital punishment is to be implemented because of the sanctity of human life. We are created in God's image. The universally binding principle is that when a murder occurs, the murderer must be put to death.

Third, the New Testament also teaches capital punishment. Romans 13:1–7 specifically states that human government, ordained by God, is to be obeyed; government does not bear the sword in vain. Human governments are given the responsibility to punish wrongdoers, and this includes murderers, who are to be given the death penalty.

Fourth, the principle of capital punishment is never specifically removed or replaced in the Bible. As already seen, Jesus and the disciples never annulled the Old Testament standard of capital punishment. Paul taught that Christians are to express grace to each other, but he also taught that human governments are to be obeyed. Capital punishment is taught in both the Old and New Testaments.

8
Drug Abuse

Nearly everywhere we look, the consequences of drug abuse can be seen. Violent street gangs, family violence, the spread of AIDS, and babies born with cocaine dependency all testify to the pervasive influence of drugs throughout the world.

The statistics are staggering. The average age of first alcohol use is twelve, and the average age of first drug use is thirteen. According to the National Institute on Drug Abuse, 93 percent of all teenagers in the United States have had some experience with alcohol by the end of their senior year of high school, and 6 percent drink daily. Almost two-thirds of all American young people try illicit drugs before they finish high school. One out of sixteen seniors smokes marijuana daily, and 20 percent have done so for at least a month sometime in their lives.[1] A recent poll found that adolescents listed drugs as the most important problem facing people their age, followed by crime and violence in school and social pressures.[2]

One survey released by the University of Colorado shows that drug use is not just a problem outside the church. The study involved nearly fourteen thousand junior-high and high-school youth and compared churched young people with unchurched young people, finding very little difference between them. For example, 88 percent of the unchurched young people reported drinking beer, compared to 80 percent of churched young people. When asked how many had tried marijuana, 47 percent of the unchurched young people had done so, compared to 38 percent of the churched youth. For amphetamines and barbiturates, 28 percent of the unchurched had tried them, while 22 percent of the church young people had tried them. And for cocaine use, the percentage was 14 percent for unchurched youths and 11 percent for churched teens.[3]

Fighting drugs may seem futile. When drug dealers are arrested, they often are released prematurely because court dockets are overloaded. Plea bargaining and paroles are standard fare as the revolving doors of justice spin faster. As the casualties mount in this war against drugs, some commentators have begun to suggest that the best solution is to legalize drugs. But a war is not won by surrendering. If drugs were legalized, addiction would increase, health costs would increase, and governments would once again capitulate to societal pressures and shirk their responsibility to establish moral law.

But if legalization is not the answer, then something must be done about the moral dilemma posed by drugs. Some drugs like alcohol are legal, while other drugs have been decriminalized (marijuana is not illegal in some states) and other drugs are illegal (cocaine, heroin). How should society deal with drug abuse? And what about the impact of drugs on society? The annual cost of drug abuse in the United States was estimated by the National Center for Health Statistics to be nearly sixty billion dollars, and the medical bill for alcohol was nearly one hundred billion dollars.

TYPES OF DRUGS

Alcohol

Alcohol is the drug most commonly used and abused by young people as well as adults. Nationwide surveys indicate that about 90 percent of the nation's youth experiment with alcohol—currently teenagers' drug of choice. An annual survey conducted by the University of Michigan has revealed the extent to which young people drink. Over 65 percent of the nation's high-school seniors currently do so, and about 40 percent reported having a heavy drinking episode within the two weeks prior to the survey.[4]

Alcohol is an intoxicant that depresses the central nervous system and can bring a temporary loss of control over physical and mental powers. The signs of drunkenness are well known: lack of coordination, slurred speech, blurred vision, and poor judgment.

In recent years debate has raged over whether alcoholism is a sin or a sickness.[5] The Bible clearly labels drunkenness as sin in such passages as Deuteronomy 21:20–21; 1 Corinthians 6:9–10; and Galatians 5:19–20. But the fact that the Bible calls drunkenness sin does not mitigate against the growing physiological evidence that certain people's biochemistry makes them more prone to addiction.

Some studies suggest that because of their body chemistry alcoholics process alcohol differently than do nonalcoholics. Acetaldehyde is the intermediate by-product of alcohol metabolism. But the biochemistry of some people makes it difficult to process acetaldehyde into acetate. Thus acetaldehyde builds up in the body and begins to affect a person's brain chemistry. The chemicals produced act much like opiates and therefore contribute to alcoholism.[6]

The social costs of alcohol are staggering. Alcoholism is the third largest health problem (following heart disease and cancer). Often alcohol-related medical problems begin before birth. More than forty thousand babies are born at risk each year because their mothers drank alcohol during pregnancy.[7]

There are an estimated 10 million problem drinkers in the American adult population, and an estimated 3.3 million teenagers are problem drinkers. Half of all traffic fatalities and one-third of all traffic injuries are alcohol-related. Alcohol is involved in 67 percent of all murders and 33 percent of all suicides.[8]

Alcohol is also a prime contributor to the breakdown of American families. A high percentage of family violence, parental abuse and neglect, lost wages, and divorce are tied to the abuse of alcohol in this country. In a George Gallup poll nearly one-fourth of all Americans cited alcohol and/or drug abuse as one of three factors most responsible for the high divorce rate in this country.[9]

Since the publication of Janet Geringer Woitiz's book *Adult Children of Alcoholics*, society has begun to understand the long-term effect of alcoholism on future generations. Children of Alcoholics (COAs) exhibit a number of traits, including having to guess what normal behavior is, having difficulty following a project from beginning to end, judging themselves without mercy, and having difficulty with intimate relationships.[10]

Thus in the fight against drugs Christians must not ignore the impact alcohol has had on Americans' lives. Alcohol is also an addictive drug and has had a profound negative effect on individuals, families, and our society.

Marijuana

Marijuana is produced from the hemp plant (*Cannabis sativa*) that grows throughout the world. It has gone from a hidden drug of the counterculture to the drug of choice for young people wanting to "get high." It has become widely available and openly used, especially in states that have decriminalized its usage.

Marijuana is regularly used by twenty million Americans, making it the most commonly used illicit drug in the country.[11] In the 1970s an alarming 10 percent of all high school seniors smoked marijuana every day. Although that percentage dropped significantly in the 1980s because of a strong anti-drug campaign, the percentage now seems to be increasing. A national survey by the National Institute on Drug Abuse in 1994 found that annual marijuana use among eighth-graders rose from 6.2 percent in 1991 to 13 percent in 1994. For tenth-graders the rise was from 16.5 percent to 30.4 percent.[12]

Marijuana is an intoxicant that is usually smoked in order to induce a feeling of euphoria that lasts from two to four hours. Many users believe it is a relatively harmless drug, but mounting scientific evidence demonstrates how dangerous marijuana can be. The short-term effects of marijuana include impairment in learning, memory, perception, judgment, and complex motor skills. Marijuana can also cause difficulty in speaking, listening effectively, thinking, retaining knowledge, problem-solving, and forming concepts.

An article in the *Journal of the American Medical Association* found that marijuana users had "55 percent more industrial accidents, 85 percent more injuries, and a 78 percent increase in absenteeism."[13] In one study of reckless drivers who were not obviously drunk from alcohol, 59 percent tested positive for cocaine or marijuana.[14] Another study found that 35 percent of all automobile accident victims had detectable levels of marijuana in their blood.[15]

Marijuana also causes many medical complications. Because most marijuana users inhale unfiltered smoke and hold it in their lungs for as long as possible, the lungs and pulmonary system are damaged. Marijuana smoke also has more cancer-causing agents than tobacco smoke.

A study reported in the *Cancer* journal reported that children of women who smoke marijuana are eleven times more likely to contract leukemia.[16] Mothers who smoke marijuana also contribute to low birth weight and developmental problems for their children and increase by as much as 500 percent the risk of abnormalities similar to those caused by fetal alcohol syndrome.[17]

Since the 1970s more than 10,500 scientific studies have demonstrated the adverse consequences of marijuana use.[18] Many of these studies were collected when most of the marijuana sold was less potent and less addictive than it is today. Former drug czar Lee Brown estimates that marijuana on the streets today is up to ten times more potent than it was a generation ago.[19]

Carlton Turner, former National Institute on Drug Abuse director and head of the Marijuana Research Project at the University of Mississippi, concludes, "There is no other drug used or abused by man that has the staying power and broad cellular actions on the body that *cannabis* [marijuana] does."[20]

Marijuana is not a safe drug. It damages brain and lung cells and adversely affects reproduction in women and fertility in men. It also adversely affects concentration. And most importantly, it has been considered a "gateway drug" because of its potential in leading young people to experiment with stronger drugs such as cocaine and heroin.

Cocaine

Cocaine occurs naturally in the leaves of coca plants and was reportedly chewed by natives in Peru as early as the sixth century. It became widely used in beverages (like Coca Cola) and medicines in the nineteenth century, but was restricted in 1914 by the Harrison Narcotics Act. Today cocaine users range from Wall Street lawyers inhaling it from fourteen-carat gold spoons to teenage junkies in back alleys smoking it in "crack" pipes.

More than thirty million Americans have used cocaine, and about five million are regular users, with the number increasing daily.[21] Every day some five thousand neophytes sniff a line of coke for the first time.[22] About one in five twelfth-graders have tried cocaine, and 30 percent of all college students have tried cocaine by their fourth year.[23]

Cocaine is a stimulant and an ego builder. Along with increased energy comes a feeling of personal supremacy—the illusion of being smarter, sexier, and more competent than anyone else. And while cocaine confidence makes a person feel indestructible, the crash from coke leaves him or her depressed, paranoid, and searching for more.

In recent years snorting cocaine has given way to smoking it. Snorting cocaine limits the intensity of the effect because the blood vessels in the nose are constricted. Smoking cocaine delivers a much more intense euphoric feeling. The smoke goes directly to the lungs and then to the heart. On the next heartbeat it is on the way to the brain.

Ann Rose Childress of the University of Pennsylvania notes that "you can become compulsively involved with snorted cocaine. We have many Hollywood movie stars without nasal septums to prove that." But when cocaine is smoked "it seems to have incredibly powerful effects that tend to set up a compulsive addictive cycle more quickly than anything that we've seen."[24]

Until recently people speaking of cocaine dependence would never call it an addiction. Cocaine's withdrawal symptoms are not physically wrenching like those of heroin and alcohol. Yet cocaine involves compulsion, loss of control, and continued use in spite of the consequences. Frequently cocaine sniffers burn a hole in their nasal septum, eventually constricting their nasal passages so that they can no longer snort the stuff. All this suggests that cocaine is indeed addicting.

Cocaine users sucked in by its siren charms describe its effect in sexual terms. Its intense and sensual effect make it a stronger aphrodisiac than sex itself. Research at the University of California at Los Angeles with apes given large amounts of cocaine showed they preferred the drug to food or sexual partners and were willing to endure severe electric shocks in exchange for large doses.[25]

Cocaine has been accorded a symbolic status that makes it all the more dangerous. It is perceived as chic, cozy, and clean. Friends snort coke with other friends and rationalize it by asking, "Who is it hurting?" But the cocaine trade is anything but cozy and clean: It is dirty and dangerous. Cocaine users implicitly acquiesce to hundreds of cocaine-related murders and gang killings each year.

The cocaine problem in this country has been made worse by the introduction of "crack," which is ordinary cocaine mixed with baking soda and water and heated. This material is then dried and broken into tiny chunks that resemble rock candy. Users usually smoke these crack rocks in glass pipes.

Crack (so-called because of the cracking sound it makes when heated) has become the scourge of the drug business. A single hit of crack provides an intense, wrenching rush in a matter of seconds. Unlike normal cocaine, which penetrates the mucous membranes slowly and circulates to the brain in minutes, crack is absorbed rapidly through the lungs and hits the brain within seconds in a dangerously concentrated form. It is the most hazardous form of cocaine and also the most addicting.

Another major difference between ordinary cocaine and crack is the cost. According to Mark Gold, founder of the nationwide cocaine hotline, the cost to an addict using crack is one-tenth the cost he would have paid for the equivalent in cocaine powder just a decade ago.[26] Since crack costs much less than normal cocaine, it is particularly appealing to adolescents. The number of twelfth-graders having tried cocaine will probably continue to increase because of the price and availability of crack.

Hallucinogens

Another category of drugs is hallucinogens. The drug of choice during the 1960s used to be LSD. People looking for the "ultimate trip" would take LSD or perhaps peyote and experience bizarre illusions and hallucinations.

In the last few decades these hallucinogens have been replaced by PCP, often known as "angel dust" or "killer weed." First synthesized in the 1950s as an anesthetic, PCP was discontinued because of its side effects but is now manufactured illegally and sold to thousands of teenagers.

PCP is often sprayed on cigarettes or marijuana and then smoked. Users report a sense of distance and estrangement. PCP creates body image distortion, dizziness, and double vision. The drug distorts reality in such a way that it can resemble mental illness. Because the drug blocks pain receptors, violent PCP episodes may result in self-inflicted injuries. Suicides, drowning, and self-mutilation are all common occurrences for PCP users.

Chronic PCP users have persistent memory problems and speech difficulties. Mood disorders such as depression, anxiety, and violent behavior are also reported. High doses of PCP can produce a coma, which can last for days or weeks.

Synthetic Drugs

So-called "designer drugs" have also made an impact on society. Manufactured in clandestine laboratories, these drugs mimic the effects of commonly abused drugs. Since they were not even anticipated when current drug laws were written, they often have existed in a legal limbo while the extent of their use has been increasing.

One drug is MDMA, also known as "ecstasy." Called "the LSD of the 1980s and 1990s," it gives the user a cocaine-like rush with a hallucinogen euphoria. Ecstasy was sold legally for a few years despite National Institute on Drug Abuse fears that it could cause brain damage. In 1985 the Drug Enforcement Agency outlawed MDMA, although it is still widely available.[27]

Other drugs have been marketed as a variation of the painkillers Demerol and Fentanyl. The synthetic variation of the anesthetic Fentanyl is considered a thousand times more potent than heroin. It is known on the street as "synthetic heroin" and "China White."

Designer drugs have become a growth industry in the 1990s. Creative drug makers in clandestine laboratories can produce these drugs for a fraction of the cost of smuggled drugs and with much less hassle from law enforcement officers. In the end these drugs may pose the greatest threat to our society in the future.

HOW TO FIGHT THE DRUG BATTLE

Society must fight America's drug epidemic on five major fronts.[28] The first battlefront is at the border. Federal agents must patrol the 8,426 miles of the deeply indented Florida coastline and the 2,067-mile border with Mexico. This is a formidable task, but vast distances are not the only problem.

The smugglers have almost unlimited funds and some of the best equipment available. Fortunately the federal interdiction forces (namely, Customs officers, Drug Enforcement Agency, and the Immigration and Naturalization Service) are improving their capabilities. Customs forces have enlisted more personnel and are getting more sophisticated equipment.

The second battlefront is law enforcement at home. Police must crack down with more arrests, more convictions, longer sentences, and more seizures of drug dealers' assets. Unfortunately law enforcement successes pale when compared to the volume of drug traffic. Even the most effective crackdowns seem to do little more than move drugs from one location to another. An effective weapon on this battlefront is a 1984 law that makes it easier to seize the assets of drug dealers before they are convicted. In some cities police have even confiscated the cars of suburbanites who drive into the city to buy crack.

But attempts to deter drug dealing have been limited by flaws in the criminal justice system. A lack of jail cells prevents significant prosecution of drug dealers. And even if this problem were alleviated, the shortage of judges would still result in the quick release of drug pushers.

A third battlefront is drug testing. Many government and business organizations are implementing testing of present and prospective employees on a routine basis. The theory is simple. Drug testing is a greater deterrent to drug use than the remote possibility of going to jail. People who know they will have to pass a urine test in order to get a job will be much less likely to dabble in drugs. In 1980, 27 percent of some twenty thousand military personnel admitted to using drugs in the previous thirty days. Five years later, when drug testing was implemented, the proportion dropped to 9 percent.[29]

But drug testing is not without its opponents. Civil libertarians feel this deterrent is not worth the loss of personal privacy. Some unions believe that random testing in the workplace would violate the Fourth Amendment's prohibition against unreasonable searches.

A fourth battleground is drug treatment. Those who are addicted to drugs need help. But who should provide the treatment? And who should pay the cost of such treatment? Private hospital programs are now a $4 billion-a-year business with a daily cost of as much as $500 per bed per day. This is clearly out of the reach of many addicts whose employers or insurance companies cannot pick up the costs.

A fifth battleground is education. Teaching children the dangers of drugs can be an important step in helping them learn to say no to drugs. The National Institute on Drug Abuse estimates that 72 percent of the nation's elementary and secondary schoolchildren are being given some kind of drug education.[30]

SHOULD WE LEGALIZE DRUGS?

Those weary of the war on drugs have suggested drugs be decriminalized. Former Surgeon General Joycelyn Elders suggested that the impact of legalizing drugs be studied. For years an alliance of liberals and libertarians have promoted the idea that legalizing drugs would reduce drug costs and drug crimes in this country. But would it? The following are some of the arguments for drug legalization.

"Legalization will take the profit out of the drug business."

Surprising as it may sound, relatively few drug dealers actually earn huge sums of money. Most in the crack business are low-level runners who make very little money. Many crack dealers smoke more crack than they sell. Drug cartels are the ones making the big profits.

Would legalizing drugs affect large drug dealers or drug cartels in any appreciable way? No. Drug cartels would still control price and supply even if drugs were legalized in this country. If the government set the price for legalized drugs, criminals could undercut the price and supply whatever drugs the government did not supply.

Addicts would not be significantly affected by legalization. Does anyone seriously believe their behavior would change just because they were using legal drugs instead of illegal drugs? They would still use theft and prostitution to support their habits.

Proponents also argue that legalizing drugs would reduce the cost of drugs and thus would reduce the supply of drugs flowing to this country. Recent history suggests that just the opposite will take place. When cocaine first hit the United States, it was expensive and difficult to obtain. But when more was dumped into this country and readily available in less expensive vials of crack, drug addiction rose and drug-related crimes rose.

"Drug legalization will reduce drug use."

Proponents argue that legalizing drugs will make them less appealing— they will no longer be "forbidden fruit." However, logic and social statistics suggest that decriminalizing drugs will actually increase drug use.

Those arguing for the legalization of drugs often point to Prohibition as a failed social experiment. But was it a failure? When Prohibition was in effect, alcohol consumption declined by 30 to 50 percent and deaths from cirrhosis of the liver fell dramatically.[31] One study found that suicides and drug-related arrests also declined by 50 percent.[32] After the repeal of the eighteenth amendment in 1933, alcoholism rose. So did alcohol-related crimes and accidents. If anything, Prohibition proves the point—decriminalization increases drug use.

Comparing alcohol and drugs actually strengthens the argument against legalization, since many drugs are even more addictive than alcohol. For example, alcohol has an addiction rate of approximately 10 percent, while cocaine has an addiction rate as high as 75 percent.[33]

Many drugs are actually "gateway drugs" to other drug addictions. A 1992 article in the *Journal of Primary Prevention* found that marijuana is essentially a "necessary" condition for the occurrence of cocaine use. Other research shows that (a) involvement with illicit drugs is a developmental phenomenon, (b) increased experimentation correlates with increasing age, and (c) cigarette and alcohol use precedes the use of marijuana.[34]

Robert DuPont, former director of the National Institute on Drug Abuse, argues that the potential market for legal drugs can be compared to the number of Americans who now use alcohol (140 million persons). If his analysis it correct, then approximately 50 million Americans would eventually use cocaine if it were a legal drug.

Great Britain's experiment with drug legalization has been a disaster. Between 1960 and 1970 the number of British heroin addicts increased thirtyfold, and during the 1980s it increased by as much as 40 percent each year. By contrast the number of heroin addicts in this country today is about the same as it was fifteen years ago—five hundred thousand.

But the real question is not, Which is worse: alcohol or drugs? The question is whether either alcohol or drugs should be legalized. Legalized alcohol currently leads to one hundred thousand deaths annually and costs ninety-nine billion dollars each year.[35] Drugs should not be legalized too!

"Legalizing drugs will reduce social costs."

"We are losing the war on drugs," say drug legalization proponents, "so let's cut the costs of drug enforcement by decriminalizing drugs."

Currently the United States spends eleven billion dollars each year to combat drug-related crime. If drugs were made legal, some crime-fighting costs might drop, but many social ills, including other forms of crime (to support drug habits), drug-related accidents, and welfare costs, would certainly increase.

Statistics from states that have decriminalized marijuana demonstrate this concern. In California, within the first six months of decriminalization of drugs, arrests for driving under the influence of drugs rose 46 percent for adults and 71.4 percent for juveniles.[36] The use of marijuana doubled in Alaska and Oregon when it was decriminalized in those states.[37]

Crime would certainly increase. Justice Department figures show that approximately one-third of inmates used drugs prior to committing their crimes.[38] And juvenile crime would no doubt increase as well. A 1990 study published in the *Journal of Drug Issues* found a strong association between the severity of the crime and the type of substance used—the more intoxicating the substance, the more serious the incident.[39]

Meanwhile both worker productivity and student productivity would decrease. The Drug Enforcement Administration estimates that drug decriminalization would cost the United States more than alcohol and tobacco-related costs combined, perhaps between $140 billion and $210 billion a year in lost productivity and job-related accidents.[40]

Government services would no doubt need to be expanded to pay for additional drug education and treatment for those addicted to legal drugs. And child protective services would no doubt have to expand to deal with child abuse. Patrick Murphy, a court-appointed lawyer for thirty-one thousand abused and neglected children in Chicago, says that more than 80 percent of the cases of physical and sexual abuse of children now involve drugs. Legalizing drugs will not reduce these crimes; it would make the problem worse.[41]

Is it accurate to say the nation is losing the war on drugs? Drug use in this country was on the decline in the 1980s because of a strong antidrug campaign. Casual cocaine use, for example, dropped from twelve million in 1985 to six million in 1991. Legalizing drugs in this country would constitute surrender in the drug war at a time when substantial evidence shows this battle can be won on a number of fronts.

"The government should not dictate moral policy on drugs."

Libertarians who promote drug legalization value personal freedom. They believe government should not dictate morals, and they fear that citizens' civil liberties may be threatened by a tougher policy against drugs.

The true threat to individual freedoms comes from the drug cartels in foreign countries, drug lords in this country, and drug dealers in our streets. Legalizing drugs would send the wrong message to society. Those involved in the drug trade often see that drugs ultimately lead to prison or death, so many begin to seek help.

Obviously some people are going to use drugs whether they are legal or illegal. Keeping drugs illegal maintains criminal sanctions that persuade most people that their lives are best lived without drugs. Legalization, on the other hand, would remove the incentive to stay away from drugs and would certainly increase drug use.

William Bennett has said, "I didn't have to become drug czar to be opposed to legalized marijuana. As Secretary of Education I realized that, given the state of American education, the last thing we needed was a policy that made widely available a substance that impairs memory, concentration, and attention span. Why in God's name foster the use of a drug that makes you stupid?"[42]

BIBLICAL PERSPECTIVES

Some people may believe the Bible has little to say about drugs, but this is not so. First, the Bible says much about the most common and most abused drug, namely, alcohol. Although drinking wine is not strictly forbidden (John 2:1–10; Psalms 104:15; 1 Timothy 5:23), Ephesians 5:18 admonishes Christians not to be drunk with wine. In many places in Scripture drunkenness is called a sin (Deut. 21:20–21; 1 Cor. 6:9–10; Gal. 5:19–20). The Bible also warns of the dangers of drinking alcohol in Proverbs 20:1; Isaiah 5:11; and Habakkuk 2:15–16. If the Bible warns of the danger of alcohol, then by implication it is also warning of the dangers of taking other kinds of drugs.

Second, drugs were an integral part of many ancient Near Eastern societies. For example, the pagan cultures surrounding Israel used drugs as part of their religious ceremonies.[43] Both the Old and New Testaments condemn sorcery and witchcraft. The Greek word translated "witchcraft" (Gal. 5:20), "magic arts" (Rev. 9:21), or "magic spell" (18:23) is *pharmakeia*, from which come the English words "pharmacy" and "pharmaceutical." In ancient times drugs were prepared by a witch or shaman.

Pagan worshipers used drugs to induce an altered state of consciousness that allowed demons to take over the minds of the users. Drug use was involved in sorcery. In our day many use drugs merely for so-called "recreational" purposes, but the occult connection cannot be discounted.

Galatians 5:19–21 says, "The acts of the sinful nature are obvious: sexual immorality, impurity and debauchery; idolatry and witchcraft [which includes the use of drugs]; hatred, discord, jealousy, fits of rage, selfish am-bition, dissensions, factions and envy; drunkenness, orgies, and the like. I warn you, as I did before, that those who live like this will not inherit the kingdom of God."

The New American Standard Bible translates the word *witchcraft* as "sor-cery" here. This involvement in witchcraft associated with drugs is a sin. The nonmedical use of drugs is considered one of the acts of a sinful na-ture. Using drugs, whether to "get a high" or to tap into the occult, is one of the acts whereby users demonstrate their depraved, carnal condition.

The psychic effects of drugs should not be discounted. A question-naire designed by Charles Tate and sent to users of marijuana documented some disturbing findings. In his article in *Psychology Today* he noted that one-fourth of the marijuana users who responded to his questionnaire reported that they were taken over and controlled by an evil person or power during their drug-induced experience. And over half of those ques-tioned said they have experienced religious or "spiritual" sensations in which they meet spiritual beings.[44]

Many proponents of the drug culture have linked drug use to spiritual values. During the 1960s Timothy Leary and Alan Watts referred to the "religious" and "mystical" experience gained through the use of LSD (along with other drugs) as a prime reason for taking drugs.[45]

No doubt drugs are dangerous, not only to the body but also to the spirit. Christians must warn our children and our society of the dangers of drugs.

HOW TO KEEP CHILDREN OFF DRUGS

Drugs pose a threat to children, but parents can protect them from much of this threat by working on the following preventive measures. First, build up your child's self-esteem. Children with a positive self-image stand a better chance against peer pressure to use drugs. Children need to know they are a special creation of God (Ps. 139:13–16) and thus are worthy of dignity and respect (8:5–8). Children need to be taught the fallacy of try-ing to conform to some group's standards by going along with their drug habits. Drugs are dumb and dangerous, not chic and cool, despite what some people might say.

Second, parents should monitor their child's friendships. Before allowing a child to spend too much time with another child, the parents should get to know the family. Does the child go home after school to an empty house? Is there adult supervision of the child's activities?

Third, parents can promote alternatives to drugs. This includes everything from "Just Say No" clubs and programs to alternative activities such as sports, school clubs, the arts, and hobbies.

Fourth, parents need to teach children about drugs. Drug education should not be left to the schools. Parents must be personally involved, letting their children know that drugs will not be tolerated. This means parents should be educated about drugs and drug paraphernalia.

Fifth, parents must set a good example. Parents who are drug-free have a much better chance of rearing drug-free children. If a parent is using drugs, he or she should stop immediately. The unconditional message to their children must be that drugs are wrong and that they will not be tolerated in their home.

WHAT TO DO IF YOUR CHILD IS ON DRUGS

All the preventive measures in the world cannot assure that children will avoid experimenting with drugs. If an adult suspects his or her child is already using drugs, these practical suggestions should be followed.

First, parents should not deny their suspicions. Drug addiction takes time, but it occurs must faster with a child than with an adult. Some of the newer drugs (like crack) can quickly lead to addiction. Denial may waste precious time. A child's life may be in danger.

Second, parents must learn to recognize the symptoms of drug abuse. Some readily noticeable physical symptoms include a pale face, imprecise eye movements, and neglect of personal appearance. Some less noticeable symptoms involving social interaction include diminished drive or reduced ambition, a significant drop in the quality of schoolwork, reduced attention span, impaired communication skills, and less care for the feelings of others.

Third, parents must be consistent. Having clear rules regarding curfew, accountability for an allowance, and knowing where one's teen spends his or her time are important. Consistent parental guidelines allow for less opportunity to stumble into sin of any kind.

Fourth, parents should open up lines of communication. Asking probing questions and becoming informed about the dangers of drugs are strong means for offsetting drug use.

Finally, parents must be tough. Fighting drugs takes patience and persistence. Unconditional love is a potent weapon against drugs.

WHAT CAN THE CHURCH DO?

The church can provide much-needed answers and help to those addicted to alcohol and other drugs. Here are just a few suggestions of how the church can help substance abusers.

First, the pastor and staff must be educated about drug abuse. Substance abuse is a medical problem, a psychological problem, and a spiritual problem. The church staff should be aware of how these various aspects of the problem interrelate.

Pastoral staff members should also know the causes, effects, and treatments. He or she must be aware of the responses of both dependents and codependents. Sometimes the abuser's family prevents recovery by continuing to deny the problem exists.

The church staff can obtain helpful drug information through local libraries and various local agencies. Fortunately more Christians are writing good material on this issue, so local Christian bookstores are also a source of help.

Second, congregations must be educated. The church should know the facts about substance abuse. This is a worthy topic for sermons and Sunday school lessons. Ignorance puts young people in particular and the congregation in general at risk. Christians must be armed with the facts to combat this scourge on our nation.

Third, a program of prevention must be put in place. The best way to fight drug abuse is to stop it before it starts. A program that presents the problem of substance abuse and shows the results is vital. It should also provide a biblical framework for dealing with the problem of drugs in society and the church.

Fourth, churches might consider establishing support groups for both drug users and their families. The success of non-church-related groups like Alcoholics Anonymous points to the need for substance abusers to be in an environment that encourages acceptance and accountability. Ideally these should be within the church and should be taught from Christian principles. Offering support can be a primary way of "bearing one another's burdens" as Christians.

9
Breakdown of the Family

Social commentators have decried the breakdown of the family for years. After all, families are the bedrock of society. When families fall apart, society falls into social and cultural decline. Ultimately the breakdown of the American family is at the root of nearly every other social problem and pathology.

Just a few decades ago most children in America (80 percent) grew up in intact, two-parent families. Today children who do so are a minority. Illegitimacy, divorce, and other lifestyle choices have radically altered the American family, and thus have altered the social landscape.

Karl Zinsmeister of the American Enterprise Institute has written, "There is a mountain of scientific evidence showing that when families disintegrate, children often end up with intellectual, physical and emotional scars that persist for life." He continued, "We talk about the drug crisis, the education crisis, and the problem of teen pregnancy and juvenile crime. But all these ills trace back predominantly to one source: broken families."[1]

Broken homes and broken hearts also account for the incumbent economic difficulties America faces as a culture. The moral foundation of society erodes as children learn the savage values of the street rather than the civilized values of culture. And government inevitably expands to intervene in family and social crises brought about by the breakdown of the family. Sociologist Daniel Yankelovich puts it this way:

> Americans suspect that the nation's economic difficulties are rooted not in technical economic forces (for example, exchange rates or capital formation) but in fundamental moral causes. There exists a deeply intuitive sense that the success of a market-based economy depends on a highly developed social morality—trustworthiness, honesty, concern for future generations, an ethic of service to others, a humane society that takes care of those in need, frugality instead of greed, high standards of quality and concern for community. These economically desirable social values, in turn, are seen as rooted in family values. Thus the link in public thinking between a healthy family and a robust economy, though indirect, is clear and firm.[2]

UNWED MOTHERS

One of the most significant factors contributing to the breakdown of the family has been the steady rise of unwed births. Since 1960, illegitimate births have increased more than 400 percent. In 1960, 5 percent of all births were out of wedlock. Thirty years later nearly 30 percent of all births were illegitimate. Among blacks two out of every three births are illegitimate.[3]

To put this astonishing increase in illegitimate births in perspective, compare 1961 with 1991. Roughly the same number of babies were born in both years (about 4 million). But in 1991, five times as many of these babies were born out of wedlock.[4] That is one million illegitimate births in one year.

Even more disturbing is the realization that the rate of illegitimacy has increased nearly 60 percent in the last decade alone. Almost one-quarter of all unmarried women in the United States become unwed mothers. And the largest proportional increase is among well-educated, affluent women, suggesting that the social stigma on illegitimacy is disappearing.[5]

Social commentator Charles Murray believes that "illegitimacy is the single most important social problem of our time—more important than crime, drugs, poverty, illiteracy, welfare, or homelessness because it drives everything else."[6] The public costs of illegitimacy are unusually high. Michael Novak wrote, "Children born out of wedlock tend to have high infant mortality, low birth weight (with attendant morbidities), and high probabilities of being poor, not completing school, and staying on welfare themselves. As a matter of public policy (not to mention biblical morality) it pays for society to approve of marriage as the best setting for children, and to discourage having children out of wedlock."[7]

While speaking to the Commonwealth Club in San Francisco, Vice President Dan Quayle argued that "it doesn't help matters when prime-time TV has Murphy Brown—a character who supposedly epitomizes today's intelligent, highly paid, professional woman—mocking the importance of fathers by bearing a child alone, and calling it just another lifestyle choice."[8]

At the time, one would have thought the vice president had uttered the greatest blasphemy of our time. Yes, he was using a fictional character to make a point. Yes, he was challenging the tolerant, politically correct conventions of the time. But he was addressing an important issue neglected by many.

Fortunately a year later *Atlantic Monthly* magazine devoted the cover story of its April 1993 issue to this problem. The article was titled, "Dan Quayle was Right." "After decades of public dispute about so-called family diversity, the evidence from social-science research is coming in: The dissolution of two-parent families, though it may benefit the adults involved, is harmful to many children, and dramatically undermines our society."[9]

The author, Barbara Dafoe Whitehead, warned Americans of the cost of ignoring the breakdown of the family. "If we fail to come to terms with the relationship between family structure and declining child well-being, then it will be increasingly difficult to improve children's life prospects, no matter how many new programs the federal government funds. Nor will we be able to make progress in bettering school performance or reducing crime or improving the quality of the nation's future work force—all domestic problems closely connected to family breakup. Worse, we may contribute to the problem by pursuing policies that actually increase family instability and breakup."[10]

TEENAGE PREGNANCIES

Every sixty-four seconds, a baby is born to a teenage mother, and every five minutes a baby is born to a teenager who already has a child.[11] More than two-thirds of these births are to teen girls who are not married.

Becoming a teenage parent significantly decreases the chance that the young mother will be able to complete high school, attend college, and successfully compete for a job. She is much more likely to rear the child in poverty than are girls who do not become mothers as teenagers. "When teenagers have babies both mothers and children tend to have problems—health, social, psychological, and economic. Teens who have children out of wedlock are more likely to end up at the bottom of the socio-economic ladder."[12]

A related trend is that a growing number of adults are having sex with teens. This is more than just Joey Buttafuoco and Amy Fisher or Woody Allen and Soon-Yi Previn. Social statistics show that adult males are fathers of two-thirds of the babies born to teenage girls.[13]

In some ways this is not a new phenomenon. In 1920, for example, 93 percent of babies born to teenagers were fathered by adults. But the difference is that pregnant teens no longer marry the fathers. Today 65 percent of teenage mothers are unmarried.[14] Many of these kids are destined to spend a lifetime in a cycle of poverty and welfare dependency.

Why teenage girls become sexually involved with adult males is sometimes difficult to discern. A desire for a mature male protector and teenage insecurity are significant reasons. Teenage girls from broken homes or abusive homes often are easy prey for adult men, which may explain why adult men seek out teenage girls. In many cases teen sex is not consensual. Girls under the age of eighteen are victims of approximately half the rapes committed each year.[15]

Thus stemming the tide of teen pregnancy and reforming the current welfare system that often encourages it are important action points. But doing so must take into account the fact that adult male behavior is a significant factor in teenage girls becoming pregnant.

Whether we look at the increase in illegitimate births in general or teenage pregnancy in particular, we see a disturbing trend. In essence, Americans have been conducting a social experiment for the last three decades. And the evidence clearly points to major problems when children are reared in families without two parents. Illegitimate births are part of the reason for the breakdown of the family; divorce (as discussed in the next chapter) is the other.

SINGLE PARENTS

The number of single-parent families in America has increased threefold. Although they are called "single-parent homes," they could just as easily be called "female-headed homes," since approximately 90 percent of single-parent homes are homes without a father.[16]

Again, comparisons to the past are instructive. According to some projections, only 6 percent of black children and 30 percent of white children born in 1980 will live with both parents through age eighteen. By comparison, for children born in 1950, 52 percent of black children and 81 percent of white children lived with both parents until the children were eighteen.[17]

Children from single-parent homes are two to three times more likely than children in two-parent families to have emotional and behavioral problems. In addition, they are more likely to drop out of high school, become pregnant as teenagers, abuse drugs, and become entangled with the law.[18]

Older teenagers from broken homes also suffer. For example, they are more likely to have poor relationships with their fathers and mothers, to show high levels of emotional and behavioral problems, to have received psychological help, and to have dropped out of high school. Disruption-related problems are more apparent in young adulthood than they were in adolescence, especially among females. Young women from disrupted families are more likely to have disturbed mother-child relationships and to receive psychological help, while males are more likely to drop out of school and to have behavior problems. Youth experiencing early disruption (before age six) are particularly at risk.[19]

Back in 1965, when Daniel Patrick Moynihan served as assistant secretary of labor, he warned of the dangers of broken homes: "From the wild Irish slums of the 19th century Eastern seaboard, to the riot-torn suburbs of Los Angeles, there is one unmistakable lesson in American history: A community that allows a large number of young men to grow up in broken families, dominated by women, never acquiring any stable relationship to male authority, never acquiring any rational expectations about the future—that community asks for and gets chaos. Crime, violence, unrest, disorder—most particularly the furious, unrestrained lashing out at the whole social structure—these are not only to be expected, they are nearly inevitable."[20]

The conclusion should be obvious. Broken homes lead to broken hearts, along with social and cultural decline. As sociologist David Popenoe concluded, "I know of few other bodies of data in which the weight of evidence is so decisively on one side of the issue: On the whole, for children, two-parent families are preferable. . . . If our prevailing views on family structure hinged solely on scholarly evidence, the current debate never would have arisen in the first place."[21]

HOW TO REBUILD THE FAMILY

Teach Sexual Abstinence

A fundamental reason for the increase in unwed births is teenage sexual promiscuity. Reduce teenage sexual activity and illegitimacy will be reduced. Fortunately the abstinence message seems to be gaining in popularity and getting the media attention it deserves.

For example, the front page of the Sunday *New York Times* "Style" section featured the surprising headline: "Proud to Be a Virgin: Nowadays, You Can Be Respected Even If You Don't Do It." And the March 1994 issue of *Mademoiselle* featured an article proclaiming "The New Chastity." The article wondered if "saying no to sex might turn out to be the latest stage in the sexual revolution." *Mademoiselle* found that views on sexuality seem to be changing. Virgins, for example, are no longer seen as individuals who are fearful or socially inept. In fact, abstinence is now being equated with strength of will and character. Those once labeled "carefree" are now considered "careless" in light of AIDS and STDs.[22]

The Bible warns of the dangers of sexual immorality and calls for sexual abstinence. The apostle Paul wrote in 1 Corinthians 6:18, "Flee from sexual immorality. All other sins a man commits are outside his body, but he who sins sexually sins against his own body." Likewise in 1 Thessalonians 4:3 Paul said to "avoid sexual immorality." Peter admonished believers "to abstain from sinful desires, which war against your soul" (1 Pet. 2:11). Christians need to be speaking out on this important issue of abstinence.

One of the most visible campaigns for abstinence has come from the "True Love Waits" campaign begun by the Southern Baptist Convention in the spring of 1993. Students make this pledge: "Believing that true love waits, I make a commitment to God, myself, my family, those I date, my future mate, and my future children to be sexually pure until the day I enter a covenant marriage relationship."

A grass-roots movement to promote abstinence through a variety of programs has been spreading throughout the country. Crisis Pregnancy Centers provide speakers to address the issue of abstinence. Other groups—with names like "Aim for Success," "Best Friends," and "Athletes for Abstinence"—are spreading the positive message of abstinence to teens who need to hear an alternative to the safe-sex message.

Target Teen Pregnancies

The problem with teenage sex is not simply that teens are having sex. As already noted, in approximately half the cases adults are having sex with teenagers. State laws governing statutory rape are often called a "fictitious chastity belt" since law enforcement often ignores the laws.

The reasons for lax enforcement of these laws vary, but they surely include the fallout from the sexual revolution and the children's rights movement. American society has come to accept the notion that even young teenagers are engaging in consensual sex. While there may be some tawdry publicity when a high-profile entertainer like Woody Allen or Kelsey Grammer is accused of sex with a teenager, generally the issue is ignored.

But the issue cannot be ignored by Christians. "Welfare reform, sex education and teen pregnancy prevention programs and welfare reform are doomed to failure when they ignore the prevalence of adult-teen sex."[23] Education about the problem and enforcement of statutory rape laws would substantially reduce the number of unwed teens.

Teach Strong Marriage Principles

Marriages are falling apart, and other marriages never begin as sexual partners choose to live together rather than get married. Churches and Christian organizations must teach marriage principles so that marriages will last. Once built on commitment, today's marriages are seen as contracts based on the idea "as long as love shall last." Sound, biblical education is necessary to put marriages back on a firm foundation.

God created marriage (Gen. 2:24) and provided clear instructions for the roles of husbands and wives (Eph. 5:22–33). Hebrews 13:4 says that "marriage should be honored by all." Churches and Christian organizations need to provide sound biblical education on marriage, especially in this day when so many conflicting messages are being given about the home and family.

Fortunately a growing number of effective organizations are providing that needed education. Family Life Ministry holds weekend Family Life conferences throughout the country and the world to packed audiences eager to learn more about how to build strong marriages and families. The Marriage Encounter program has been providing the same important teaching in church and retreat settings. Also books, tapes, videos, and other seminars are focusing needed attention on the principles that will build a strong marriage and allow it to flourish.

Emphasize Fatherhood

As more and more children grow up in single-parent homes, fathers appear irrelevant and superfluous. Not only are they seen as expendable; they are often seen as part of the problem.

Yet the consequences of fatherless homes are devastating. "More than 70 percent of all juveniles in state reform institutions come from fatherless homes."[24] Children who grow up without fathers are more likely to be involved in criminal behavior because they lack a positive male role model in their lives. Fathers are not irrelevant. They may indeed spell the difference between success and failure for their children.

Often fatherless homes feed the cycle of illlegitimacy itself. "Young white women who grow up without a father in the home are more than twice as likely to bear children out of wedlock. And boys living in a single-parent family are twice as likely to father a child out of wedlock as boys from intact homes."[25]

Psychologist Christopher Bacorn, writing in *Newsweek* magazine, had one strong message to fathers: "Dear Dads: Save Your Sons." He laments the hundreds of angry, sullen, troubled teenage boys he sees who are brought in by anguished mothers trying to raise a son without a father. As one disappointed mother turned to leave with her troubled teenage son, Bacorn says he "was filled with a measure of hopelessness. But anger was there too, anger at the fathers of these boys. Anger at fathers who walk away from their children, leaving them feeling confused, rejected, and full of suffering. What's to become of boys like this? What man will take an interest in them? I can think of only one kind—a judge."[26]

He is right. "The likelihood that a young male will engage in criminal activities doubles if he is raised without a father and triples if he lives in a neighborhood with a high concentration of single-parent families."[27] The relationship between fatherlessness and crime should remind us of the importance of building strong families, *with fathers.*

Fortunately there are many ministries encouraging men to stand with their families. Gatherings like the Promise Keepers conferences are highly visible symbols of a much greater movement of men (in individual churches or parachurch organizations) who have dedicated themselves to running their families on biblical principles.

Groups like MAD DADS (Men Against Destruction Defending Against Drugs and Social Disorder) have been organized to encourage fathers in high-crime urban areas. Especially critical are young urban (often black) youths who do not have strong male role models to emulate. One organizer said, "They saw pimps and hustlers and dope dealers and gang bangers and hypersexual individuals who like to make babies but didn't assume the responsibility of taking care of them—so why should the kids? And so our first goal was just to mobilize strong, black fathers who were drug-free, who were willing to stand up and be role models, giving our kids another group of men they could look at."[28]

Building strong families must include building families with fathers.

Fatherlessness is one of the primary causes of social disintegration. Parenting cannot be left to mothers and grandmothers. Fathers are essential.

Modify the Tax System

The United States tax code should be pro-family, but it is not. "In the early 1950s the average family of four paid only about 5 percent of family income in taxes to Uncle Sam. Most of the rest was take-home pay. But in the 1990s, that same family pays roughly 24 percent of its earnings in federal income and payroll taxes."[29] Parents trying to meet these financial burdens have had to work longer hours, and it is no coincidence that as the tax burden has gone up, time with families has gone down. But the tax code affects families in other ways.

Our current tax code discourages marriage. This is what legislators have called a "marriage penalty." Some couples who are married pay more in taxes (often thousands of dollars more) than they would if they just lived together. The "marriage penalty" must be removed from the tax code.

There is also a "family penalty." Our current tax code also undervalues children. The personal dependent exemption has not kept pace with inflation. Economists estimate that the personal dependent exemption should be increased from the current $2,650 to $7,000.

Reform the Welfare System

Welfare and illegitimacy are inextricably connected. Breaking the cycle of poverty requires attention to both components. Our current welfare system supports and even encourages illegitimacy. On the other hand, illegitimacy can often begin the cycle of poverty and dependency. Nearly half of unwed teenage mothers go on welfare within one year after the birth of a first child. And by the time that child is five years old, 72 percent of white teens and 84 percent of black teens have received Aid for Dependent Children.[30] Social scientists have also found that the impact affects the next generation. "Children born outside of marriage are three times more likely to depend on welfare themselves when they reach adulthood."[31]

One University of Toledo economist estimates that about half of the rise in black illegitimacy has resulted from expanded welfare eligibility and benefits.[32] And University of Washington researchers found that states that pay higher welfare benefits have higher rates of illegitimacy.[33]

Welfare reform must work to discourage teenage pregnancies. Reform must also discourage mothers on welfare from having additional children they cannot afford to care for. (Of course, such reform ought not to encourage abortions as a means of reducing childbirths.) Finally, welfare reform must encourage fathers to take a greater responsibility for their illegitimate children.

Remove Major Obstacles to Adoption

As the illegitimate birthrate increases, lawmakers are considering adoption as one solution. Currently there are nearly five hundred thousand children in America's foster-care system. Nearly half of those who "graduate" from foster care (i.e., they turn eighteen without being placed in an adoptive family) will end up on welfare.[34] Unfortunately the social welfare bureaucracy only clears about fifty thousand kids for adoption each year.

Pregnancy counselors often ignore discussions about adoption with their pregnant clients, and social agencies mired in paperwork move too slowly in placing foster children in permanent, loving homes. Some have suggested that the simplest solution may be for states to place the job of finding suitable parents in the hands of private adoption services. Congress is also considering granting adopting parents a tax credit of up to five thousand dollars to pay for the substantial costs involved in the process of adoption. It is considering legislation as well that would mandate that pregnancy counselors provide clear, accurate information on the benefits of adoption.

America's families are falling apart, and society is falling into social and cultural decline. We must rebuild marriages and families. We must fight the rising rates of divorce and illegitimacy. And we must provide alternatives to the current welfare system, which often encourages and even subsidizes illegitimacy.

In the background is another crucial battleground: the sexual revolution. Rampant sexual immorality fuels the rising rates of unwed births as well as the rising numbers of sexually transmitted diseases. Christians must address the issue of sex in our society.

10
Divorce

MARRIAGES AND FAMILIES are falling apart in record numbers, and divorce is usually the reason. But often the impact of divorce is overlooked because of its subtle yet insidious erosion of the family structure. When the divorce rate increased in the 1960s, few would have predicted the dire consequences decades later. Divorce quickly moved from the margins to the mainstream and changed both the structure and the impact of the family.

This is the conclusion of not just Christians but also of researchers working in the field of social science. Clinical psychologist Diane Medved, for example, set out to write a book to help couples facing transitions due to divorce. She began her book with this startling statement:

> I have to start with a confession: This isn't the book I set out to write. I planned to write something consistent with my previous professional experience—helping people with decision making. . . . For example, I started this project believing that people who suffer over an extended period in unhappy marriages ought to get out. . . . I thought that striking down taboos about divorce was another part of the ongoing enlightenment of the women's, civil-rights, and human potential movements of the last twenty-five years. . . . To my utter befuddlement, the extensive research I conducted

for this book brought me to one inescapable and irrefutable conclusion: I had been wrong.[1]

She titled her book *The Case against Divorce.*

Until recently, divorce has been a relatively rare phenomenon. Certainly there have always been some couples who have considered divorce an option. But fundamental changes in our society in the last few decades have changed divorce from rare to routine.

During the 1970s the divorce rate doubled (and the number of divorces tripled from 400,000 in 1962 to 1.2 million in 1981).[2] To put this in perspective, compare the two most recent generations of women. Just 14 percent of caucasian women who married in the 1940s eventually divorced. But, almost half of those married in the late sixties and early seventies have already divorced.[3] Essentially the increase in the divorce rate has come not from older couples but from the baby-boomer generation. One Stanford University sociologist calculated that while men and women in their twenties comprised only about 20 percent of the population, they contributed 60 percent of the growth in the divorce rate in the 1960s and early 1970s.[4]

This increase is due to at least two major factors: attitude and opportunity. The baby-boomers' attitudes toward such issues as fidelity, chastity, and commitment are strikingly different from that of their parents. Their parents would stay in a marriage in order to make it work. Baby boomers, however, are less committed to the ideal of marriage and are quite willing to end what they feel is a bad marriage and move on with their lives. While their parents might have kept a marriage going "for the sake of the kids," the baby-boomer generation as a whole is much less concerned about such issues.

Economic opportunities also seem to be a significant factor in divorce. The rise in divorce closely parallels the increase in the number of women working. Women with a paycheck are less likely to stay in a marriage that is not fulfilling to them. Armed with a measure of economic power, many women have less incentive to stay in a marriage and work out their differences with their husbands. Sociologist David Popenoe, surveying a number of studies on divorce, concluded that "nearly all have reached the same general conclusion. It has typically been found that the probability of divorce goes up the higher the wife's income and the closer that income is to her husband's."[5]

The divorce rate is also affected by age, religious faith, and family background. Divorce rates are highest among those who marry young, and the divorce rate is three times greater for those who never attend religious services.[6] Marital failure often breeds marital failure. One study shows that adult children of divorced parents are four times more likely to get divorced than adult children of intact couples.[7]

DIVORCE MYTHS

Two statistical myths surrounding divorce need to be discussed. First, the divorce rate is *not* 50 percent. The percentage comes from comparing two fairly reliable social statistics: the number of marriage licenses issued and the number of divorce decrees issued. The problem arises from comparing the two numbers inappropriately.

In any given year there are approximately two million marriages and one million divorces. Comparing these two numbers produces the frequently cited 50 percent figure. But only a very small percentage of the people who married in any given year were also divorced in that same year. Comparing divorces to marriages in this way is a case of statistically mixing apples and oranges.

A better way to estimate the divorce rate is to take the percent of the total adult population who are currently or ever have been married (72 percent) and compare that to the number of people who are currently divorced (9 percent). This produces a 13 percent current divorce rate.

The second myth is related to the first: Most marriages *do not* end in divorce. While there has been much concern and hand-wringing over the rising divorce rate, we should not lose sight of the fact that a majority of marriages do not end in divorce court. Substantial media attention on divorce overlooks the fact that approximately 50 million established marriages are "flowing along like Ol' Man River."[8] These marriages may run into white water and the ride may be bumpy at times, but they continue to flow along the channel of marital stability and fidelity.

DIVORCE AND FAMILIES

Although the divorce rate is not as rampant as advertised, it is still having a devastating impact on both adults and children. Every year, parents of over one million children divorce. These divorces effectively cut one generation off from another. Children are reared without the presence of one of their parents. They are often forced to take sides in the conflict between their parents. And children often carry the scars of conflict and frequently blame themselves for the divorce.

One demographer, looking at this ominous trend of divorce and reflecting on its impact, acknowledged "No one knows what effect divorce and remarriage will have on the children of the baby boom. A few decades ago, children of divorced parents were an oddity. Today they are the majority. The fact that divorce is the norm may make it easier for children to accept their parents' divorce. But what will it do to their marriages in the decades ahead? No one will know until it's too late to do anything about it."[9]

What little is known about the long-term impact of divorce is disturbing. In 1971, Judith Wallerstein began a study of sixty middle-class families in the midst of divorce. Her ongoing research has provided a longitudinal study of the long-term effects of divorce on parents and children.

Like Diane Medved, Judith Wallerstein had to revise her previous assumptions. According to the prevailing view at the time, divorce was seen as a brief crisis that would resolve itself. Her book, *Second Chances: Men, Women and Children a Decade after Divorce*, vividly illustrates the long-term psychological devastation wrought not only on the children but also on the adults.[10] Here are just a few of her findings of the aftershocks of divorce:

- Three out of five children felt rejected by at least one parent.

- Five years after their parent's divorce, more than one-third of the children were doing markedly worse than they had been before the divorce.

- Half grew up in settings in which the parents were warring with each other even after the divorce.

- One-third of the women and one-fourth of the men felt that life had been unfair, disappointing, and lonely.

Some have criticized the Wallerstein study because it was not a representative study. For example, more than three-fourths of both mothers and fathers in her study had at least some college training, many with advanced degrees. But the fact that the study was unrepresentative makes her conclusions all the more shocking. Caucasian, educated, upper-middle-class children whose lives before divorce were relatively untroubled economically and emotionally should (at least theoretically) have had the least problems with divorce. Their long-term conflicts clearly demonstrate that the emotional tremors register on the psychological Richter scale many years after the divorce.

Researcher Robert Coombs has come to similar conclusions about the impact of divorce on adults. He has found that:

- Divorced men and women experience far greater health problems than their married or never-married counterparts.

- A greater number of divorced men and women are admitted for psychiatric care than married or single people, and their treatments are less successful.[11]

One review of thirty-two studies on the long-term effects of divorce concluded, "Adults of divorced parents have more problems and lower levels of well-being than adults whose parents stay married. They are depressed more frequently, feel less satisfied with life, get less education, and have less prestigious jobs. Even their physical health is poorer."[12]

For children the emotional impact also has an educational impact. One researcher came to these conclusions about the impact of divorce on children:

- Children of divorce do poorer in school, exhibit greater behavioral problems at home and in school, and engage in sexual activity and criminal behavior earlier in life than children whose parents remain married.[13]

- Compared with those from intact families, adults who experienced divorce as children have poorer psychological adjustment, lower socioeconomic attainment, and greater marital instability.[14]

One national study found an overall average of one lost year of education for children in single-parent families.[15]

The fragmented family left after divorce is significantly affected by the demise of the marriage. Family rules, relationships, and traditions suffer. By their own reports, divorced mothers are less likely to read to their children, share meals with them, and supervise school activities than married mothers. Compared with married mothers, single mothers exercise less control and have fewer rules about bedtimes, television watching, homework, and household chores.[16]

These fragmented families are also affected economically. After divorce the income of households with children declines, and a sizable percentage of divorced and separated women with kids live in poverty. In fact, the working middle class in this country has been rocked by the one-two punch of divorce and illegitimacy, creating what has been called the "feminization of poverty." Census Bureau statistics show that single mothers are five times more likely to be poor than are their married sisters.[17]

Remarriage after divorce adds another twist to modern relationships. Nearly half of all marriages in 1990 involved at least one person who had been down the aisle before, up from 31 percent in 1970.[18]

These changing family structures complicate relationships. Divorce and remarriage shuffle family members together in foreign and awkward ways. Clear lines of authority and communication get blurred and confused in these newly revised families. One commentator trying to get a linguistic handle on these arrangements called them "neo-nuclear" families.[19] The rules for these neo-nukes are complex and ever-changing. Children looking for stability are often insecure and frustrated. One futuristic commentator imagined this possible scenario: "On a spring afternoon, half a century from today, the Joneses are gathered to sing "Happy Birthday" to Junior. There's Dad and his third wife, Mom and her second husband, Junior's two half brothers from his father's first marriage, his six stepsisters from his mother's spouse's previous unions, 100-year-old Great Grandpa, all eight of Junior's current "grandparents," assorted aunts, uncles-in-law and stepcousins. While one robot scoops up the gift wrappings and another blows out the candles, Junior makes a wish . . . that he didn't have so many relatives."[20]

The stress on remarried couples is difficult enough, but it intensifies when stepchildren are involved. Conflict between a stepparent and a stepchild is inevitable and can often threaten the stability of a remarriage. According to one study, remarriages that involve stepchildren are more likely to end in divorce than those that do not.[21] Fully 17 percent of marriages that are remarriages for both husband and wife and that involve stepchildren break up within three years.[22] (Of course, a good number of first-time marriages end in divorce within three years too.)

NO-FAULT DIVORCE

Historically the laws governing marriage were based on the traditional Judeo-Christian belief that marriage was for life. Marriage was intended to be a permanent institution. Thus the desire for divorce was not held to be self-justifying. Legally the grounds for divorce had to be circumstances that justified making an exemption to the assumption of marital permanence. The spouse seeking a divorce had to *prove* that the other spouse had committed one of the "faults" recognized as justifying the dissolution of the marriage. In most states the classic grounds for divorce were cruelty, desertion, and adultery.

This legal foundation changed when California enacted a statute in 1969 that allowed for no-fault divorce. Before 1969, society erected a formidable barrier to prevent (or at least hinder) the dissolution of marriage. The legal change to no-fault divorce effectively led to what could now be called "divorce-on-demand." One by one, various state legislatures enacted no-fault divorce laws so that today this concept has become the de facto legal principle in every state.

Although marriage was to be "for better or worse, for richer or poorer," no ethic of self-sacrifice was likely to endure the self-indulgent 1960s. Perhaps the rise in divorce was inevitable, but the changes in the divorce law made it more certain. Obviously the increase in the divorce rate could not be solely explained by the implementation of no-fault divorce laws. The divorce rate was already going up when many states passed no-fault provisions. But these laws no doubt contributed to the increase. A University of Oklahoma study found that in the three years after no-fault was instituted, the divorce rates in forty-five of fifty states jumped.[23]

Arguments for no-fault divorce seemed compelling at the time. They were hailed as an overdue reform of a hypocritical system rife with conflict and lurid accusations. It was promised that no longer would partners have to prove fault with clandestine photographs and private investigators. Proponents of no-fault divorce promised that marital separation would be more amicable.

The fault-based system of divorce law had its roots in the view that marriage was a sacrament and was indissoluble. The current no-fault provisions have changed this perception. Marriage is no longer viewed as a covenant; it is seen instead as a contract. But legally it is an even less reliable contract than a standard business contract.

Classic contract law holds that a specific promise is binding and cannot be broken merely because the promisor changes his or her mind. In fact, the concept of "fault" in divorce proceedings is more like tort law than contract law in that it implies a binding obligation between two parties which has been breached, thus leading to a divorce. When state legislatures implemented no-fault divorce provisions, they could have replaced the fault-based protections with contract-like protections. Unfortunately they did not. In just a few decades we have moved from a position where divorce was permitted for a few reasons to a position in which divorce is permitted for *any* reason, or no reason at all.

Robert Plunkett, vice-dean of the Southern California Institute of Law, described the case against no-fault divorce in this way: "The wedding vow has devolved from being the most serious and solemn oath a typical person ever made into being less than a contract. An oral contract made with a two-year-old is more binding than the contract of marriage; it at least binds one party, the adult. A marriage contract is binding on no one."[24]

The impact on the institution of marriage has been devastating. Marginal marriages are much easier to dissolve, and couples who once might have tried to stick it out and work out their problems instead opt for a no-fault divorce.

But all marriages (not just marginal marriages) are at risk. After all, marriages do not start out marginal. Most marriages start out on a solid footing. But after the honeymoon comes the more difficult process of learning to live together harmoniously. The success of the process is affected by both internal factors (such as willingness to meet each other's needs) and external factors (such as the availability of divorce). But even these factors are interrelated. If the law gives more protection to the marriage contract, a partner may be more likely to love sacrificially and invest effort in the marriage. If the law gives less protection, a partner may be more likely to adopt a "looking out for number one" attitude.

The breakdown of marriage and family through divorce has eroded the social significance of the institution of marriage. Russian sociologist Pitirim Sorokin predicted decades ago that "divorces and separations will increase until any profound difference between socially sanctioned marriages and illicit sex-relationships will disappear."[25]

With millions of people divorced and millions more unwed couples living together, social acceptance for nontraditional lifestyles and relationships rises. Just as bad money drives out good money, so do these relationships cheapen the sacred institution of marriage.

In her book *The Abolition of Marriage*, Maggie Gallagher writes, "The law now forbids private individuals from distinguishing between married and unmarried couples in many cases. For example, many landlords and home mortgage companies, for a host of sound business as well as social reasons, once showed a certain favoritism for married couples and intact families. But with the rise in divorce rates, legislatures and courts established laws forbidding discrimination in housing or credit on the basis of marital status."[26]

Under the current laws and the current social climate, marriage is but one of many social lifestyles and options.

Various divorce reform bills have been proposed to rectify the current legal situation regarding divorce. Here are a few of the provisions found in many of these bills:

1. *Proving fault*: When one spouse opposes the divorce, the other spouse must prove fault.

2. *Family counseling*: All parties in uncontested divorces must seek therapy and counseling. In contested cases, therapy would be at the court's discretion.

3. *Family plan:* Divorcing parents must establish a plan for their children's physical care and financial future.

4. *Prenuptial counseling*: Premarital counseling would be required for couples.

Before no-fault divorce was instituted, women held a potent weapon. If a man wanted his freedom, he would have to pay for it. Usually the wife gained a measure of economic security through bargaining. Currently, under no-fault divorce laws, one spouse (even over the objections of the other) can obtain a divorce for essentially any reason at any time. By giving all the legal clout to the party that wants to break the marriage (and virtually none to the party that wants to preserve it), less culpable parties are forced to seek concessions from their estranged spouses. Often this takes the form of women being forced to accept insufficient child-support payments.

Returning to a fault basis for divorce would level the playing field and reduce the number of divorces. Currently 80 percent of divorces in this country are unilateral rather than truly mutual decisions.[27] Putting couples through the bother of offering proof of fault is also a good way of separating the cases where both mutually desire to divorce from cases where the noninitiating party has merely given up.

BIBLICAL PERSPECTIVE

The Bible speaks to the issue of divorce in both the Old and New Testaments. The most important Old Testament passage on divorce is Deuteronomy 24:1–4. "If a man marries a woman who becomes displeasing to him because he finds something indecent about her, and he writes her a certificate of divorce, gives it to her and sends her from his house, and if after she leaves his house she becomes the wife of another man, and her second husband dislikes her and writes her a certificate of divorce, gives it to her and sends her from his house, or if he dies, then her first husband, who divorced her, is not allowed to marry her again after she has been defiled. That would be detestable in the eyes of the Lord. Do not bring sin upon the land the Lord your God is giving you as an inheritance."

These verses were not intended to endorse divorce. The intention was to regulate the existing custom of divorce, not to put forth God's ideal for marriage. Jesus taught that this was a concession to human sinfulness and "hardness of heart" (Matt. 19:8).

Divorce was widespread in the ancient Near East. The certificate of divorce apparently was intended to protect the reputation of the woman and gave her the right to remarry. This public declaration protected her from charges of adultery. The Mishnah, for example, stated that a divorce certificate was not valid unless the husband explicitly said, "You are free to marry any man."[28]

Key to understanding this passage is the definition of "something indecent." It probably did not mean adultery, since that was subject to the penalty of death (Deut. 22:22), or premarital intercourse with another man (22:20–21), since that carried the same penalty. The precise meaning of the phrase is unknown and was subject to some debate even during the time of Christ. The conservative school of Shammai understood it to mean a major sexual offense. The liberal school of Hillel taught that it referred to anything displeasing to the husband (including something as trivial as spoiling his food). The apparent purpose of this law was to prevent frivolous divorce and to protect a woman who was divorced by her husband. The passage in no way encourages divorce; instead it regulates the consequences of divorce.

Another significant Old Testament passage is Malachi 2:10–16. "Have we not all one Father? Did not one God create us? Why do we profane the covenant of our fathers by breaking faith with one another? . . . Has not the LORD made them one? In flesh and spirit they are his. And why one? Because he was seeking godly offspring. So guard yourself in your spirit, and do not break faith with the wife of your youth. 'I hate divorce,' says the LORD God of Israel." This passage deals with breaking a prior agreement or covenant. It specifically addresses the issue of illegal intermarriage and the issue of divorce. Malachi taught that husbands and wives are to be faithful to each other because they have God as their Father. The marriage relationship is built on a solemn covenant. While God may tolerate divorce under some of the circumstances described in Deuteronomy 24, the instructions were given to protect the woman if a divorce should occur. This passage in Malachi reminds us that God hates divorce.

The Book of Matthew gives the clearest teachings by Jesus on the subject of divorce. "It has been said, 'Anyone who divorces his wife must give her a certificate of divorce.' But I tell you that anyone who divorces his wife, except for marital unfaithfulness, causes her to commit adultery, and anyone who marries a woman so divorced commits adultery" (Matt. 5:31–32).

"I tell you that anyone who divorces his wife, except for marital unfaithfulness, and marries another woman commits adultery" (19:9).

In these passages Jesus challenged the views of both of the two schools of Jewish thought (Shammai and Hillel), teaching that marriage is for life and should not be dissolved by divorce.

Defining the word *porneia* (translated "marital unfaithfulness") is a key element in seeking to understand these passages. While some commentators teach that this word refers to incestuous relationships or sexual promiscuity during the betrothal period, most scholars believe the word applies to relentless, persistent, and unrepentant adultery. Among those holding to this exception clause for adultery, some believe remarriage is possible while others do not.

The other significant section of teaching on divorce in the New Testament can be found in Paul's teaching on divorce in 1 Corinthians 7:10–15.

> To the married I give this command (not I, but the Lord): A wife must not separate from her husband. But if she does, she must remain unmarried or else be reconciled to her husband. And a husband must not divorce his wife. To the rest I say this (I, not the Lord): If any brother has a wife and she is not a believer and she is willing to live with him, he must not divorce her. And if a woman has a husband who is not a believer and he is willing to live with her, she must not divorce him. For the unbelieving husband has been sanctified through his wife, and the unbelieving wife has been sanctified through her believing husband. Otherwise your children would be unclean, but as it is, they are holy. But if the unbeliever leaves, let him do so. A believing man or woman is not bound in such circumstances; God has called us to live in peace.

In the first section Paul addressed Christians married to one another. Paul was obviously aware of the prevalence of divorce in the Greek world and of the legal right a wife had to initiate a divorce. He gave the command for believers to stay married.

In the next section Paul addressed the issue of mixed marriages. He said that even though there is religious incompatibility in such a marriage, the believing spouse is not to seek a divorce. Some divorces may have been initiated because of the command of Ezra to the Israelites in Jerusalem after the exile to divorce their pagan spouses (Ezra 10:11). Paul again affirmed the biblical principle: Do not seek divorce. However, if the unbelieving spouse insists on divorce, the believer may have to concede to those proceedings and is not bound in such circumstances.

Based on the preceding passages we can therefore conclude that a Christian can acquiesce to divorce in cases of marital infidelity by the other spouse or in cases of desertion by an unbelieving spouse. Yet even in these cases the church should not encourage divorce. Certainly in very troubling cases that involve mental, sexual, or physical abuse, legal separation is available as a remedy to protect the abused spouse. God hates divorce; therefore Christians should never be in the position of encouraging or promoting divorce. Instead they should be encouraging reconciliation.

One final question is whether a divorced person is eligible for a leadership position within the church. First Timothy 3:2 calls for a church leader to be above reproach and "the husband of one wife." Rather than prohibiting a divorced person from serving in leadership, the language of this verse actually focuses on practicing polygamists. Polygamy was practiced in the first century and was even found among Jewish and Christian groups. The phrase is literally "a one-woman man," that is, a man who is faithful to and focused on his wife. If Paul intended to prohibit a divorced person from leadership, he could have used a much less ambiguous term.

As Christians in a society where divorce is rampant, we must come back to these important biblical principles concerning marriage. Christians should work to build strong marriages. Pastors must frequently preach and teach about the importance of marriage. Christians should encourage others to attend various marriage-enrichment seminars and ministries in their communities.

Christians should also reach out to those who have been divorced and communicate Christ's forgiveness to them in the midst of their shattered lives. They need counseling and support groups. Many times they also need financial help and direction as they begin to put together the pieces of their lives.

Churches must be careful that their ministry to divorced people does not compromise their theology. Christians must reach out with both biblical convictions and biblical compassion. Marriage for life is God's ideal (Gen. 2); nevertheless millions of people have been devastated by divorce and need the compassionate outreach of Christians.

Churches have unfortunately erred on one side or another. Most churches have maintained a strong stand on marriage and divorce. While this strong biblical stand is admirable, it should also be balanced with compassion toward those caught in the throes of divorce. Strong convictions without compassionate outreach often seem to communicate that divorce is the unforgivable sin.

On the other hand, some churches in their desire to minister to divorced people have compromised their theological convictions. By starting without biblically based convictions about marriage and divorce, they have let their congregation's circumstances influence their theology.

Marriage for life is God's ideal, but divorce is a reality in our society. Christians should reach out with Christ's forgiveness to those whose lives have been shattered by divorce.

11
Pornography

PORNOGRAPHY is tearing apart the very fabric of modern society. Yet Christians are often ignorant of its impact and apathetic about the need to control this menace.

Pornography is an eight-billion-dollar-a-year business with close ties to organized crime.[1] The wages of sin are enormous when pornography is involved. Purveyors of pornography reap vast profits through sales in so-called "adult bookstores" and showing of films and live acts at porno theaters.

Pornography involves books, magazines, videos, and mechanical devices and has moved from the periphery of society into the mainstream through the renting of videocassettes, sales of so-called "soft-porn" magazines, and the airing of sexually explicit movies on cable television. To some, pornography is nothing more than a few pictures of scantily clad women in seductive poses. But pornography has become much more than just photographs of nude women.

Nearly nine hundred theaters in our country show pornographic films and more than fifteen thousand "adult" bookstores and video stores offer pornographic material. Adult bookstores outnumber McDonald's restaurants in the United States by a margin of at least three to one.[2] In 1985 nearly one hundred full-length pornographic films were distributed to "adult" theaters, providing estimated annual box-office revenues of fifty million dollars.[3]

DEFINITIONS OF PORNOGRAPHY

The 1986 Attorney General's Commission on Pornography defined pornography as material that "is predominantly sexually explicit and intended primarily for the purpose of sexual arousal." Hard-core pornography "is sexually explicit in the extreme, and devoid of any other apparent content or purpose."[4]

Another important term is "obscenity." The current legal definition of obscenity is found in the 1973 case of *Miller v. California.* "According to the *Miller* case, material is obscene if all three of the following conditions are met: (1) the average person, applying contemporary community standards, would find that the work, taken as a whole, appeals to the prurient interests. (2) The work depicts or describes, in a patently offensive way, sexual conduct specifically defined by the applicable state (or federal) law, and (3) The work, taken as a whole, lacks serious artistic, political, or scientific value."[5]

TYPES OF PORNOGRAPHY

The first type of pornography we will discuss is adult magazines. These are primarily (but not exclusively) directed toward adult male readers. The magazines with the widest distribution (e.g., *Playboy* and *Penthouse*) do not violate the *Miller* standard of obscenity and thus can be legally distributed. But other magazines which do violate these standards are still readily available in many adult bookstores.

Another type of pornography is videocassettes. These are rented or sold in most adult bookstores and have become a growth industry for pornography. People who would never go into an adult bookstore or watch a pornographic movie in a public theater can obtain these videocassettes through bookstores or in the mail and watch them in the privacy of their homes. Usually these videos display a high degree of hard-core pornography and portrayal of illegal acts.

A third type of pornography is motion pictures. Ratings standards are being relaxed, and many pornographic movies carrying R and X ratings are being widely shown and distributed. Many of these so-called "hard R" rated films would have been considered obscene just a decade ago.

A fourth type of pornography is television. As in the case of motion pictures, standards for commercial television have been continuously lowered. But cable television poses an even greater threat. The Federal Communications Commission does not regulate cable in the same way it does public access stations. Thus many pornographic movies are shown on cable television. Like videocassettes, cable television provides the average person with easy access to pornographic material. People who would never go to an adult bookstore can now view the same sexually explicit material in their homes, making cable television "the ultimate brown wrapper."

A fifth type of pornography is "cyberporn," or pornography on computers and through modems. Hard-core pictures, movies, online chat, and even live sex acts can now be downloaded and viewed by virtually anyone through the Internet. Sexually explicit images can be found on Web pages and in news groups and are far too readily available for anyone of any age. What was once only available to a small number of people willing to drive to the bad side of town can now be viewed at any time in one's home at a nominal cost.

A sixth type of pornography is audio porn. This includes "Dial-a-porn" telephone calls, the second fastest growth market of pornography. Although most of the messages fall within the *Miller* definition of obscenity, these businesses continue to thrive and are often used by children.

According to Henry Boatwright, chairman of the U.S. Advisory Board for Social Concerns, approximately 70 percent of the pornographic magazines sold end up in the hands of minors. WAP (Women Against Pornography) estimates that about 1.2 million children are annually exploited in commercial sex (child pornography and prostitution).

THE DOCUMENTED EFFECTS OF PORN

Defenders of pornography argue that it is not harmful and thus should not be regulated or banned. In 1970 the Presidential Commission on

Obscenity and Pornography concluded there was no relationship between exposure to erotic material and subsequent behavior. But more than a decade of research, as well as the production of more explicit and violent forms of pornography, has shown that pornography can have profound effects on human behavior.

The 1986 *Final Report of the Attorney General's Commission on Pornography* examined five classes of material: sexually violent material; nonviolent materials depicting degradation, domination, subordination, or humiliation; nonviolent and nondegrading materials; nudity; and child pornography. The first two categories demonstrated negative effects, the third showed mixed results, the fourth was not found harmful but commissioners agreed it was morally objectionable, and the fifth involves sexual exploitation and is already outlawed.

Psychological Effects

Psychologist Edward Donnerstein, of the University of Wisconsin, found that brief exposure to violent forms of pornography can lead to antisocial attitudes and behavior. Male viewers of pornography tend to be more aggressive toward women, less responsive to the pain and suffering of rape victims, and more willing to accept various myths about rape.[6]

Researchers have found that exposure to pornography (especially violent pornography) can produce an array of undesirable effects, including rape and sexual coercion,[7] increased fantasies about rape,[8] and desensitization to sexual violence and trivialization of rape.[9]

In an attempt to isolate the role of violence from sex in pornography-induced situations, James Check, of York University in Canada, conducted an experiment in which men were exposed to different degrees of pornography—some violent, some not. All groups exhibited the same shift in attitude, namely, a higher inclination to use force as part of sex.[10]

In another study researchers Dolf Zillman and Jennings Bryant investigated the effects of nonviolent pornography on sexual callousness and the trivialization of rape. They showed that continued exposure to pornography had serious adverse effects on beliefs about sexuality in general

146

and on attitudes toward women in particular. They also found that pornography desensitized people to rape as a criminal offense.[11] These researchers also confirmed that massive exposure to pornography encouraged a desire for increasingly deviant materials that promote violence (such as sadomasochism and rape).[12]

Zillman measured the impact of viewing pornography on the subjects' views as to what constitutes normal sexual practice. The group that saw the largest amount of pornography gave far higher estimates of the incidence of oral sex, anal sex, group sex, sadomasochism, and bestiality than did the other two groups.[13]

One study demonstrated that pornography can diminish a person's sexual happiness.[14] The researchers found that people exposed to non-violent pornography reported diminished satisfaction with their sexual partner's physical appearance, affection, curiosity, and sexual performance. They were also inclined to put more importance on sex without emotional involvement.

In a nationwide study University of New Hampshire researchers Larry Baron and Murray Strauss found a strong statistical correlation between circulation rates of pornographic magazines and rape rates.[15] They found that in states with high circulation rates of pornography literature, rape rates were also high. In states with low circulation rates, rape rates also tended to be low.

Of course, a statistical correlation does not prove that pornography causes rape. Certainly not everyone who uses pornography becomes a rapist. And it is possible that rape and pornographic consumption are only indirectly related through other factors, like social permissiveness and "macho" attitudes among men. In fact, Baron and Strauss did examine some of these factors in their study and did not find any significant correlation.

Subsequent studies have had similar results. Ohio State University researchers Joseph Scott (who testifies frequently for pornographers in court) and Loretta Schwalm examined even more factors than Baron and Strauss (including the circulation of nonsexual magazines) and could not eliminate the correlation between pornography and rape.[16]

Michigan state police detective Darrell Pope found that in 41 percent of the thirty-eight thousand sexual assault cases in Michigan between 1956 and 1979, pornographic material was viewed just before or during the crime. This corroborates with research done by psychotherapist David Scott, who found that "half the rapists studied used pornography to arouse themselves immediately prior to seeking out a victim."[17]

Addiction to Pornography

Researcher Victor Cline has documented in his research how men become addicted to pornographic materials and begin to desire more explicit or deviant material, ending up acting out what they have seen.[18]

In fact, psychologists have identified a five-step pattern in pornographic addiction. The first step is *exposure*. Addicts have been exposed to pornography in many ways, ranging from sexual abuse as children to looking at widely available pornographic magazines.

The second step is *addiction*. People who continually expose themselves to pornography "keep coming back for more and more" in order to get new sexual highs. James L. McCough, of the University of California at Irvine, says that "experiences at times of emotional or sexual arousal get locked in the brain by the chemical epinephrine and become virtually impossible to erase."[19]

A third step is *escalation*. Previous sexual highs become more difficult to attain; therefore users of pornography begin to look for more exotic or deviant forms of sexual behavior to bring them stimulation.

A fourth step is *desensitization*. What was initially shocking becomes routine. Shocking and disgusting sexual behavior is no longer avoided but is sought out for more intense stimulation. Concern about pain and degradation gets lost in the pursuit of the next sexual experience.

A fifth step is *acting out* the fantasies. People do what they have seen and found sexually stimulating. Not every pornography addict will become a serial murderer or a rapist. But many do look for ways to act out their sexual fantasies.

The *Final Report of the 1986 Attorney General's Commission on Pornography* includes a full chapter of testimony from victims whose assailants had previously viewed pornographic materials. The adverse effects range from physical harm (rape, torture, murder, sexually transmitted diseases) to psychological harm (suicidal thoughts, fear, shame, nightmares).

Social Effects

Defining the social effects of pornography has been difficult because of some of the prevailing theories of its impact. One view is that it actually performs a positive function in society by acting like a "safety valve" for potential sexual offenders.

The most famous proponent of this view was Berl Kutchinsky, a criminologist at the University of Copenhagen. His famous study on pornography found that when the Danish government lifted restrictions on pornography, the number of sex crimes decreased.[20] His theory was that the availability of pornography siphons off dangerous sexual impulses. But when the data for his "safety-valve" theory was further evaluated, many of his research flaws began to show.

For example, Kutchinsky failed to distinguish between different kinds of sex crimes (such as rape and indecent exposure) and instead merely lumped them together. This effectively masked an increase in rape statistics. He also failed to take into account that increased tolerance for certain crimes (e.g., public nudity and sex with a minor) may have contributed to a drop in the reported crimes.

Proving cause and effect in pornography is virtually impossible because ethically researchers cannot do certain kinds of research. As researcher Dolf Zillman says, "Men cannot be placed at risk of developing sexually violent inclinations by extensive exposure to violent or nonviolent pornography, and women cannot be placed at risk of becoming victims of such inclinations."[21]

Deborah Baker, a legal assistant and executive director of an anti-obscenity group, agrees that conclusively proving a connection between pornography and crime would be very difficult.

> The argument that there are no established studies showing a connection between pornography and violent crime is merely a smokescreen. Those who promote this stance well know that such research will never be done. It would require a sampling of much more than a thousand males, exposed to pornography through puberty and adolescence, while the other group is totally isolated from its influence in all its forms and varying degrees. Each group would then have to be monitored—through the

commission of violent crimes or not. In spite of the lack of formal research, though, the FBI's own statistics show that pornography is found at 80 percent of the scenes of violent sex crimes, or in the homes of the perpetrators.[22]

Nevertheless a number of compelling statistics suggest that pornography does have profound social consequences. For example, of the fourteen hundred child sexual-molestation cases in Louisville, Kentucky between July 1980 and February 1984, adult pornography was connected with each incident and child pornography with the majority of them.[23] Extensive interviews with sex offenders (rapists, incest offenders, and child molesters) have uncovered a sizable percentage of offenders who use pornography to arouse themselves before and during their assaults.[24] Police officers have seen the impact pornography has had on serial murders. In fact, pornography consumption is one of the most common profile characteristics of serial murders and rapists.[25]

Professor Cass Sunstein, writing in the *Duke Law Journal*, says that some sexual violence against women "would not have occurred but for the massive circulation of pornography." Citing cross-cultural data, he concludes, "The liberalization of pornography laws in the United States, Britain, Australia, and the Scandinavian countries has been accompanied by a rise in reported rape rates. In countries where pornography laws have not been liberalized, there has been a less steep rise in reported rapes. And in countries where restrictions have been adopted, reported rapes have decreased."[26]

In his introduction to a reprint of the *Final Report of the Attorney General's Commission on Pornography*, columnist Michael McManus noted the following: "The FBI interviewed two dozen sex murderers in prison who had killed multiple numbers of times. Some eighty-one percent said their biggest sexual interest was in reading pornography. They acted out sex fantasies on real people. For example, Arthur Gary Bishop, convicted of sexually abusing and killing five young boys, said, 'If pornographic material would have been unavailable to me in my early states, it is most probable that my sexual activities would not have escalated to the degree they did.' He said pornography's impact on him was 'devastating. . . . I am a homosexual pedophile convicted of murder, and pornography was a determining factor in my downfall.'"28

James Dobson interviewed Ted Bundy, one of this nation's most notorious serial killers. On the day before his execution Bundy said that the "most damaging kinds of pornography are those that involve violence and sexual violence. Because the wedding of those two forces, as I know only too well, brings about behavior that is just, just too terrible to describe."28

CENSORSHIP AND FREEDOM OF SPEECH

Attempts to regulate and outlaw pornography within a community are frequently criticized as censorship and a violation of the First Amendment. But the U.S. Supreme Court clearly stated in *Roth v. United States* (1957) that obscenity was not protected by the First Amendment. Federal, state, and local laws apply to the sale, display, distribution, and broadcast of pornography. Pornographic material, therefore, can be prohibited if it meets the legal definition of obscenity.

The Supreme Court ruled in the case of *Miller v. California* (1973) that a legal definition of obscenity must meet the three-part test previously discussed. If it appeals to the prurient interest, is patently offensive, and lacks serious value (artistically, politically, or scientifically) then the material is considered obscene and is illegal.

The Supreme Court further ruled in *Paris Adult Theatre v. Slaton* (1973) that material legally defined as obscene is not accorded the same protection as free speech in the First Amendment. The court ruled that even if obscene films are shown only to "consenting adults," this did not grant them immunity from the law.

In the case of *New York v. Ferber* (1982) the Supreme Court ruled that child pornography was not protected under the First Amendment even if it was not legally defined as obscene under their three-part test. Since children cannot legally consent to sexual relations, child pornography constitutes sexual abuse. Congress also passed the Child Protection Act in 1984, which provided tougher restrictions on child pornography.

Cable television is presently unregulated since it is not technically "broadcasting" as defined in the Federal Communications Act. Thus cable television is able to show pornographic movies with virtual impunity. The Federal Communications Act must be amended so that the Federal Communications Commission can regulate cable television.

BIBLICAL PERSPECTIVE

God created men and women in His image (Gen. 1:27) as sexual beings. But because of sin in the world (Rom. 3:23), sex has been misused and abused (1:24–25).

Pornography attacks the dignity of men and women created in the image of God. Pornography also distorts God's gift of sex, which should be shared only within the bounds of marriage (1 Cor. 7:2–3). When the Bible refers to human sexual organs, it often employs euphemisms and indirect language. Although there are some exceptions (a woman's breasts and womb are sometimes mentioned), generally Scripture maintains a basic modesty toward a man's or woman's sexual organs.

Moreover, Scripture specifically condemns the practices that result from pornography, such as sexual exposure (Gen. 9:21–23), adultery (Lev. 18:20), bestiality (18:23), homosexuality (18:22 and 20:13), incest (18:6–18), and prostitution (Deut. 23:17–18).

A biblical perspective of human sexuality must recognize that sexual intercourse is exclusively reserved for marriage for the following purposes. First, it establishes the one-flesh union (Gen. 2:24–25; Matt. 19:4–6). Second, it provides for sexual intimacy within the marriage bond. The word "know" indicates a profound sense of sexual intimacy (Gen. 4:1). Third, sexual intercourse is for the mutual pleasure of husband and wife (Prov. 5:18–19). Fourth, sexual intercourse is for procreation (Gen. 1:28).

The Bible also warns against the misuse of sex. Premarital and extramarital sex is condemned (1 Cor. 6:13–18; 1 Thess. 4:3). Even thoughts of sexual immorality (often fed by pornographic material) are condemned (Matt. 5:27–28).

Moreover, Christians must realize that pornography can have significant harmful effects on the user. These include a comparison mentality, a performance-based sexuality, a feeling that only forbidden things are sexually satisfying, increased guilt, decreased self-concept, and obsessional thinking.

Christians therefore must do two things. First, they must work to keep themselves pure by fleeing immorality (1 Cor. 6:18) and thinking on things that are pure (Phil. 4:8). As a man thinks in his heart, so is he (Prov. 23:7, NKJV). Christians must make no provision for the flesh (Rom. 13:14). Pornography will fuel the sexual desire in abnormal ways and can eventually lead to even more debase perversion. We therefore must "abstain from fleshly desires which war against the soul" (1 Pet. 2:11, KJV). Second, Christians must work to remove this sexual perversion of pornography from society.

STEPS TO COMBAT PORNOGRAPHY

First, parents must teach a wholesome, biblical view of sex to their children. Helpful aids can be obtained from groups like Focus on the Family and Josh McDowell Ministries.

Second, we must evaluate our exposure to media (magazines, television shows, rock music) with inappropriate sexual themes. Parents should set a positive example for their children, taking time to discuss these stories, programs, and songs with them from a Christian perspective.

Third, pastors should warn their congregations about the dangers of pornography and instruct them in a proper view of sexuality. Like Joseph in the Old Testament, we should flee immorality and enticement into sin. Sermons should also be given to help members build a strong Christian home.

Fourth, parents should block cyberporn with software available for this purpose. There are many commercial services as well as special software programs that can screen and block areas children may try to investigate. These programs will block out sexual hot spots on the Internet and can detect an offending phrase that might be used in an online chat room. Parents should also try to be readily available to their children when they are online and should ask them about their online computing. Extensive late-night use by children and teens may be an indication of a problem.

Fifth, individual Christians should get involved with national (National Coalition Against Pornography, Enough Is Enough) or local decency groups organized to fight pornography. These groups have been effective in many localities in ridding their communities of the porno plague.

Sixth, we should express our concern to local officials (through letters and petitions) about adult movie houses and bookstores in our communities. Seventh, if we receive pornographic material in the mail, it should be reported to the local postmaster with the request that federal agents take action. Eighth, Christians should not patronize stores that sell pornographic materials. Boycotts and pickets can be organized to get community attention focused on the problem.

Christians can make a difference in this area. Following these common sense procedures can begin to rid our communities of the porno plague and return a standard of decency to our society.

12
Gambling

G AMBLING used to be what a few unscrupulous people did with the aid of organized crime. But gambling fever now seems to affect nearly everyone as more and more states are legalizing various forms of gambling. Legalized gambling currently exists in forty-seven states and the District of Columbia. More Americans are gambling than ever before, and they are also gambling more of their money. The total amount of money legally wagered in the United States has risen by 3,000 percent since 1974.[1] The momentum seems to be on the side of those who want legalized gambling as a way to supplement state revenues. But these states and their citizens often ignore the costs that are associated with legalized gambling. The social and economic costs are enormous.

BAD SOCIAL POLICY

Legalized gambling is bad social policy. At a time when Gamblers Anonymous estimates that there are at least twelve million compulsive gamblers, it does not make a lot of sense to have the state promoting gambling. State sponsorship of gambling makes it harder, not easier, for compulsive gamblers to reform. Since about 96 percent of those gamblers began gambling before the age of fourteen,[2] we should be especially concerned about the message such a policy sends to young people.

The economic costs that gamblers themselves incur are significant. The average compulsive gambler has debts exceeding eighty thousand dollars.[3] And this figure pales in comparison with other social costs that surface because of family neglect, embezzlement, theft, and involvement in organized crime. Compulsive gamblers damage the lives of their family, friends, and business associates. Some of the consequences of gambling are marital disharmony, divorce, child abuse, substance abuse, and suicide attempts.

Proponents argue that state lotteries are an effective way to "raise taxes" painlessly. But the evidence shows that legalized gambling often hurts those who are poor and disadvantaged. A national task force on gambling found that those in the lowest income bracket lost more than three times as much money to gambling (as a percentage of income) as those at the wealthiest end of the spectrum.[4] One New York lottery agent reported that "seventy percent of those who buy my tickets are poor, black, or Hispanic."[5] And a National Bureau of Economic Research "shows that the poor bet a much larger share of their income."[6]

A major study on the effect of the California lottery came to the same conclusions. The Field Institute's California poll found that 18 percent of the state's adults bought 71 percent of the tickets sold. These heavy lottery players (who bought more than twenty tickets each in the contest's first forty-five days) were "more likely than others to be black, poorer and less educated than the average Californian."[7]

Studies also indicate that gambling increases when economic times are uncertain and people are concerned about their future. Joseph Dunn, director of the National Council on Compulsive Gambling, says, "People who are worried about the factory closing take a chance on making it big. Once they win anything, they're hooked."[8]

The social impact of gambling is often hidden from the citizens who decide to legalize gambling. But later these costs show up in the shattered lives of individuals and their families. Psychologist Julian Taber warns, "No one knows the social costs of gambling or how many players will become addicted. . . . The states are experimenting with the minds of the people on a massive scale."[9] Families of gamblers are torn apart by strife, divorce, and bankruptcy. Boydon Cole and Sidney Margolius, in their book *When You Gamble—You Risk More Than Your Money*, conclude, "There is no doubt of the destructive effect of gambling on the family life. The corrosive effects of gambling attack both the white-collar and blue-collar families with equal vigor."[10]

The impact on crime is also significant. The crime rate in gambling communities is nearly double the national average.[11] Researchers calculate that for every dollar the state receives in gambling revenues, it costs the state at least three dollars in increased social costs (for criminal justice and social welfare).[12]

BAD GOVERNMENTAL POLICY

Legalized gambling is also bad governmental policy. Government should promote public virtue, not seduce its citizens to gamble in state-sponsored vice. Government is supposed to be the servant of God according to Romans 13, but its moral stance is compromised when it enters into a gambling enterprise.

Citizens would be outraged if their state government began enticing its citizens to engage in other potentially destructive behavior (such as taking drugs). But those same citizens see no contradiction when government legalizes and even promotes gambling. Instead of being a positive moral force in society, government contributes to the corruption of society.

Ross Wilhelm, professor of business economics at the University of Michigan, says, "State lotteries and gambling games are essentially a rip-off and widespread legalization of gambling is one of the worst changes in public policy to have occurred in recent years. . . . The viciousness of the state-run games is compounded beyond belief by the fact that state governments actively advertise and promote the games and winners."[13]

The corrosive effect legalized gambling has on government itself is also a cause for concern. As one editorial in the *New York Times* noted, "Gambling is a business so rich, so fast, so powerful and perhaps inevitably so unsavory that it cannot help but undermine government."[14]

LEGAL AND ILLEGAL GAMBLING

One of the standard clichés used by proponents of legalized gambling is that by instituting legal gambling, illegal gambling will be driven out. This argument makes a number of faulty assumptions. First, it assumes that people are going to gamble anyway, and so the state might as well get a piece of the action. Second, it assumes that, given the choice, people would rather gamble in a state-sponsored program because it will be regulated. They believe the state will make sure that the program is fair and that each participant has an equal chance of winning. Third, it assumes that if the state enters the gambling arena, it will drive out illegal gambling because it will be a more efficient competitor for gamblers' dollars.

Although the arguments seem sound, they are not. Although some people do gamble illegally, most citizens do not. Legalized gambling entices people to gamble who normally would not gamble at all. Duke University researchers have found that the lottery is a "powerful recruiting device" because one-fourth of those who otherwise would not gamble at all do bet on lotteries.[15]

Second, legal gambling does not drive out illegal gambling. If anything, just the opposite is true. As legalized gambling comes into a state, it provides additional momentum for illegal gambling. The Organized Crime Section of the Department of Justice found that "the rate of illegal gambling in those states which have some legalized form of gambling was three times as high as those states where there was not a legalized form of gambling."[16] And one national review found that "In states with different numbers of games, participation rates increase steadily and sharply as the number of legal types of gambling increases. Social betting more than doubles from 35 percent in states with no legal games to 72 percent in states with three legal types; the illegal gambling rate more than doubles from nine percent to 22 percent; and commercial gambling increases by 43 percent, from 24 to 67 percent."[17]

We can see that legalized gambling in various states has been a stimulator of illegal gambling, not a competitor to it.

The reasons for the growth of illegal gambling in areas where legalized gambling exists are simple. First, organized crime syndicates often use the free publicity of state lotteries and parimutuel betting to run their own numbers games. The state actually saves them money by providing publicity for events involving gambling. Second, many gamblers would rather bet illegally than legally. When they work with a bookie, they can bet on credit and do not have to report their winnings to the government, two things they cannot do if they bet on state-sponsored games. This explains why illegal gambling thrives in states with legalized gambling.

Another important issue is the corrupting influence legalized gambling can have on society. First, legalized gambling can have a very corrupting influence on state government. In the last few years there have been numerous news reports of corruption and fraud in state lotteries. Second, there is the corrupting influence on the citizens themselves. Gambling breeds greed. Research has shown that the number of compulsive gamblers increases between 100 and 550 percent when legalized gambling is brought into an area.[18] Every day otherwise sane people bet large amounts of money in state lotteries because they hope they will win the jackpot. Moreover, states and various gambling establishments produce glitzy ads that appeal to people's greed in order to entice them to risk even more than they can afford.

The government should be promoting positive social values like thrift and integrity rather than negative ones like greed and avarice. It should be promoting the public welfare rather than seducing citizens to engage in state-sponsored vice.

ECONOMIC COSTS

Legalized forms of gambling (state lotteries, parimutuel betting, and casinos) are often promoted as good economic policy. Proponents say they are painless ways of raising billions of dollars in state revenue. But there is another economic side to legalized gambling.

First, the gross income statistics for legalized gambling are much higher than the net income. State lotteries are one example. Although about half the states in the U.S. have lotteries and the figures vary from state to state, we can work with some average figures. Generally, the cost of management, advertising, and promotion is approximately sixty cents of each dollar. In other words, for every dollar raised in a lottery, only forty cents goes to the state budget. By contrast, direct taxation of the citizens costs only about one cent on the dollar, so that for every dollar raised by taxes, ninety-nine cents goes to the state.

Second, gambling adversely affects a state economy. Legalized gambling depresses businesses because it diverts money that could have been spent in the capital economy into gambling that does not stimulate the economy. Boarded-up businesses surrounding casinos are a visible reminder of this, but the effect on the entire economy is even more devastating than may be apparent at first. Money that could be invested, loaned, and recycled through the economy is instead risked in a legalized gambling scheme.

Legalized gambling siphons off a lot of money from the economy. More money is wagered on gambling than is spent on elementary and secondary education ($286 billion versus $213 billion in 1990).[19] Historian John Ezel concludes in his book *Fortune's Merry Wheel*, "If history teaches us anything, a study of over 1,300 legal lotteries held in the United States proves . . . they cost more than they brought in if their total impact on society is reckoned."[20]

SPORTS GAMBLING

Although sports gambling is illegal in almost every state, there has been a push over the last few years to legalize it. One concern is how sports gambling has affected the integrity of the game. Illegal gambling has already adversely affected sports; legalizing it would simply make matters worse.

One issue revolves around how sports betting is carried out. Betting is done against a point spread. A team is picked to win by so many points. The point-spread issue has become a large part of the game. At some sporting events people in the stands are disappointed when their team does not beat the point spread. Even though the team won, some of the fans became upset because they did not defeat the team by enough points to cover the spread.

True fans are concerned if the team wins or loses. Gamblers, however, are concerned with whether the team was able to beat the point spread. Winning by one point is not enough if the point spread was three.

Sportswriters and sports broadcasters routinely announce that a team is favored by a certain number of points. They argue that reporting such information is appropriate because it is relevant to the game. But is it? When the headlines of a newspaper boldly state, for example, "Denver Broncos Favored by Six Points," they have gone far beyond merely reporting about a sporting event and are actually promoting sports gambling.

Sports gambling has also affected sports by introducing organized crime into the sporting arena. Past scandals at Boston College and Tulane University illustrate how gambling has adversely affected the integrity of athletes, coaches, and colleges. Players have been involved in point-shaving scandals. It is clear the problem could only become worse in an environment in which sports gambling is legalized.

Another area of ethical concern is how government might become involved in sports gambling. Once sports gambling is legalized, the possibility of governmental investigation is opened up. A wise sports decision might be questioned by a government-oversight body. Suppose a football team were picked to win by more than three points and was leading by one point with less than a minute left. Even if they were on their opponent's twenty-yard-line, they might decide not to kick a field goal. To do so would risk the possibility of a blocked kick. A wise coach would tell his team to sit on the ball and let the clock run out. The team would win but not beat the point spread. Citizens who lost money would certainly call for an investigation to see if fraud was involved.

Obviously sports gambling takes place, even though it is illegal. But good reasons argue against legalizing it. It is bad social policy, it is bad economic policy, and it is bad governmental policy. Sports gambling is bad not only for these reasons but also because it could adversely affect the integrity of the game.

BIBLICAL PERSPECTIVE ON GAMBLING

Even though the Bible does not directly address gambling, a number of principles can be derived from Scripture. First, the Bible emphasizes a number of truths that conflict with gambling. The Bible, for example, emphasizes the sovereignty of God (Matt. 10:29–30). Gambling, however, is based on chance. The Bible admonishes people to work creatively and for the benefit of others (Eph. 4:28), while gambling fosters a something-for-nothing attitude. The Bible condemns materialism (Matt. 6:24–25), while gambling promotes it.

Gambling breeds a form of covetousness, whereas the tenth commandment (Exod. 20:17) admonishes people not to covet. Coveting, greed, and selfishness are the base emotions that entice individuals to gamble. Christians should be concerned about gambling, if for no other reason than the effect it has on the "weaker brother" and how it will affect the compulsive gambler. State-sponsored gambling makes it more difficult for compulsive gamblers to reform. Legalized gambling thus becomes an institutionalized form of greed and a pioneer of addictive behavior.

Second, gambling destroys the work ethic. Two key biblical passages deal with the work ethic. In Colossians 3:23–24 the apostle Paul wrote, "Whatever you do, work at it with all your heart, as working for the Lord, not for men, since you know that you will receive an inheritance from the Lord as a reward. It is the Lord Christ you are serving." And in 2 Thessalonians 3:7 and 10 he stated, "For you yourselves know how you ought to follow our example. . . . For even when we were with you, we gave you this rule: 'If a man will not work, he shall not eat.'"

The Twentieth Century Fund research group commented, "Gambling's get-rich-quick appeal appears to mock capitalism's core values: Disciplined work habits, thrift, prudence, adherence to routine, and the relationship between effort and reward."[21] These core values of the work ethic are all part of the free enterprise system as well as part of the Christian life. Gambling corrupts these values and replaces them with greed and selfishness. Rather than depending on hard work, gamblers depend on luck and chance.

Third, gambling destroys families. Gambling is a major cause of family neglect. Many of the social costs associated with gambling come from a get-rich-quick mind-set. As people get caught up in a gambling frenzy, they begin to neglect their families. Money spent on lottery tickets or at horse tracks is frequently not risk capital but is income that should be spent on family needs. According to 1 Timothy 5:8 a person who refuses to care for his family is worse than an unbeliever. Parents must provide for their children (2 Cor. 12:14) and eat the bread of their labors (2 Thess. 3:12). When gambling is legalized, it causes people to neglect their God-mandated responsibility to care for their families, and many of those families then end up on welfare.

Fourth, gambling is a form of state-sponsored greed. Romans 13:1–4 teaches that government is to be a servant of God, providing order in society and promoting public virtue. Legalized gambling undercuts the government's proper role and subverts the moral fabric of society through greed and selfishness promoted by a state-sponsored vice.

Since gambling undermines the moral foundations of society and invites corruption in government, Christians must stand against attempts to legalize gambling.

13
Homosexuality

WITHIN THIRTY YEARS homosexuality has moved from the margins of society to the mainstream. Though many homosexuals may not be "out of the closet," homosexuality is. In the years following the beginning of the gay rights movement in 1969, homosexuality has been publicly debated and promoted in almost every arena.

Homosexuality has become an issue of public policy and morality. Homosexuals march for equal treatment under the law, comparing their plight to that of disadvantaged minorities. They call for total acceptance of the gay lifestyle and for freedom from criticism and condemnation.

Against these claims the Bible provides signposts that warn people away from the dangers of sexual relations outside of God's ordained plan. All sexual sins (fornication, adultery, homosexuality) represent an attempt by mankind to deviate from God's best and to trespass into dangerous areas. Unfortunately many in the homosexual community have tried to alter the biblical teaching on homosexuality. They argue that the Bible does not condemn homosexuality at all.

GENESIS AND THE SIN OF SODOM

Foundational to a Christian understanding of sexuality is God's plan in creation found in Genesis 1 and 2. He created humans as male and female in His image and likeness (1:27). Human sexuality is manifested in two genders, not three, four, or five.[1] The Bible teaches that it was not good that man was alone (2:18), so God created woman to be man's counterpart and colaborer.

Homosexuality cannot fulfill the unitive and the procreative aspects of human sexuality as ordained by God. This is precisely why in various passages the Bible refers to homosexual relations as unnatural. Homosexuality is a violation of the natural process God intended for human sexuality.

The first reference to homosexuality in the Bible is in Genesis 19. Lot entertained two angels who came to the city to investigate its sins. In the evening all the men from every part of the city of Sodom surrounded Lot's house and ordered him to bring out the visitors so that "we may know them" (19:5, NKJV). The men of Sodom did not know they were angels. The Hebrew word for "know" (*yādaʿ*) means that the men of the city wanted to have sex with the visitors. This is why the New International Version renders the clause, "so that we can have sex with them."

More recently, proponents of homosexuality argue that biblical commentators misunderstand the story of Sodom.[2] They argue that the men of the city merely wanted to meet these visitors. Some commentators argue that the men were anxious to extend Middle Eastern hospitality, whereas other commentators say they wanted to interrogate the visitors and make sure they were not spies. In either case, homosexuals argue, the passage has nothing to do with homosexuality. They say the sin of Sodom was inhospitality, not homosexuality.

Prohomosexuality commentators point out that the Hebrew word *yādaʿ* can mean "to get acquainted with" as well as mean "to have intercourse with." In fact, the word appears over nine hundred times in the Old Testament, and only twelve times does it mean "to have sex with" someone. Therefore they conclude that the sin of Sodom had nothing to do with homosexuality.

The problem with this argument is the context. Statistics is not the same as exegesis. Word count is not the sole criterion for determining the meaning of words. And even if a statistical count should be used, the argument backfires. Of the twelve times the word "to know" is used in the Book of Genesis, it means "to have sexual intercourse with" in ten of the twelve occurrences.

Second, the context does not warrant the interpretation that the men of Sodom only wanted to get acquainted with the strangers. This is borne out by Lot's reply. "So Lot went out to them through the doorway, shut the door behind him, and said, 'Please my brethren, do not do so wickedly! See now, I have two daughters who have not known a man; please let me bring them out to you, and you may do to them as you wish; only do nothing to these men, since this is the reason they have come'" (Gen. 19:6–8, NKJV). One can sense Lot's panic as he foolishly offered his virgin daughters to the crowd instead of the foreigners. This is not the action of a man responding to the crowd's request "to become acquainted with" the men.

Lot described his daughters as women who "have not known a man." Clearly this implies sexual intercourse and does not mean "to be acquainted with." It is unlikely that the first use of the word "to know" (v. 5) differs from the second use of the word (v. 8). Both times the words "to know" mean "to have intercourse with" or "to have sex with." This is the only consistent translation for the passage.

Third, Jude 7 provides a fitting commentary on Genesis 19. The New Testament reference clearly states that the sin of Sodom involved "sexual immorality and perversion." The word "perversion" (rendered "strange flesh" in the NKJV) could imply homosexuality or even bestiality,[3] and provides further evidence that the sin of Sodom was homosexuality, not inhospitality.

MOSAIC LAW

Homosexual practices are condemned in the Mosaic Law. Two passages in Leviticus call it detestable (or "an abomination," NKJV): "Do not lie with a man as one lies with a woman; it is detestable" (18:22), and "If a man lies with a man as one lies with a woman, both of them have done what is detestable" (20:13). The word for "detestable" or "abomination," used several times in Leviticus 18, is a strong term of disapproval, implying that something is abhorrent to God.

Commentators see these verses as an expansion of the seventh commandment. Though not an exhaustive list, the sexual sins listed in Leviticus are representative of the common sinful practices of nations surrounding Israel.

Prohomosexual commentators have more difficulty dealing with these clear passages, but they usually offer one of two responses. Some argue that these verses appear in the "holiness code" of Leviticus and therefore they apply only to the priests and ritual purity.[4] Therefore, according to this perspective, these are religious prohibitions, not moral prohibitions. Others argue that these prohibitions were merely for the Old Testament theocracy and are not relevant today. They suggest that if Christians wanted to be consistent with the Old Testament law code in Leviticus, they should avoid eating rare steak, wearing mixed fabrics, and having marital intercourse during the wife's menstrual period.[5]

Do these passages apply merely to ritual purity rather than moral purity? Part of the problem comes from making the two issues distinct. The priests were to model moral behavior within their ceremonial rituals. Moral purity and ritual purity cannot be so easily separated, especially when discussing the issue of human sexuality. To hold to this rigid distinction would imply that such sins as adultery were not immoral (see Lev. 18:20) or that bestiality was morally acceptable (see 18:23).

The second argument concerns the relevance of the Mosaic Law today. Few Christians today keep kosher kitchens or balk at wearing clothes made of more than one kind of fabric. But the logical extension of the argument that the Old Testament admonition against homosexuality is irrelevant today would be that bestiality and incest are also morally acceptable, since prohibitions against these two sins surround the prohibition against homosexuality. If the Mosaic Law is irrelevant to homosexuality, then it is also irrelevant to having sex with animals (18:23) or having illicit sex with someone's daughter (18:17).

More to the point, to say that the Mosaic Law has ended is not to say that God has no laws or moral codes for mankind. Even though the ceremonial law has passed, the moral law remains. The New Testament speaks of the "law of the Spirit" (Rom. 8:2) and the "law of Christ" (Gal. 6:2). One cannot say that something that was sin under the Law is not sin under grace. Ceremonial laws concerning diet or wearing mixed fabrics no longer apply, but moral laws (including those rooted in God's creation order for human sexuality) continue. Moreover, these prohibitions against homosexuality can also be found in the New Testament.

NEW TESTAMENT PASSAGES

Three key New Testament passages concerning homosexuality are Romans 1:26–27; 1 Corinthians 6:9–10; and 1 Timothy 1:10. Of the three, the most significant is the one in Romans because it deals with homosexuality within the larger cultural context. It says, "Because of this, God gave them over to shameful lusts. Even their women exchanged natural relations for unnatural ones. In the same way the men also abandoned natural relations with women and were inflamed with lust for one another. Men committed indecent acts with other men, and received in themselves the due penalty for their perversion."

Here the apostle Paul set forth the gentile world's guilt before a holy God and focused on the arrogance and lust of the Hellenistic world. Gentiles turned away from the true worship of God, so that "God gave them over to shameful lusts." Rather than follow God's instruction in their lives, they "suppress the truth by their wickedness" (1:18), following passions that dishonor God.

Another New Testament passage dealing with homosexuality is 1 Corinthians 6:9–10. "Do you not know that the wicked will not inherit the kingdom of God? Do not be deceived: Neither the sexually immoral nor idolaters nor adulterers nor male prostitutes nor homosexual offenders nor thieves nor the greedy nor drunkards nor slanderers nor swindlers will inherit the kingdom of God." Making use of the "abuse" argument, prohomosexual commentators point out that Paul was only singling out homosexual *offenders*. In other words, they argue that Paul was condemning homosexual abuse rather than responsible homosexual behavior.

In essence, these commentators suggest that Paul was calling for temperance rather than abstinence. But this approach could not be applied to other sins listed in 1 Corinthians 6 or 1 Timothy 1. Was Paul calling for responsible adultery or responsible prostitution? Is there such a thing as moral theft and swindling? Obviously the argument breaks down. Scripture never condones sex outside of marriage (including premarital sex, extramarital sex, and homosexual sex). God created man and woman for the institution of marriage (Gen. 2:24).

BIOLOGICAL CAUSES FOR HOMOSEXUALITY

Is there a biological cause or causes for homosexuality? The answer is not as simple as homosexual activists would have us believe. Human sexuality is influenced by a complex set of factors. Therefore it is impossible to provide a single cause for homosexuality. There is no such thing as a "typical homosexual," and it is doubtful we would ever find a single causal factor for homosexuality. Physiological, psychological, and spiritual factors all play a part.

For years scientists have been looking for biological causes of homosexuality. Finding such a factor (e.g., hormones or a gay gene) would give support to the frequently heard homosexual cliché that "I was born this way." It gives credence to the concept that homosexuality is not a sin but a biological condition entitled to legal and social recognition.[6] The three most prominent studies have been a brain study (by Simon LeVay), a twins study (by Michael Bailey and Richard Pillard), and a genetic study (by Dean Hamer).

Simon LeVay, a neuroscientist at the Salk Institute, has argued that homosexuals and heterosexuals have notable differences in the structure of their brains. In 1991 he studied forty-one cadavers (nineteen homosexual men, sixteen heterosexual men, six heterosexual women). He found that a specific portion of the hypothalamus, the area of the brain that governs sexual activity, was consistently smaller in homosexuals than in heterosexuals.[7] He therefore argued that there is a distinct physiological component to sexual orientation. In other words, "biology is destiny."

Numerous problems exist with this study, however. First, there was considerable range in the size of the hypothalamic region. In a few homosexual men this region was the same size as that of the heterosexuals, and in a few heterosexuals this region was as small as that of the homosexuals. So the statistical correlation is not as strong as news reports of the initial study might lead one to believe.

Second is the chicken-and-egg problem. When there is a difference in brain structure, is the difference the *cause* of sexual orientation or is it the *result* of sexual orientation? Researchers, for example, have found that when people who become blind begin to learn Braille, the area of the brain controlling the reading finger actually grows larger. Could this be a possible explanation for the size difference between the hypothalami of homosexuals and heterosexuals?

Third, LeVay later had to admit that he did not know the sexual orientation of some of the cadavers in the study. He acknowledged that he was not sure if the heterosexual males in the study were actually heterosexual. Since some of those he identified as "heterosexual" had died of AIDS, critics have raised doubts about the accuracy of his study.

Fourth, there was the potential for bias in this study. LeVay has said he was driven to study the potential physiological roots of homosexuality after his homosexual lover died of AIDS. He even admitted that if he failed to find a genetic cause for homosexuality he might walk away from science altogether.[8] Later he did just that, moving to West Hollywood to open up a small, unaccredited "study center" focusing on homosexuality.

In December 1991 Michael Bailey of Northwestern University joined Richard Pillard of the Boston University School of Medicine in publishing a study of homosexuality in twins. They surveyed homosexual men for information about their brothers and found statistics they believed proved that sexual orientation is biological. Of the homosexuals who had identical twin brothers, 52 percent of those twins were also homosexual; 22 percent of those who had fraternal male twins said that their twin was gay; and only 11 percent of those who had adopted siblings said their adopted brothers were also homosexual. They attributed the differences in those percentages to the differences in genetic material shared.

Though this study has also been touted as proving a genetic basis to homosexuality, there are significant problems with it. First, this theory is not new. It was first proposed in 1952. Since that time three other separate research studies have come to very different conclusions.[9] Therefore the conclusions of the Bailey-Pillard study should be evaluated in the light of other contradictory studies.

Second, most published reports did not mention that only 9 percent of the nontwin brothers of homosexuals were homosexuals. Fraternal twins share no more genetic material than nontwin brothers, yet homo-sexuals are more than twice as likely to share their sexual orientation with a fraternal twin than with a nontwin brother. Whatever the reason, the answer cannot be genetic.

Third, why are not nearly all identical twin brothers of homosexuals also homosexual? In other words, if biology is determinative, why are nearly half of the identical twins *not* homosexual? Bailey admitted that "there must be something in the environment to yield the discordant twins."[10] And that is precisely the point: There is something (perhaps everything) in the environment to explain sexual orientation.

Fraternal incest, for example, has been statistically shown to be much higher for twins than nontwins.[11] Could the social and emotional close-ness of twins explain similar sexual orientation? An identical twin of a homosexual that sleeps in the same bed or bedroom is more apt to be physically closer to his twin. As one biologist put it, "In order for such a study to be at all meaningful, you'd have to look at twins raised apart. It's such badly interpreted genetics."[12]

Fourth, there was potential for bias in the twins study. Bailey is a homo-sexual and has been an outspoken proponent of a pro-gay agenda in science. While the study should be evaluated on its merits, it nevertheless is important to be aware of potential bias in any scientific study.

The third major study usually cited as proving a biological cause for homosexuality is the so-called "gay gene" study. In 1993 a team of re-searchers led by Dean Hamer of the National Cancer Institute announced "preliminary" findings from research into the connection between homo-sexuality and genetic inheritance.[13] In a sample of seventy-six homosexual males, the researchers found a statistically higher incidence of homosexu-ality in their male relatives (brothers, uncles) on their mother's side of the family. This suggested a possible inherited link through the X chromosome. A follow-up study of forty pairs of homosexual brothers found that thirty-three shared a variation in a small section of the X chro-mosome.

Although this study was promoted by the press as evidence of the dis-covery of a gay gene, some of the same concerns raised with the previous two studies apply here. First, the findings involve a limited sample size and are therefore sketchy. Even the researchers acknowledged that these were "preliminary" findings. In addition to the sample size being small, there was no control testing done for heterosexual brothers. Insufficient research done on the social histories of the families was also raised by critics as a major concern with the study.

Second, similarity does not prove cause. Just because thirty-three pairs of homosexual brothers share a genetic variation does not mean that variation causes homosexuality. And what about the other seven pairs that did not show the variation but were homosexuals? Some of the same concerns raised about the Bailey-Pillard study are relevant here.

Third, research bias may again be an issue. Hamer and at least one of his other team members were homosexual. It seems that this was deliberately kept from the press and was revealed only later. Hamer, it turns out, was not merely an objective observer. He has presented himself as an expert witness on homosexuality, and he stated that he hoped his research would give comfort to men feeling guilty about their homosexuality.[14]

Each of these three studies looking for a biological cause for homosexuality had its flaws. Does that mean there is no physiological component to homosexuality? Not at all. Actually it is probably too early to say conclusively. Scientists may indeed discover a clear biological predisposition to sexual orientation. But a predisposition is not the same as a determination. Maintaining this difference leads to some key distinctions, acording to Sherwood Cole.

> Assuming that biological influences on homosexuality are "predisposing" rather than "determining" also allows one to make some additional important distinctions. For example, "predisposing" influences are much more likely to influence one's orientation (desires, attitudes, preferences, attractions, and fantasies) than one's behavior. While these influences are not to be treated lightly, it may or may not result in the overt expression of homosexual behavior. Since the Bible's condemnation and prohibition of homosexuality (Lev. 18:22; 20:13; Rom. 1:26–27; 1 Cor. 6:9; 1 Tim 1:10) address behavioral practices, not orientation, this distinction is important to the debate. The individual who, in spite of a homosexual orientation, refrains from the practice of this lifestyle is to be commended, not condemned.[15]

The social and moral implications of this distinction are also relevant. Some people may inherit a predisposition for anger, depression, or alcoholism, yet society does not condone these behaviors. And even if violence, depression, or alcoholism were proven to be inborn (determined by genetic material), would we accept them as normal and refuse to treat them? Of course not. The Bible has clear statements about such things as anger and alcoholism. Likewise the Bible has clear statements about homosexuality.

PSYCHOLOGICAL CAUSES FOR HOMOSEXUALITY

Because human sexuality is so complex, finding a single cause for homosexuality is unlikely. There is, however, growing evidence that a number of environmental factors in a family or an individual's experience seem to influence one's sexual orientation.

Since the time of Sigmund Freud, counselors have noticed a pattern of family relationships that frequently appears in a homosexual person's family of origin: a domineering mother and a passive or absent father. Though this is a stereotype with obvious exceptions, the pattern still manifests itself in the lives of many homosexual men. One counselor summarized the various research findings in this way: "In his book *Male Homosexuality* (Yale University Press, 1988) Dr. Richard Friedman cites 13 independent studies from 1959 to 1981 on the early family lives of homosexuals. Out of these 13, all but one concluded that, in the parent-child interactions of adult homosexuals, the subject's relationship with the parent of the same sex was unsatisfactory, ranging from a distant, nonintimate relationship to an outright hostile one."[16]

Another factor is early sexual experience. Many homosexuals cite backgrounds of being sexually molested or having had sexual experiences early in their childhood. These experiences may range from sexual abuse (from another homosexual and/or a family member) to an early childhood sexual experience that could be described as pleasurable. In an attempt to rationalize the feelings that surface from this experience the child often begins to act on those feelings and pursue similar sexual experimentation.

Much less research has been done on lesbian women, but sexual abuse does seem to be a frequent pattern in the history of women with homosexual tendencies. This abuse may be physical, sexual, and/or emotional. When the abuse comes at the hand of a man, the women may view men as tyrants and avoid them. When the abuse comes at the hand of a woman, she may grow up longing for the womanly love and protection she did not receive.

Psychologists have identified certain emotional needs everyone has. Homosexuals report that one or more of these emotional needs are unmet.[17] Is it possible that homosexuals attempt to meet these legitimate needs by relating to same-sex persons in illegitimate ways? Three human emotional needs are relevant to this discussion.

The first is the need for gender identity. In other words, what does it mean to be male or female? Boys with gender-identity problems do not feel masculine. Showing "effeminate" behavior is not femininity; it is a lack of confidence of the ability to be masculine. Often this derives from a lack of bonding with the same-sex parent ("I'm unacceptable to my father, so I must be unacceptable to other males"). For lesbians, the trigger will be the opposite of the homosexual man. In other words, while the trigger for the male can be a weak father, the trigger for a female may be a distant mother.

The second need is for a healthy role model. How does an emotionally healthy man or woman act? Children learn what masculinity and femininity are by watching how this is modeled in the lives of those close to them. When the role models are missing, the cues and influences may be missing or mixed, thereby leading to a different sense of identity and sexual orientation.

The third need is for same-sex bonding. Bonding with members of one's own sex is a basic psychological need. This would include bonding with a nurturer (usually a parent), a mentor (a coach, a teacher, a discipler), and comrades (peers and friends of the same sex). Research shows that only after the need for bonding with the same sex has been fulfilled can relationships move on to the opposite sex. Often, however, bonding with others of the same sex does not happen. A boy, for example, may bond with the women in his life, or with no one at all. Some counselors suggest that people struggling with homosexual feelings are not so much having a sexual problem as much as they are having a relational problem. This same-sex "deficit" may be an explanation for homosexual behavior.

SPIRITUAL CAUSES FOR HOMOSEXUALITY

Ultimately homosexuality is a manifestation of the sin nature that strikes us all (Rom. 3:23). Because of the Fall (Gen. 3) God's creation was spoiled and human behavior has fallen into degrading passions (Rom. 1:24). Sin has spoiled every aspect of our being (spiritual, intellectual, emotional, physical, sexual). Therefore we should not be surprised that anyone (heterosexual or homosexual) could have sexual fantasies and temptations in this area. Those who choose to act on those feelings and temptations are acting outside God's plan for human sexuality.

A society that turns from God's plan accelerates sexual irresponsibility. Homosexuals are told they "were born that way" and should celebrate their sexuality. Heterosexuals are encouraged to experiment and expand their sexual choices. People with guilt feelings over their sexual experiences and temptations are encouraged to accept their feelings with the cliché "once gay, always gay." The ultimate problem is not physiological or even psychological, but an unwillingness to deal with the spiritual problem of sin. Psychological and spiritual counsel, therefore, is the answer to homosexuality.

ONCE GAY, ALWAYS GAY?

One of the most frequent clichés heard in homosexual circles is "once gay, always gay." In a sense it is a corollary cliché to the slogan "You are born gay." Secular counselors routinely tell patients struggling with homosexual feelings that they were born that way, that they cannot change, and that they should simply learn to affirm their feelings.

Despite such clichés and counseling there is hope for the person struggling with homosexual feelings. Groups like Exodus International provide a network of ninety organizations that specialize in helping homosexuals leave their lifestyle and change their sexual orientation. Consider this sampling of quotations from experts in the sexual counseling field.

- "Some people do change their sexual orientation" (Dr. John Money).[18]

- "Despite the rhetoric of homosexual activists, all studies which have attempted conversion from homosexuality to heterosexuality have had significant success" (Dr. Glenn Wood and Dr. John Dietrich).[19]

- "I have recently had occasion to review the result of psychotherapy with homosexuals and have been surprised by the findings—a considerable percentage of overt homosexuals became heterosexual" (Dr. Ruben Fine).[20]

The success rate for homosexual counseling varies, depending on the approaches and circumstances. William Masters and Virginia Johnson reported successful results in 71.6 percent of all cases after a six-year follow-up period.[21] Others have reported similar success rates.

The time for treatment can also vary. Joseph Nicolosi reported, "I have worked with about 175 men to date and I can say in terms of claims of cure that when the men stay with me in a matter of months they begin to experience change in their life."[22]

Ultimately it is Christ's loving act of redemption that can free someone bound by the ropes of sexual addiction (heterosexual or homosexual). Some people experience no further homosexual temptations, but most struggle with their sexual temptations in the process of sanctification. Individual Christians and churches must find creative ways to reach out to those caught in the bondage of homosexuality by learning to love the sinner while hating the sin.

14
Technology

TECHNOLOGY is the systematic modification of the environment for human ends. Often it is a process or activity that extends or enhances a human function. A microscope, for example, extends one's visual perception. A tractor extends one's physical ability. A computer extends a person's ability to calculate. Technology also includes devices that make physical processes more efficient. The many chemical processes we use to make products also fit this definition of technology.

The biblical mandate for developing and using technology is stated in Genesis 1:28. God gave mankind dominion over the land, and we are obliged to use and manage these resources wisely in serving the Lord. God's ideal was not to have a world composed exclusively of primitive areas. Before the Fall Adam was to cultivate and keep the Garden of Eden (Gen. 2:15). After the Fall the same command pertains to the application of technology to this fallen world, a world that "groans" in travail (Rom. 8:22). Technology can benefit mankind in exercising proper dominion (such as curing disease, breeding livestock, or growing better crops), and thus remove some of the effects of the Fall.

Technology is neither good nor evil in itself. The worldview behind each particular technology determines its value. In the Old Testament, technology was used both for good (e.g., the building of the ark, Gen. 6) and for evil (e.g., the building of the Tower of Babel, Gen. 11). Therefore the focus should not be so much on the technology itself as on the philosophical motivation behind its use. Three important principles that should be considered.

First, technology should be seen as a tool, not as an end in itself. There is nothing sacred about technology. Unfortunately Western culture tends to rely on it more than is appropriate. If a computer, for example, proves a particular point, people have a greater tendency to believe it than if the answer was a well-reasoned conclusion given by a person. If a machine can do the job, employers are prone to mechanize, even if human labor does a better or more creative job. Often our society unconsciously values machines over man. Humans become servants to machines rather than the other way around.

There is a tendency to look to science and engineering to solve problems that in reality may be due to human sinfulness (wars, prejudice, greed), the fallenness of the world (death, disease), or God's curse on Adam (finite resources). In Western culture especially, we tend to believe that technology will save us from our problems, and thus we use technology as a substitute for God. As Christians we must not fall into this trap, but instead must exhibit our ultimate dependence on God. We must also differentiate between problems that demand a technological solution and ones that can be remedied by a social or spiritual one.

Second, technology should be applied in different ways, according to differing circumstances. For example, there are distinctions between man and animal that, because we are created in God's image (Gen. 1:26–27), call for different applications of medical science. Using artificial insemination to improve the genetic fitness of livestock does not justify using it on human beings. Christians should resist the idea that just because we *can* do something we *should* do it. Technological ability does not automatically grant moral permission.

Another important aspect of this principle is to recognize the diversity of cultural and social contexts when implementing technology. American farmers may use a high-energy, green-revolution type of agriculture, but that does not mean it is the best form of agriculture to export worldwide.

Many commentators, most notably E. F. Schumacher, have focused on the notion of appropriate technology.[1] In Third World countries, for example, sophisticated energy-intensive and capital-intensive forms of agriculture may be inappropriate for the culture as it presently exists. Industrial advance often brings social disruption and increasing havoc to a society. Developing countries must use caution in choosing the appropriate steps to industrialize, lest they be greatly harmed in the process.

Third, ethics rather than technology must determine the direction of our society. Jacques Ellul has expressed the concern that technology moves society instead of vice versa.[2] Our society today seems all too motivated by a technological imperative in the culture. The technological ability to do something is not the same as a moral imperative to do it. Technology should not determine ethics, particularly for Christians.

Though scientists may possess the technological ability to be gods, they nevertheless lack the wisdom to act as God. Too often man has tried to use technology to become God. He uses it to work out his own physical salvation, to enhance his own development, or even to attempt to create life. Christians who take human fallenness seriously will humbly admit that we often do not know enough about God's creation to use technology wisely. The reality of human sinfulness means that society should be careful to prevent the use of technology for greed and exploitation.

Technology's fruits can be both sweet and bitter. C. S. Lewis writes in *The Abolition of Man*, "From this point of view, what we call Man's power over Nature turns out to be power exercised by some men over men with Nature as its instrument. . . . There neither is nor can be any simple increase of power on Man's side. Each new power won *by* man is a power *over* man as well. Each advance leaves him weaker as well as stronger. In every victory, besides being the general who triumphs, he is also the prisoner who follows the triumphal car."[3]

Christians must bring a strong biblical critique to each technological advance and analyze its impact. The goal should be to liberate the positive effects of technology while restraining negative effects by setting up appropriate constraints against abuse.

COMPUTERS AND THE INFORMATION REVOLUTION

The information revolution is the latest technological advance Christians must consider. The shift to computers and an information-based society has been swift as well as spectacular. The first electronic digital computer ENIAC weighed thirty tons, had eighteen thousand vacuum tubes, and occupied a space as large as a boxcar.[4] Less than forty years later, many hand-held calculators had comparable computing power for a few dollars. Today most people have a computer on their desk containing more computing power than engineers could imagine just a few years ago.

The impact of computers on our society was probably most vividly seen when in 1982 *Time* magazine picked the computer as its "Man of the Year"—actually listing it as "Machine of the Year."[5] It is hard to imagine a picture of the *Spirit of St. Louis* or an Apollo lander on the magazine cover under a banner "Machine of the Year." This perhaps shows how influential the computer has become for Americans.

The computer has become helpful in managing knowledge at a time when the amount of information is expanding exponentially. The information stored in the world's libraries and computers doubles every eight years.[6] In a sense the computer age and the information age go hand in hand.

The rapid development and deployment of computing power, however, has also raised some significant social and moral questions. Christians in this society need to think clearly about these issues, but often the ignore them or become confused.

One key ethical issue to consider is computer crime. In a sense computer fraud is merely a new field encountering old problems. Computer crimes are often nothing more than fraud, larceny, and embezzlement carried out by more sophisticated means. The crimes usually involve falsifying addresses, records, or files. In short, they are old-fashioned crimes using newfangled technology.

Another concern arises from the centralization of information. Governmental agencies, banks, and businesses use computers to collect information on citizens and customers. For example, it is estimated that the federal government has on average about fifteen files for each American.[7] Nothing is inherently wrong with collecting information if the information can be kept confidential and is not used for immoral actions. Unfortunately this is often difficult to guarantee.

In an information-based society, the centralization of information can be as dangerous as the centralization of power. Given sinful man in a fallen world, we should be concerned about the collection and manipulation of vast amounts of personal information.

In the past, centralized information processing has certainly been used for persecution. When Adolf Hitler's Gestapo began rounding up millions of Jews, information about their religious affiliation was stored in shoe boxes. U.S. Census Bureau punch cards were used to round up Japanese Americans living on the West Coast at the beginning of World War II.[8] Modern technology makes this kind of task much easier. Governmental agencies routinely collect information about citizens' ethnic origin, race, religion, gross income, and even political preference.

Moreover, the problem is not limited to governmental agencies. Many banking systems, for example, utilize electronic funds-transfer systems. Plans to link these systems together into a national system could also provide a means of tracking the actions of citizens. A centralized banking network could fulfill nearly every information need a malevolent dictator might have. This is not to say that such a thing will happen. It does mean, however, that governments that want to monitor their citizens will be able to do so more efficiently with computer technology than ever before.

A related problem arises from the confidentiality of computer records. Computer records can be abused, like any other system. Reputations built up over a lifetime can be ruined by computer errors, and often there is little recourse for the victim. Congress passed the 1974 Privacy Act to allow citizens to find out what records federal bureaucracies have on them and to correct any errors.[9] But more legislation is needed than this particular act.

The proliferation of computers has presented another set of social and moral concerns. In the recent past most of that information was centralized and required the expertise of the "high priests of FORTRAN" to utilize it. Now many people can have access to information because of the increased numbers of personal computers and increased access to information through the Internet. This access to information will have many interesting sociological ramifications, and it is also creating a set of troubling ethical questions. The proliferation of computers that can tie into other computers provides more opportunities for computerized crime.

The news media frequently carry reports about computer "hackers" who have been able to gain access to confidential computer systems and obtain or interfere with the data banks. Although these were supposed to be secure systems, enterprising computer hackers broke in anyway. In many cases this merely involved curious teenagers. Nevertheless computer hacking has become a developing area of crime. Criminals might use computer access to forge documents, change records, or draft checks. They can even use computers for blackmail by holding files for ransom and threatening to destroy them if their demands are not met. Unless better methods of security are developed, professional criminals will begin to crack computer security codes and gain quick access into sensitive files.

As with most technological breakthroughs, the engineers have outrun the lawmakers. Computer deployment has created a number of legal questions. First, there is the problem of establishing penalties for computer crime. Typically, intellectual property has had a unique status in our criminal justice system. Legal scholars should reevaluate the notion that ideas and information need not be protected in the same way as property. Legislators need to enact computer information protection laws that will deter criminals, or even curious computer hackers, from breaking into confidential records.

A second legal problem arises from the question of jurisdiction. Telecommunication technology allows information to be shared across state and even national borders. Few federal statutes govern this area, and fewer than half the states have laws dealing with information abuse.

Enforcement of laws will be a problem for several reasons. One reason is the previously stated problem of jurisdiction. Another is that police departments rarely train their personnel in computer abuse and fraud. A third reason is lack of personnel. Computers are nearly as ubiquitous as telephones or photocopiers.

Computer fraud also raises questions about the role of insurance companies. How do companies insure an electronic asset? What "value" does computer information have? These questions will also need to be addressed.

COMPUTER ETHICS AND BIBLICAL PRINCIPLES

The following few principles are suggestive of a biblical foundation for computer ethics. The first principle is that one should never do with computers what he or she would consider immoral without them. An act does not gain morality because a computer has made it easier to achieve. If it is unethical for someone to rummage through your desk, then it is equally unethical for that person to search your computer files. If it is illegal to violate copyright law and photocopy a book, then it is equally wrong to copy a disk of computer software.

A second principle is to treat information as something that has value. People who use computers to obtain unauthorized information often do not realize they are doing something wrong. Since information is not a tangible object and can be shared, it does not seem to them like stealing since it does not seem to deprive someone of something. Yet in an information-based society, information itself is a valuable asset. Stealing information should carry similar legal penalties to stealing tangible objects.

A third principle is to remember that computers are merely tools to be used, not technology to be worshiped. God's mandate is to use technology wisely within His creation. Many commentators express concern that within an information society such as ours, people may be tempted to replace ethics with statistics.

Massive banks of computer data already exert a powerful influence on public policy. Christians must resist society's tendency to undermine the moral basis of right and wrong with facts and figures. Unfortunately growing evidence indicates that the computer revolution has been a contributing factor in the change from a moral foundation to a statistical one. The adoption of consensus ethics ("51 percent make it right") and the overuse of cost-benefit analysis (a modernized form of utilitarianism) give evidence of this shift.

Fourth, computers should not replace human intelligence. In *The Society of Mind* Marvin Minsky, professor at the Massachusetts Institute of

Technology, says that "the mind, the soul, the self, are not a singly ghostly entity but a society of agents, deeply integrated, yet each one rather mindless on its own."[10] He dreams of being able ultimately to reduce mind (and therefore human nature) to natural mechanisms. Obviously this is not an empirical statement but a metaphysical one that attempts to reduce everything (including mind) to matter.

The implications, however, are profound. Besides lowering humans to the level of mere material processes, it begins to elevate machines to the levelof human life. One article asked the question, Would an intelligent computer have a "right to life?"[11] Granting computers rights might be something society would consider, since many are already willing to grant certain rights to animals.

In a sense the question is whether an intelligent computer would have a soul and therefore access to fundamental human rights. As bizarre as the question may sound, it is no doubt inevitable. When seventeenth-century philosopher Gottfried Wilhelm von Leibniz first described a thinking machine, he was careful to point out that this machine would not have a soul—fearful perhaps of reaction from the church.[12] But already scientists predict that computer intelligence will create "an intelligence beyond man's" and provide wonderful new capabilities.[13] One of the great challenges in the future will be how to manage new computing power that will outstrip human intelligence.

The Bible teaches that humans are more than bits and bytes, more than blood and bones. Created in the image of God, human beings have a spiritual dimension. They are more than just complex computers. Computers should be used for what they do best: to analyze discrete data with objective criteria. Computers may be a wonderful tool, but they should not replace human intelligence and intuition.

15
Ecology and the Environment

Eᴄᴏʟᴏɢʏ ɪs ᴛʜᴇ sᴛᴜᴅʏ of relationships among organisms. Man, as one of those organisms, is having the greatest impact on the environment. In one sense, that should be expected. Mankind's dominance over other species is part of God's plan for creation (Gen. 1:28). But never before have humans had the technology to exercise so much power over creation as today. Forests can be cleared in a day, rivers can be tamed by dams and levees, and crops can be planted on land never before considered arable.

Advanced technology coupled with an ever-increasing population has clearly put strains on the biosphere. Discussions about deforestation, topsoil loss, toxic wastes, and greenhouse gases are just a few of the concerns that routinely fill newspapers and nightly newscasts. Unfortunately these discussions often take place without an adequate understanding of the scientific issues involved. Environmental debates are an arena filled with hyperbole and misinformation.

It is not the purpose of this chapter to sort through the scientific claims and counterclaims about environmental issues. Instead the focus is on what the key ecological issues are and how Christians should respond. What does the Bible say about ecology and the environment? Is there an ethical obligation to preserve the environment? These are key

187

questions for Christians to answer as we seek to exercise stewardship over God's creation.

THE EXTENT OF ENVIRONMENTAL PROBLEMS

Given the diverse nature of environmental issues, it is helpful to have a framework for discussing the extent of these problems. Calvin DeWitt has developed a framework of seven degradations of the creation. Presented in his book *The Environment and the Christian*,[1] these were later adapted by the Evangelical Declaration on the Care of Creation. Though not without controversy, this framework provides a brief but comprehensive survey of the extent of the environmental problems facing mankind.

The first degradation is *land conversion and habitat destruction*. Approximately two billion acres of natural lands in this country have been converted to human uses, in addition to the more than three billion acres of cropland. While much of this land conversion has been very beneficial to mankind (in planting crops and irrigating desert regions), some has been detrimental. Examples of detrimental effects include the building of homes on prime farmland, draining wetland areas, and tropical deforestation.

In the past few centuries, pioneers in this country cleared the land for farming, thus making a positive contribution to society and the environment. However, today's destruction of habitat and conversion of land far exceed any environmental action that preceded it. It may well impact the long-term sustainability of the environment and mankind. The current situation is reminiscent of Isaiah's warning, "Woe to you who add house to house and join field to field till no space is left and you live alone in the land" (Isa. 5:8).

The second degradation is *species extinction*. How many species go extinct? Unfortunately the answer to that question is elusive. Harvard biologist Edward Wilson has published varying claims that four thousand or fifty thousand species become extinct every year.[2] Al Gore apparently chose to use the higher figure when he said in his book *Earth in the Balance* that one hundred species become extinct every day.[3] Most scientists feel such estimates for species extinction are much too high. Estimating the extinction rate is made more difficult since scientists are uncertain as to how many millions of species actually exist on this planet. The revitalization of certain species in this country (e.g., alligators and bald eagles) should not obscure the fact that many other species worldwide are becoming extinct. Reasons for extinction are many, including destruction of habitat, overharvesting (as in hunting and fishing), and the introduction of new species into an environment. And many are preventable.

Third is *land degradation.* Much of what was formerly tall-grass prairie in the United States is today known as the corn belt. Agronomists estimate that two bushels of topsoil are lost for every bushel of corn produced.[4] Green-revolution agriculture (using fertilizers, herbicides, and pesticides) has made it possible to plant corn (or any crop) year after year on the same land. The principles of crop rotation that preserved topsoil and were used by previous generations have been largely abandoned. Intensive forms of agriculture (single crops, cattle feedlots) have dramatically altered the land, destroying the natural fauna and creating an ecological desert. Earthworms are less abundant on farmland and the number of birds has been diminished by the removal of fencerows and hedgerows. Contrast the current state of agriculture with God's command to obey a sabbath rest for the land: "When you enter the land I am going to give you, the land itself must observe a sabbath to the LORD. For six years sow your fields, and for six years prune your vineyards and gather their crops. But in the seventh year the land is to have a sabbath of rest, a sabbath to the LORD. Do not sow your fields or prune your vineyards" (Lev. 25:2–4). While Christians are not under the Mosaic Law, the principles in these verses should be considered.

A fourth degradation is *resource conversion* and *waste and hazard production.* Scientific experiments and industrial processes have produced approximately seventy thousand kinds of chemicals. The biological impact of these chemicals on the flora and fauna of this planet can be devastating. The products and by-products of industrial manufacturing have polluted the air and water. Some chemicals designed to destroy one form of life, such as herbicides and pesticides, may have unintended consequences in other parts of the environment. Various gases produced in manufacturing—such as carbon dioxide, methane, ozone, and chlorofluorocarbons—affect the air and may even alter the earth's energy exchange and global temperature. Ezekiel 34:18 raises questions about the impact of degradation from one part of the environment to another part: "Is it not enough for you to feed on the good pasture? Must you also trample the rest of your pasture with your feet? Is it not enough for you to drink clear water? Must you also muddy the rest with your feet?"

A fifth degradation is *global toxification.* Weather and the physical systems (e.g., rivers, oceans) on this planet are dynamic, not static. Chemical substances (whether toxic or not) are transported thousands of miles from their origin, so that it is becoming more difficult to talk about a *local* polluter of a *local* environment. Pesticides have been found in the fat of Antarctic animals. Toxic wastes leach into groundwater. Pollutants can be measured in the upper atmosphere. In essence, environmental problems have become a global problem.

Sixth is *alteration of planetary exchange.* The earth is in a dynamic balance of light and energy within this solar system. The earth's temperature is merely the sum of energy coming from the sun minus the energy radiated back into outer space. Changing that energy equation will change the temperature of the earth.

Many scientists warn that the production of certain greenhouse gases (like carbon dioxide) alter earth's energy equation, which will lead to catastrophic results such as the melting of polar icecaps or other climate modifications. Critics, however, question the assumptions of the climatic models that lead to such predictions. Others warn that certain chemicals, like chlorofluorocarbons (CFCs), may be destroying the earth's ozone layer, which provides protection from harmful ultraviolet radiation. While it is beyond the scope of this chapter to consider all the scientific evidence for and against such threats, these concerns do remind us of the human potential for disrupting the earth's energy exchange with the biosphere.

Seventh is *human and cultural degradation.* Cultures that have lived in harmony with the land have been affected by social pressures and environmental problems. In this country Amish and Mennonite farming communities face social, economic, and political pressures that force some to abandon their farms, altering their three-hundred-year-old communities. Many tropical cultures are wiped off the land because of deforestation, mining, or the use of political force. Thus rich cultural heritages disappear and vital information is lost (e.g., the use of various tropical plants for medicinal purposes).

These seven environmental degradations illustrate the possible extent of the current environmental crisis. A creation that God pronounced as good (Gen. 1:31) fell into decay at the Fall. Although mankind was given dominion over the world (1:28), benevolent stewardship of the earth has not always been practiced. Thus an environmental crisis has developed.

THE ENVIRONMENT AND HUMAN SINFULNESS

Environmentalists trying to discover the reason for our current environmental crisis have pointed to various culprits. Many blame the modern industrial mind-set that allows companies virtually to rape global resources. They call for a paradigm shift and the adoption of a pantheistic view of the world, which views nature as a living organism. James Lovelock, for example, rejects the biblical concept of God and replaces it with a pagan worldview centered on Gaia.[5] In essence, he and some other environmentalists are calling for worship of Gaia (or some version of the idea of Mother Earth) by becoming one with nature.

Other critics lay the blame on Christianity. Lynn White, in his classic essay in *Science* magazine, said that Christianity established a "dualism of man and nature" which allowed mankind to exploit the environment. He believes the ecological crisis will continue "until we reject the Christian axiom that nature has no reason for existence save to serve man."[6]

The proper biblical response is to understand that God is both transcendent (apart from nature) and immanent (involved with the creation). God is both the Creator and the Sustainer of the creation. Nature should not be worshiped, nor should technology be used to destroy the environment. God's command to humankind to "subdue" the earth does not mean to exploit it for selfish gain.

The root of the environmental crisis is human sinfulness. Those looking to assess blame should remember the Pogo cartoon that said, "We have met the enemy and he is us." Francis Schaeffer said that human sinfulness manifests itself in the environmental crisis in two ways: greed and haste. He used the example of strip-mining to illustrate his point. "If the strip-miners would take bulldozers and push back the topsoil, then rip out the coal, put back the soil, and replace the topsoil, in ten years after the coal was removed there would be a green field, and in fifty years a forest. But . . . as it stands, for an added profit above what is reasonable in regard to nature, man turns these areas into deserts—and then cries out that the topsoil is gone, grass will not grow, and there is no way to grow trees for hundreds of years."[7]

He pointed out that "if you treat the land properly, you have to make two choices." It costs more money and takes more time to treat the land properly. Ultimately, Schaeffer said, the question is, "Are we going to have an immediate profit and an immediate savings of time, or are we going to do what we really should do as God's children?" He concluded that the Christian community must "refuse men the right to ravish the land, just as we refuse them the right to ravish our women."[8] A proper Christian response comes from proper Christian theology concerning the environment.

BIBLICAL PERSPECTIVES

A Christian view of ecology strikes a balance between naturalistic and pantheistic extremes. A naturalistic view is wrong because it alienates humans from nature so that we deny our link with the rest of creation. When people are estranged from nature, any action can be justified and environmental exploitation results. Progress becomes the highest goal, thereby unleashing a wholesale rape of the resources.

A pantheistic view is wrong because it too closely identifies God and humans with nature. Pantheists often see killing animals or cutting down trees as improper since they believe humanity is one with nature.

What is a Christian view toward the environment? The natural beginning point is God, the Creator and Sustainer of the world. He brought the universe and earth into existence. He gave Adam dominion over the creation, but also commanded him to till the earth and keep the garden (Gen. 1:1–28; 2:15). The following principles demonstrate how God's creation of man and the world applies to ecology.

First, God is the Owner of the world. Psalm 24:1 says, "The earth is the LORD's, and everything in it, the world, and all who live in it." God owns all of the creation, and man is merely the steward of that creation. To emphasize that point, God said to Job, "Everything under heaven belongs to me" (Job 41:11). In another passage, the Lord declared, "I have no need of a bull from your stall or of goats from your pens, for every animal of the forest is mine, and the cattle on a thousand hills. I know every bird in the mountains, and the creatures of the field are mine. If I were hungry I would not tell you, for the world is mine, and all that is in it" (Ps. 50:9–12).

Second, God is the Sustainer of the world. His Son is "sustaining all things by his powerful word" (Heb. 1:3). Colossians 1:17 says that Christ "is before all things, and in him all things hold together." Besides being active in the origin of the world, God is also continually active in the operation of the world.

Although the forces of nature operate according to physical laws affected by the Fall, Scripture nevertheless identifies God's influence within these forces. For example, His hand is seen in the storms, the thunder, and the rain (Ps. 77:17–18). He causes the wind and the darkness (Amos 4:13). He is the Sustainer of life and all the forces within the world.

Third, God has a covenant with the world. After the Flood in Noah's day, God made a covenant with "all living creatures" (Gen. 9:16). This covenant was made not just with mankind, but with all animals. "This is the sign of the covenant I am making between me and you and every living creature with you, a covenant for all generations to come: I have set my rainbow in the clouds, and it will be the sign of the covenant between me and the earth. Whenever I bring clouds over the earth and the rainbow appears in the clouds, I will remember my covenant between me and you and all living creatures of every kind. Never again will the waters become a flood to destroy all life" (9:12–15).

Fourth, human beings are to exercise dominion over the creation. God placed man in the Garden of Eden to take care of it (2:15). He further charged mankind with the responsibility of exercising dominion. God said, "Be fruitful and increase in number; fill the earth and subdue it. Rule over the fish of the sea and the birds of the air and over every living creature that moves on the ground" (1:28).

Two words are important in understanding the concept of dominion: subdue and rule. The Hebrew word for "subdue" (kābaš) means to tread down or bring into bondage. This word describes the image of a conqueror and implies that humankind is to have control over nature. The Hebrew word for "rule" (rādâ) means to prevail over. This also describes the idea of being victorious.

Mankind is also to care for the environment. "The LORD God took the man and put him in the Garden of Eden to work it and take care of it" (2:15). The Hebrew word for "care" (šamar) means to keep or preserve. Having dominion over the creation is not a license to rape the resources; rather it is a solemn responsibility to keep and care for the environment.

Fifth, God gave specific commands for exercising stewardship of the environment. In the Old Testament theocracy God commanded Israel to care for the land (Lev. 25:1–12), to treat domesticated animals properly, and to respect wildlife (Deut. 25:4; 22:6). They were also to conserve trees (20:19–20) and bury their wastes (23:13). God judged those who misused the land (Isa. 5:8–10).

Sixth, God promised the Israelites He would restore their land when they were obedient. Deteronomy 28:1–4 says, "If you fully obey the LORD your God and carefully follow all his commands I give you today. . . . The fruit of your womb will be blessed, and the crops of your land and the young of your livestock—the calves of your herds and the lambs of your flocks." God honors faithful obedience to His principles. God also brought worldwide restoration of all the earth's creatures. Noah was commanded to preserve the earth's creatures from the Flood (Gen. 6–7). Therefore if people are faithful to God's principles toward creation, God will bring about restoration.

ACTION STEPS FOR ENVIRONMENTAL STEWARDSHIP

Christians must be good stewards of the creation. The following are a few suggestions for individuals and churches in responding to environmental concerns.

First, Christians should study what the Bible says about stewardship of resources. Often this has been a neglected area of study for the Christian community. One Yale University study found that "knowledge of the creatures, respect for the creation and understanding ecological relationships was inversely related to frequency of church attendance."[9] In other words, dedicated Christians were the least likely to be interested in ecological issues.

Why do Christians seem to be so apathetic toward the environment? Two reasons seem to relate. For one thing Christians often see the world as evil and corrupted by sin. Often they are hesitant to enter the political arena for this reason. Perhaps they believe that the world is not worth protecting, especially since a Christian's ultimate destiny is heaven. Such belief, however, clearly contradicts God's direct command for mankind to care for the environment. Also, some Christians may fear the prevailing pantheistic influence on the environmental movement. But New Age influence in environmentalism may be due in large part to the withdrawal of Christians from this arena. When Christianity did not fill this void, pantheism and other worldviews filled it instead.

Second, churches should integrate biblical concepts about creation in their preaching and teaching. Some churches steer away from discussing creation because they do not want to engage in a debate about evolution. This attitude not only leaves the congregation confused about the issue of the world's origins, but it also keeps them from learning vital truths about a Christian's responsibility toward the creation.

Third, parents should see that their children are educated properly about the environment. Many schools do teach ecology, but often from a pantheistic perspective. Parents should check the curriculum to see if it teaches about Gaia, Mother Earth, or globalism. A good place for Christian-based environmental education is at Christian camps, many of which provide extensive outdoor education programs.

Fourth, Christians should practice sound ecological principles. This would include such actions as recycling, which helps reduce the amount of resources used up and trash produced. People in their workplaces and homes should develop practices that help the environment. Applying these principles will make a positive impact on the environment as Christians seek to be good stewards of God's creation.

16
Media

Mᴏᴅᴇʀɴ ᴍᴇᴅɪᴀ—radio, television, and movies—are so much a part of our lives that it is hard to remember they are a relatively recent addition to society. Today the various forms of media are ubiquitous. Television is just one example. More homes have TV sets (98 percent) than have indoor plumbing. In the average home the television set is on for more than six hours a day.

The positive benefits brought by media are significant. First, they broaden viewers' horizons and bring us in contact with a broad array of events and cultures. Marshall McLuhan envisioned the emergence of a "global village" in which all mankind would be brought together through electronic circuitry.[1] In a sense that global village has already been ushered in by the vast number of existing electronic outlets (radio, television, satellites, the Internet). Second, the media unify the nation and even the world around major events (e.g., presidential inaugurations, Super Bowl football games, Olympic games). Third, they provide educational input and are powerful tools for dispensing news and information.

Yet the media also have negative effects that can influence our thinking and shape our worldview. Because of the prior selection of programs, scripts, and news events by reporters and editors, we see only part of the picture. Christians must therefore make sure we are not *conformed* to this media image but instead are *transformed* by the renewing of our minds in Christ (Rom. 12:1–2).

The media have largely replaced the home as a socializing unit. Cultural values used to be passed down from one generation to the next through the home, school, and church. Electronic communication has begun to change that. In his book *The Disappearance of Childhood* Neil Postman said that this changed with the first form of electronic communication (the telegraph) and continues on today with television and other forms of electronic media. "The maintenance of childhood depended on the principles of managed information and sequential learning. But the telegraph began the process of wrestling control of information from the home and school. It altered the kind of information children could have access to, its quality and quantity, its sequence, and the circumstances in which it would be experienced."[2]

Today media are *the* socializing units in our culture. Many (perhaps most) social values are transmitted by the popular culture through the media. Values are no longer learned while sitting at the feet of grandpa rocking on the front porch; they are learned in front of a television screen, movie screen, or computer screen. And many American holidays, such as Thanksgiving and the Fourth of July, are celebrated with television rather than just with the family.

Christians should not only analyze the medium; they should also analyze its message. First, the media frequently present an unreal view of our world. As documented in detail later in this chapter, heavy viewers of television and movies tend to overestimate their likelihood of being involved in a crime, the number of people involved in white-collar occupations, and the percentage of Americans in relation to the rest of the world. The world of television and film is not the real world, and heavy viewers often have false perceptions.

Second, the media present an oversimplified view of life. The predictable plots of characters in television and film hardly mirror reality. Life for them is relatively easy; they are unhindered by the difficulties of life or their problems are readily solved. Their world is less ambiguous and complex than real life .

Third, the media often desensitizes its viewers. Yesterday's sensation can become tomorrow's ho-hum. Television and film producers reach for bigger, better, more explicit scenes to build and keep audiences. Over time, viewers become desensitized to the sex and violence in the media. What was shocking ten years ago is generally accepted fare today.

SEX IN THE MEDIA

Is there too much sex on television and in film? Many American people seem to think so. A survey conducted in 1994 found that 75 percent of Americans felt that television had "too much sexually explicit material." Moreover, 86 percent believed that television had contributed to "a decline in values."[3] And no wonder. Scanning the ads for movies or surfing through television channels reveals plots celebrating premarital sex, adultery, and even homosexuality. The amount of sexual promiscuity portrayed in the media appears to be at an all-time high.

The chapter on pornography should provide ample warning to Christians about the dangerous effects of sex, especially when linked with violence. Neil Malamuth and Edward Donnerstein document the volatile impact of sex and violence in the media. "There can be relatively long-term, anti-social effects of movies that portray sexual violence as having positive consequences."[4] In a message given by Donnerstein, he concluded with this warning and observation: "If you take normal males and expose them to graphic violence against women in R-rated films, the research doesn't show that they'll commit acts of violence against women. It doesn't say they will go out and commit rape. But it does demonstrate that they become less sensitized to violence against women, they have less sympathy for rape victims, and their perceptions and attitudes and values about violence change."[5]

It is important to remember that these studies are applicable not just to hard-core pornography. Many of the studies used films that are readily shown on television (especially cable television) any night of the week. And many of the movies shown today in theaters are much more explicit than those shown just a few years ago.

Social commentator Irving Kristol asked this question in a *Wall Street Journal* column: "Can anyone really believe that soft porn in our Hollywood movies, hard porn in our cable movies and violent porn in our 'rap' music is without effect? Here the average, overall impact is quite discernible to the naked eye. And at the margin, the effects, in terms most notably of illegitimacy and rape, are shockingly visible."[6] Sexual images in the media do have an impact on us and so do violent images in the media.

VIOLENCE IN THE MEDIA

Violence has always been a part of the human condition because of our sin nature (Rom. 3:23), but modern families are exposed to a level of violence never seen before. Any night of the week, the average viewer can see levels of violence exceeding those found in the Roman gladiatorial games.

Does this have an effect? The Bible teaches that "as a man thinks in his heart, so is he" (Prov. 23:7, NKJV). What we view and what we think about affect our actions. And while this is true for adults, it is especially true for children. They grow up in a scary world of violence. The daily news is rife with reports of child molestations and abductions, as well as nightly tallies of murder, rape, and robbery. An article in *Newsweek* magazine concluded: "It gets dark early in the Midwest this time of year. Long before many parents are home from work, the shadows creep up the walls and gather in the corners, while on the carpet a little figure sprawls in the glow emanating from an anchorman's tan. There's been a murder in the Loop, a fire in a nightclub, an indictment of another priest. Red and white lights swirl in urgent pinwheels as the ambulances howl down the dark streets. And one more crime that never gets reported, because there's no one to arrest. Who killed childhood? We all did."[7]

Some in the entertainment industry argue that violence in the media has no effect on its viewers. They contend that televised imagery does not make people violent or callous to suffering. But if televised imagery does not affect human behavior, then the TV networks should refund billions of advertising dollars to TV sponsors.

In essence, TV executives are talking out of both sides of their mouths. On the one hand, they try to convince advertisers that a thirty-second commercial can influence consumer behavior. On the other hand, they deny that a one-hour program wrapped around the commercials can influence social behavior. Obviously this is a contradiction, especially when there is so much documentation on the harmful effects of violence in the media. Violence in film and television has a devastating impact.

Violence in the Movies

The level of violence in film has reached an all-time high. Who would have imagined just a few years ago that the top dollar-producing films would be replete with blood, gore, and violence? No wonder some film critics now say that the most violent place on earth is the Hollywood set.

In one sense violence has always been a part of moviemaking, but until recently really violent movies were only seen by the fringe of mass culture. Violence now has gone mainstream. Bloody films are being watched by more than just punk rockers. Family station wagons and vans pull up to movie theaters showing R-rated slasher films, and middle America watches these same programs a few months later on cable television or on video. Many of the movies seen at home would not have been shown in theaters ten to twenty years ago.

The brutal imagery of movies should concern all of us. Even if the appalling assault on our senses is not concern enough, we should at least wonder if these visual images contribute to an increasingly dangerous society.

Nevertheless most Americans show an ambivalent attitude toward violence. Apparently there is a contradiction between our walk and our talk. We certainly talk about the potential danger of violence in the media. One Gallup poll, for example, shows that 40 percent of Americans think movie violence is a "very great" cause of real violence, and an additional 28 percent see it as a "considerable" factor.[8] Nevertheless many of those same people who express concern will stand in block-long lines to see the latest violent action film or horror film.

Movie violence these days is louder, bloodier, and more anatomically precise than ever before. When a bad guy was shot in an old black-and-white Western, the most the audience saw was a puff of smoke and a few drops of fake blood. Now the sights, sounds, and special effects are often more jarring than the real thing. Slow motion, pyrotechnics, and a penchant for leaving nothing to the imagination all conspire to make movies and TV shows more gruesome than ever.

Movie thrillers used to emphasize the deductive powers of detective or police investigators. These have now given way to plots about police investigators or action heroes with quick fingers who track down villains who are increasingly psychotic and demonic.

Children especially confront an increasingly violent world that portrays few limits. When, for example, was the last time a child was turned away from a theater for being underage? Moreover, what is to prevent a child from buying a ticket for a PG-rated film and then walking into an R-rated film? And now any child can turn on a cable movie or pop a video into the VCR and watch violent movies at home.

Children are seeing increasingly violent films at younger and younger ages. Purdue University researcher Glenn Sparks surveyed five- to seven-year-old children in suburban Cleveland, Ohio. He found that 20 percent said they had seen "Friday the thirteenth" and 48 percent had seen "Poltergeist."[9]

Violence on Television

Children's greatest exposure to violence comes from television. TV shows, movies edited for television, and video games expose young children to a level of violence unimaginable just a few years ago. The American Psychological Association says the average child watches eight thousand televised murders and one hundred thousand acts of violence before finishing elementary school.[10] That number more than doubles by the time he or she reaches age eighteen.

One study claims that television is "considerably more violent" today than it was just two years ago. The Washington-based Center for Media and Public Affairs found that television violence increased "across the board" for cable and broadcast networks alike in both fiction and nonfiction programming.[11]

Network executives disputed this study because it looked at all programs, including news and promotional ads, rather than focusing on just the content of network programming. But their criticism actually makes the point. It is the totality of TV programming that affects families, and especially young children. The violent content of television includes more than just the twenty-two-minute programs produced by the networks. At a very young age, children are seeing a level of violence and mayhem that in the past may have been seen only by a few police officers and military personnel. TV brings hitting, kicking, stabbings, shootings, and dismemberment right into homes on a daily basis.

The impact on behavior is predictable. Two prominent reports by the Surgeon General in the last two decades link violence on television and aggressive behavior in children and teenagers. In addition the National Institute of Mental Health issued a ninety-four-page report, "Television and Behavior: Ten Years of Scientific Progress and Implications for the Eighties." They found "overwhelming" scientific evidence that "excessive" violence on television spills over into the playground and the streets.[12] In one five-year study of 732 children, "several kinds of aggression—conflicts with parents, fighting and delinquency—were all positively correlated with the total amount of television viewing."[13]

Long-term studies are even more disturbing. University of Illinois psychologist Leonard Eron studied children at age eight and then again at eighteen. He found that television habits established at the age of eight influenced aggressive behavior throughout childhood and adolescent years. The more violent the programs preferred by boys in the third grade, the more aggressive their behavior, both at that time and ten years later. He therefore concluded that "the effect of television violence on aggression is cumulative."[14]

Twenty years later Eron, along with Rowell Huesmann, found the pattern continued. They and their researchers found that children who watched significant amounts of TV violence at the age of eight were consistently more likely to commit violent crimes or engage in child or spouse abuse at thirty.[15] They concluded, "Heavy exposure to televised violence is one of the causes of aggressive behavior, crime and violence in society. Television violence affects youngsters of all ages, of both genders, at all socioeconomic levels and all levels of intelligence."[16]

Since the 1980s MTV has come on the scene, offering even more troubling images. Adolescents already listen to an estimated 10,500 hours of rock music between the seventh and twelfth grades. Now they also spend countless hours in front of MTV, seeing the visual images of rock songs that depict violence, rebellion, sadomasochism, the occult, drug abuse, and promiscuity. MTV reaches fifty-seven million cable households, and its video images are even more lurid than the ones shown on regular TV.[17] Music videos filled with sex, rape, murder, and other images of mayhem assault the senses of our youth. And MTV cartoons like *Beavis and Butt-Head* assault the sensibilities while enticing young people to start fires and commit other acts of violence.[18] Critics count eighteen acts of violence on the average in each hour of MTV videos.[19]

PSYCHOLOGICAL IMPACT OF VIOLENT MEDIA

What is the effect of these violent programs on children? It turns out that some of the greatest dangers of television are the more subtle and insidious ones. Simply watching television for long periods can skew their view of the world.

George Gerbner and Larry Gross, working at the Annenberg School of Communications in the 1970s, found that heavy television viewers live in a scary world. "We have found that people who watch a lot of TV see the real world as more dangerous and frightening than those who watch very little. Heavy viewers are less trustful of their fellow citizens, and more fearful of the real world."[20] They defined heavy viewers as those adults who watch an average of four or more hours of television a day. Approximately one-third of all American adults fit that category.

Gerbner and Gross found that violence on prime-time TV exaggerated heavy viewers' fears about the threat of danger in the real world. Heavy viewers, for example, were less likely to trust others than light viewers. Heavy viewers also tended to overestimate their likelihood of being involved in a violent crime.

And if this is true of adults, imagine how television violence affects children's perceptions of the world. Gerbner and Gross said, "Imagine spending six hours a day at the local movie house when you were 12 years old. No parent would have permitted it. Yet, in our sample of children, nearly half the 12-year-olds watch an average of six or more hours of television per day." This would mean that a large portion of young people fit into the category of heavy viewers. Their view of the world must be profoundly shaped by TV. Gerbner and Gross therefore concluded, "If adults can be so accepting of the reality of television, imagine its effect on children. By the time the average American child reaches public school, he has already spent several years in an electronic nursery school."[21]

Television violence affects both adults and children in subtle ways. We must not ignore the growing body of data that suggests that televised imagery does affect our perceptions and behaviors in unhealthy ways.

THE WORLDVIEW OF THE NEWS MEDIA

Of all the forms of media, news media has become a primary shaper of our perspective on the world. Also the rules of journalism have changed in the last few decades. It used to be assumed that reporters or broadcasters would attempt to look at events with the eyes of the average reader or viewer. It was also assumed they would not use their positions in the media to influence the thinking of the nation but merely attempt to report objectively the facts of an event. Things have changed dramatically in the news business.

The fact that people in the media are out of step with the American people should be a self-evident statement. But for anyone who does not believe this, there is abundant empirical evidence to support it.

Probably the best-known research on media bias was first published in the early 1980s by professors Robert Lichter and Stanley Rothman. Their research, published in the journal *Public Opinion*[22] and later collected in the book *The Media Elite*,[23] demonstrated that reporters and broadcasters in the prestige media differ in significant ways from their audiences.

They surveyed 240 editors and reporters of the media elite—*New York Times, Washington Post, Time, Newsweek*, ABC, NBC, and CBS. Their research confirmed what many suspected for a long time. The media elite have a liberal, secular, and humanistic bias.

People have always complained about the liberal bias in the media. But what was so surprising was how liberal members of the media actually were. When asked to describe their own political persuasion, 54 percent of the media elite described themselves as left of center. Only 19 percent described themselves as conservative. When asked whom they voted for in presidential elections, more than 80 percent always voted for the Democratic candidate.

Media personnel were also very secular in their personal outlooks. The survey found that 86 percent of the media elite seldom or never attended religious services. In fact 50 percent of them had no religious affiliation at all.

This bias is especially evident when the secular press tries to cover religious events or religious issues. Most of them do not attend church, nor do they even know people who do. Instead, they live in a secularized world and therefore tend to underestimate the significance of religious values in American life and to paint anyone with Christian convictions as a "fundamentalist."

The media elite are also humanistic in their outlook on important moral issues. For example, only 15 percent of the media elite felt that adultery is morally wrong. Thus the media may be less inclined to cover the adulterous affair of a prominent politician except when the issue can no longer be ignored (as in the cases of Wilbur Mills, Gary Hart, or as alleged against President Bill Clinton).

Ninety percent of the media elite support a woman's so-called "right to an abortion." No wonder pro-life groups have such a difficult time getting their message to the American people. Usually the issue is framed in terms of whether government has the right to infringe on a woman's right to privacy.

On the issue of homosexuality the media elite also differ from the general population. Only 24 percent of the media elite agreed or strongly agreed that "homosexuality is wrong," and that percentage has probably dropped significantly since the survey. Favorable and extensive coverage of gay issues and the AIDS issue are examples of this bias.

For a time, members of the media elite argued against these studies. They suggested that the statistical sample was too small. But when Robert Lichter began to enumerate the 240 members of the news media personnel interviewed, that tactic was quickly set aside. Others tried to argue that though the media might be liberal, secular, and humanistic, it did not affect the way the press covered the news. Later studies by a variety of media watchdogs began to erode the acceptance of that view.

A second significant study on media bias was a 1996 survey conducted by the Freedom Forum and the Roper Center.[24] Their survey of 139 Washington bureau chiefs and congressional correspondents showed a decided preference for liberal candidates and causes.

The journalists were asked for whom they voted in the 1992 election. The results were these: 89 percent said Bill Clinton, 7 percent George Bush, 2 percent Ross Perot. But in the election 43 percent of Americans voted for Clinton and 37 percent voted for Bush.

Another question they were asked was, "What is your current political affiliation?" Fifty percent said they were Democrats, 4 percent Republicans. In answer to the question, "How do you characterize your political orientation?" 61 percent said they were liberal or moderately liberal, and 9 percent were conservative or moderately conservative.

The reporters were also asked about their attitudes toward their jobs. They said they see their coverage of news events as a mission. No less than 92 percent agreed with the statement, "Our role is to educate the public." And 62 percent agreed with the statement, "Our role is sometimes to suggest potential solutions to social problems."

How Does Bias Show Up?

Bias in the news usually results from the different perspectives of most secular newspeople. People in the news business tend to be more liberal, more secular, and more humanistic than the rest of the nation, and their stories and programs reflect that orientation.

How does bias show up? While reading an article or watching a program, people need to be aware of the media's "tricks of the trade." Although these might seem like subtle, insignificant issues, they can change the whole perspective of a story.

The most important tool is language. The power of words and labels is compelling. Abortionists are called pro-choice advocates, abortion providers, or family-planning consultants. Pro-lifers are instead given labels such as anti-abortionists, militant moralists, or "self-proclaimed soldiers in God's army."

Frequently the media will allow the liberal cause to label itself but will deny the conservative cause the same right. Thus the press uses the labels "pro-choice" and "anti-abortion" (rather than "pro-life"). In countries attempting to win liberation (e.g., Afghanistan and Nicaragua), military forces fighting for freedom are rarely called "freedom fighters." Instead they are referred to as rebels, insurgents, or contras.

Another tool of journalists and broadcasters is inclusion and/or exclusion. By continuously reporting some incidents, the press increases the perceived importance of some issues and decreases the importance of others. If the press extensively covers a feminist march or an environmental protest, then those causes appear to viewers to be more important. If they ignore a pro-life rally or a march against pornography, those causes seem less important.

Another journalistic tool is placement. Even when journalists and broadcasters attempt to give fair treatment, editors can change the perception of a story. A front-page story with a headline or the lead story in a broadcast is considered more important. A story buried in the back of the paper or given a single sentence later in the broadcast is perceived as less important.

Interviewing is another tool. When reading a story or watching a broadcast, individuals need to be aware that only a small part of the interview appears in the final story. Key comments may have preceded the quote that was printed or broadcast. The interviewers may have even asked the same question several times before they got the answer they were looking for.

Reporters and broadcasters may have interviewed only people with whom they agree. In fact good reporters usually know the answers they will get from most of the people they interview before they interview them. Thus by interviewing people they agree with, they can turn what is supposed to be an objective story into a platform for their own views.

Still another tool is the use of experts. Often in controversial stories, a reporter will interview a spokesperson from one side and then a spokesperson from the other. Then many stories will end with an "expert." This person is called in to resolve the issue or set the record straight. But the expert may have a bias, too, even if he or she is a professor at a major university or works at a prominent think tank.

Bias in Other Media

Although bias is easier to spot in news reporting, it is also prevalent in other forms of media. When Robert Lichter and Stanley Rothman were interviewing those in the news media, they were also interviewing prominent people in television and film. They interviewed 104 of Hollywood's most influential television writers, producers, and executives.[25] Many of these individuals had been honored with Emmy Awards, and a few were considered household names. As with the news media, they found that those working in television were very different from the rest of the public.

In addition to being white (99 percent), and male (98 percent), they were also affluent and bicoastal. They found that 63 percent had an annual income over two hundred thousand dollars and that 82 percent grew up in large metropolitan areas. Few made the fabled journey from small-town America to Hollywood. And 73 percent came from California or the Boston-Washington corridor.

They were very liberal. Seventy-five percent described themselves as left of center, compared to only 14 percent who placed themselves to the right of center. Like the news media, at least 80 percent always voted for the Democratic candidate for president.

They were also very secular. Nearly all (93 percent) had a religious upbringing (including 59 percent who were brought up in the Jewish faith) in childhood. But 45 percent currently claimed no religious affiliation, and 93 percent said they seldom or never attended religious services.

The values of those in television were similar to those in the news media, but even more significant was their attitude toward television. For example, when asked if there was too much sex on TV, only 30 percent agreed or strongly agreed. When asked if TV was too critical of traditional values, only 12 percent agreed or strongly agreed.

A similar pattern emerged for those making major motion pictures. Lichter and Rothman interviewed 149 writers, producers, and directors from the fifty top money-producing films from 1965 through 1982.[26] Sixty-four percent of those contacted completed the questionnaire, and those included the most successful of Hollywood's moviemakers.

They were white (99 percent), male (99 percent), and from metropolitan sectors of society (81 percent). Most were from the West Coast or the Northeast (73 percent), and nearly two-thirds (64 percent) had an annual income over two hundred thousand dollars. They were also very secular, with 55 percent claiming no religious affiliation and 96 percent admitting that they seldom or never attended religious services.

The conclusion should be self-evident. When reading a newspaper or news magazine, listening to radio, or watching television or a movie, people must be aware that the potential for bias is present. Those who make up the media elite (in news, television, and film) have a worldview that differs from that of the average American and is often contrary to biblical principles. Christians then must read, listen, and watch with discernment.

SUGGESTIONS FOR DEALING WITH THE MEDIA

Christians must address the influence of the media on our society. It can be a dangerous influence that can conform us to the world (Rom. 12:2). Therefore we should do all we can to protect our families against its influence and to use the media for good. Christians should strive to apply the following two passages to their lives as they seek discernment concerning the media. Philippians 4:8 says, "Finally, brothers, whatever is true, whatever is noble, whatever is right, whatever is pure, whatever is lovely, whatever is admirable—if anything is excellent or praiseworthy—think about such things." Colossians 3:2–5 admonishes Christians, "Set your minds on things above, not on earthly things. For you died, and your life is now hidden with Christ in God. When Christ, who is your life, appears, then you also will appear with him in glory. Put to death, therefore, whatever belongs to your earthly nature: sexual immorality, impurity, lust, evil desires and greed, which is idolatry." The following are suggestions for action based on these passages:

First, control the quantity and quality of media input. Parents should set guidelines and help select television programs for the family at the start of the week and ensure that children watch only those. Parents should also set guidelines for movies, music, and other forms of media. Families should also evaluate the location of their television set so that it is not too easy to just sit and watch TV for long hours.

Second, watch TV with children. One way to encourage discussion with children is to watch television with them. The plots and actions of the programs provide a natural context for discussion. The discussion might focus on how cartoon characters or TV characters could solve their problems without resorting to violence. What are the consequences of violence? TV often ignores the consequences. What are the consequences of promiscuous sex in real life?

Third, set a good example. Parents should not be guilty of saying one thing and doing another. Neither adults nor children should spend long periods of time in front of a video display (television, video game, computer). Parents can teach their children by example that there are better ways to spend time.

Fourth, work to establish broadcaster guidelines. No TV or movie producer wants to disarm all the actors on their screens for fear that viewers will watch other programs and movies. Yet many of these TV and movie producers would like to tone down the violence, even though they do not want to be the first to do so. National standards demanded by citizens who speak up can achieve what individuals cannot do by themselves in a competitive market.

Fifth, make your opinions known. Writing letters to programs, networks, and advertisers can make a difference over time. A single letter may not make a difference, but large numbers of letters can change even editioral policy. Consider joining with other like-minded people in seeking to make a difference in the media.

While the media in our culture has a tremendous potential for good, it can also have some very negative effects. Christians need wisdom and discernment to utilize the positive aspects of media and to guard against its negative effects.

17
Government and Civil Disobedience

W HAT IS THE FUNCTION OF GOVERNMENT? Should Christians ever disobey their government? If so, under what circumstances? These are key questions for Christians with biblical convictions who seek to influence society for good.

To answer these questions adequately, we must first look at the structure and function of government. Government is not the invention of man but is a divinely ordained institution meant to bring order and justice to a fallen world. Biblically based obedience is required, but there are exceptions when civil disobedience is permitted.

A CHRISTIAN VIEW OF GOVERNMENT

Government affects our lives daily, yet few citizens take time to consider its basic function. What is a biblical view of government? Why do we have government? What kind of government does the Bible allow?

Developing a Christian view of government is difficult since the Bible does not provide an exhaustive treatment of government. This itself is perhaps instructive and provides some latitude for these institutions to reflect the needs and demands of particular cultural situations. Because the Bible does not speak directly to every area of political discussion,

213

Christians often hold different views on particular political issues. However, Christians are not free to believe whatever they want. Christians should not abandon the Bible when they begin to think about these issues, because there is a great deal of biblical material that can be used to judge particular political options.

The Old Testament provided clear guidelines for the development of a theocracy in which God was the head of government. These guidelines, however, were written for particular circumstances involving a covenant people chosen by God. These guidelines do not necessarily apply today because our modern governments are not the direct inheritors of the promises God made to Israel.

Apart from that unique situation, the Bible does not propose nor endorse any specific political system. The Bible, however, does provide a basis for evaluating various political philosophies because it clearly delineates a view of human nature. Every political theory rests on a particular view of the nature of humanity.

The Bible describes two elements of human nature. This viewpoint is helpful in judging government systems. Because humans are created in the image of God (Gen. 1:26–27), they are able to exercise judgment and rationality. However, humans are also fallen creatures (Gen. 3). This human sinfulness (Rom. 3:23) has therefore created a need to control evil and sinful human behavior through civil government.

Many theologians have suggested that the only reason we have government today is to control sinful behavior because of the Fall. But there is every indication that government would exist even if we lived in a sinless world. For example, there seems to have been some structuring of authority in the Garden of Eden (Gen. 1–2). The Bible also speaks of the angelic host as being organized into levels of authority and function.

In the creation God ordained government as the means by which human beings are ruled. The rest of the created order is governed by instinct (Prov. 30:24–28) and God's providence. Insect colonies, for example, may show a level of order, but this is due merely to genetically controlled instinct.

Human beings, on the other hand, are created in the image of God and thus are responsible to the volitional commands of God. We are created by a God of order (1 Cor. 14:33); therefore we also seek order through governmental structures.

A Christian view of government differs significantly from views proposed by many political theorists. The basis for civil government is rooted in our created nature. We are rational and volitional beings. We are not determined by fate, as the Greeks would have said, nor are we determined by our environment, as modern behaviorists say. We have the power of choice. Therefore we can exercise delegated power over the created order. Thus a biblical view of human nature requires a governmental system that acknowledges human responsibility.

While the source of civil government is rooted in human responsibility, the need for government derives from the necessity of controlling human sinfulness. God ordained civil government to restrain evil (cf. Gen. 9). Anarchy, for example, is not a viable option—because all have sinned and are in need of external control.

Since civil government is necessary and divinely ordained by God (Rom.13:1–7), it is ultimately under God's control. It has been given three political responsibilities: the sword of justice (to punish criminals), the sword of order (to thwart rebellion), and the sword of war (to defend the state).

As citizens, Christians have been given a number of civil responsibilities.We are called to render service and obedience to the government (Matt. 22:21). Because it is a God-ordained institution, we are to submit to civil authority (1 Pet. 2:13–17) as we would to other institutions of God. As discussed later in this chapter, Christians are not to give total and final allegiance to the secular state, however. Other God-ordained institutions exist in society alongside the state. Christians' final allegiance must be to God. We are to obey civil authorities (Rom.13:5) in order to avoid anarchy and chaos, but there may be times when we are forced to disobey (Acts 5:29).

Because government is a divinely ordained institution, Christians have a responsibility to work within governmental structures to bring about change. Government is part of the created order and is a "minister" of God (Rom. 13:4). Christians are to be the salt of the earth and the light of the world (Matt. 5:13–16) in the midst of the political context.

Although governments may be guilty of injustice, Christians should not stop working for justice or cease being concerned about human rights. We do not give up on marriage as an institution simply because there are so many divorces, and we do not give up on the church because of its many internal problems. Each God-ordained institution manifests human sinfulness and disobedience. Our responsibility as Christians is to call political leaders back to this God-ordained task. Government is a legitimate sphere of Christian service, and so we should not look to government only when our rights are being abused. We are to be concerned with social justice and should see governmental action as a legitimate instrument to achieve just ends.

A Christian view of government should therefore be concerned with human rights. Human rights in a Christian system are based on a biblical view of human dignity. A bill of rights, therefore, does not *grant* rights to individuals but instead acknowledges these rights as already existing. The writings of John Locke, along with the Declaration of Independence, capture this idea by stating that government is based on the inalienable rights of individuals. Government based on humanism, however, does not see rights as inalienable, and thus this opens the possibility for the state to redefine what rights its citizens may enjoy. The rights of citizens in a republic, for example, are articulated in terms of what the government is forbidden to do. But in totalitarian governments, while the rights of citizens may also be spelled out, power ultimately resides in the government and not the people.

A Christian view of government recognizes the need to limit the influence of sin in society. This is best achieved by placing certain checks on governmental authority. These protect citizens from the abuse or misuse of governmental power that results when sinful individuals are given too much governmental control.

The greatest threat to liberty comes from the exercise of power. History has shown that power is a corrupting force when placed in human hands. In the Old Testament theocracy there was less danger of abuse because the head of state was God. The Bible amply documents the dangers that ensued when power was transferred to a single king. Even David, a man after God's own heart (1 Sam. 13:14; Acts 13:22), abused his power, and thus Israel experienced great calamity (2 Sam. 11–21).

We must be aware that the abuse and misuse of power characterize human governments. The contribution of modern democratic theory was to recognize human sinfulness and to devise an ingenious method to tame its effects. John Locke, James Madison, and others recognized that since we cannot rid human nature of sinful behavior, the only solution is to use human nature to control itself.

GOVERNMENTAL AUTHORITY

A key question in political theory is how to determine the limits of governmental authority. With the remarkable growth in the size and scope of government in this century, it is necessary to define clearly the lines of governmental authority. The Bible provides some guidelines.

However, it is often difficult to set limits or draw lines. As already noted, the Old Testament theocracy differed from our modern democratic government. Although human nature is still the same, drawing biblical principles from an agrarian, monolithic culture and applying them to our technological, pluralistic culture requires discernment.

Part of this difficulty can be eased by separating two issues. First, should government legislate morality? We will discuss this in the section on social action. Second, what are the limits of governmental sovereignty? The following are a few general principles to help determine the limits of governmental authority.

As Christians, we recognize that God has ordained other institutions besides government which exercise authority in their particular sphere of influence. This is in contrast to political views that see the state as the sovereign agent over human affairs, exercising sovereignty over every other human institution. A Christian view is different.

For Christians the first institution is *the church* (1 Pet. 2:9–10; Heb. 12:18–24). Jesus taught that the government should work in harmony with the church and should recognize its sovereignty in spiritual matters (Matt. 22:21).

The second institution is *the family* (Eph. 5:22–32, 1 Pet. 3:1–7). The family is an institution under God and His authority (Gen.1:26–28; 2:20–25). When the family breaks down, the government often has to step in to protect the rights of the spouse (in cases of spouse abuse) or children (in cases of child abuse or adoption). The biblical emphasis, however, is not so much on rights as it is on responsibilities and mutual submission within the family (Eph. 5:21).

A third institution is *education*. Children are not the wards of the state, but belong to God (Ps.127:3) and are given to parents as a gift from God. Parents are to teach their children (Deut. 4:9) and may also entrust them to tutors (Gal. 4:2).

In a humanistic system of government, the institutions of church and family are usually subordinated to the state. In an atheistic system, ultimately the state becomes a substitute god and is given additional power to adjudicate disputes and bring order to society. Since institutions exist by permission of the state, there is always the possibility that a new social contract will allow government to intervene in areas such as church and family.

A Christian view of government recognizes the sovereignty of these spheres. Governmental intervention into the spheres of church and family is necessary in certain cases where there is threat to life, liberty, or property. Otherwise civil governments should recognize the sovereignty of other God-ordained institutions.

But what should Christians do if government exceeds its authority? Do Christians have a right and responsibility to disobey? Those who would quickly dismiss this question as irrelevant should realize the implications of civil disobedience on Christian discipleship and obedience to God's law. Francis Schaeffer stated that "one either confesses that God is the final authority, or one confesses that Caesar is Lord."[1] If there is never a circumstance under which a Christian would disobey the state, then ultimately the state has become god. Therefore civil disobedience must be permitted. But under what circumstances is it permissible?

A HISTORY OF CIVIL DISOBEDIENCE

Civil disobedience has a long history in this country, starting with the American Revolution. Civil disobedience continued through the the nineteenth century (e.g., abolition movement protests preceding the Civil War)

218

and surfaced in the latter part of the twentieth century in the civil rights movement, the environmental movement, and the peace movement (including protests against the Vietnam war and protests against nuclear arms). Today civil disobedience surfaces in many ways. In the Pacific Northwest, environmentalists have placed steel spikes in trees. When a high-speed chain saw hits a buried spike, the saw shatters, sending pieces of metal out like shrapnel. In New York, homosexual activists have disrupted church services and blocked access to churches because of their public stance on homosexuality. Animal-rights activists have broken into laboratories to destroy equipment and release animals.

The modern debate on civil disobedience has been heavily influenced by the nineteenth-century writer Henry David Thoreau. Beginning from a humanistic perspective, he set forth a case for disobeying government. His famous essay "On the Duty of Civil Disobedience" was written after his night in the Concord, Massachusetts, jail in July 1846.[2] He had refused to pay his poll tax as a protest against a government that supported slavery. During the night someone paid the tax and he was released.

The essay grew out of his experience and has influenced many who consider similar actions. For example, Mahatma Gandhi printed and distributed Thoreau's essay and carried a copy with him during his many imprisonments.

Thoreau challenged the prevailing notion of the day that obedience to government was more important than obedience to conscience. Most citizens would have argued that if a conflict existed between moral law and the government, one should obey the government. Thoreau insisted that moral principle should come first and that civil disobedience was required, even if it meant refusing to pay taxes or going to jail.

Thoreau's basic principle, however, leaves a question. Who is to decide when to disobey the government? According to Thoreau each individual should follow his or her innate sense of goodness. Thus each person must decide what he or she thinks is right and which laws he or she will obey or disobey. This could result in moral anarchy, because Thoreau did not believe in an absolute standard of right and wrong.

Christians, however, have a transcendent set of standards to follow. The Bible lays out clear biblical principles that should be followed when a believer feels a conflict between God and government.

The best articulation of these biblical principles can be found in Samuel Rutherford's essay *Lex Rex*.[3] Arguing that governmental law was founded on the law of God, he rejected the seventeenth-century idea of the "divine right of kings." The king was not the ultimate authority; God's law was (hence the title *Lex Rex,* "The law is king"). If the king and the government disobeyed the law, then they were to be disobeyed. He argued that all men, including the king, were under God's law and not above it. According to Rutherford the civil magistrate was a "fiduciary figure" who held his authority in trust for the people. If that trust was violated, the people had a political basis for resistance. Not surprisingly *Lex Rex* was banned in England and Scotland because it was seen as treasonous and fomenting political rebellion.

BIBLICAL EXAMPLES

The Bible provides a number of prominent examples of civil disobedience. When Pharaoh commanded the Hebrew midwives to kill all male Hebrew babies, they lied to Pharaoh and did not carry out his command (Exod. 1–2).

The Book of Daniel contains a number of instructive examples. For example, when Shadrach, Meshach, and Abednego refused to bow down to Nebuchadnezzar's golden image, they were cast into a fiery furnace (Dan. 3). Later the commissioners and satraps persuaded King Darius to make a decree that no one could petition any god or man for thirty days. Daniel nevertheless continued to pray to God three times a day and was cast into the lion's den (Dan. 6).

In the New Testament the most dramatic example of civil disobedience is recorded in Acts 4–5. When Peter and John were commanded not to preach the gospel, their response was, "We must obey God rather than men" (5:29).

These examples each include at least two common elements. First, a direct, specific conflict arose between God's law and man's law. Pharaoh commanded the Hebrew midwives to kill male Hebrew babies. Nebuchadnezzar commanded his subjects to bow before the golden image. King Darius ruled that no one could pray. And in the New Testament the high priest and the Sanhedrin forbade the apostles to proclaim the gospel.

Second, in choosing to obey God's higher law, believers paid the normal consequence for disobedience. Although several of them escaped the consequence through supernatural intervention, we know from biblical and secular history of many others who paid for their disobedience with their lives.

Some critics argue that civil disobedience is prohibited by the clear admonition in Romans 13:1, "Let every person be in subjection to the governing authorities. For there is no authority except from God, and those which exist are established by God" (NASB). Yet even this passage seems to provide a possible argument for disobeying a government that has exceeded its authority.

The verses following these speak of the government's role and function. The ruler is to be a "servant of God," and government should reward good and punish evil. Government that fails to do so is outside God's mandated authority and function. Government is not autonomous; it has delegated authority from God. It is to restrain evil and punish wrongdoers. When it does violate God's delegated role and refuses to reward good and punish evil, it has no proper authority.[4]

The apostle Paul called for believers to "be subject" to government, but he did not instruct them to "obey" every command of government. When government issues an unjust or unbiblical injunction, Christians have a higher authority. One can be "subject" to the authority of the state but still refuse to "obey" a specific law which is contrary to biblical standards.

THE PRO-LIFE EXAMPLE

Although civil disobedience has been debated in various arenas, the primary discussion of its use among Christians recently has been in the abortion debate. Millions of unborn babies are killed every year, and political means to redress this evil have often been stymied (see chapter 1). Pro-life Christians, therefore, have debated whether civil disobedience is an appropriate action.

Proponents argue that we cannot wait for the political process since unborn babies are currently dying. Therefore we should "rescue those being led away to death" (Prov. 24:11). They further argue that Christians must follow the dictates of James 4:17: "Therefore, to one who knows the right thing to do, and does not do it, to him it is sin" (NASB).

The range of activities proposed under civil disobedience varies depending on the philosophy of each pro-life group and its leaders. Possible action would include picketing abortion clinics and providing sidewalk counseling to women considering abortions. Others propose picketing the homes of abortionists. Some call for physical intervention in the form of blockading clinics and some call for even stronger uses of force.

Critics of the use of civil disobedience usually draw the line with trespassing and the use of physical intervention (e.g., blockading clinics). Four criticisms usually surface in their critique of the use of civil disobedience to protest abortion.

First, the law being broken has nothing to do with abortion. Those arrested are not being arrested because they are protesting abortion; they are being arrested for trespassing. Critics note that if certain anti-God protesters blocked the entrance to their church, they would use the same ordinance to have the protestors arrested.

Second, *Roe v. Wade* neither requires abortions nor prohibits them, but makes them permissible with certain restrictions. Women who choose to have an abortion are free moral agents responsible before God for their actions, including the protection of the rights of their innocent, unborn child. The Christian's role is to use moral arguments to save the life of the unborn child, but using physical intervention is not a valid option.

Third, Christians are not permitted to disobey a just law in order to minimize the effects of other unjust laws. When there is a clear contradiction between God and Caesar, Christians must obey God. But in other cases, Christians should render obedience to civil authority. If they did not, then a state of anarchy would quickly develop in which each person would do what he felt was right in his own eyes.

Christians must resist our culture's tendency to rebel at the first provocation, especially in light of the numerous scriptural admonitions to obey those in authority. These verses place the burden of proof on those advocating civil disobedience. If they do not or cannot prove their case for breaking the law, then we should obey civil authority.

This should especially be true in light of our sin nature (Rom. 3:23).

All of us have some rebellion in us because of our sin nature, so we want to break the law. A good check on our carnal nature (7:14) is to ask if breaking a civil law is biblically required. If not, we should give obedience to the law the benefit of the doubt.

Fourth, opponents have objected to the use of physical force. Is it proper to use physical force? Proponents believe that physical force should be used to restrain the evil of abortion. But this raises two questions. One question is: What are the limits to the use of physical force? If blocking clinics is justified, what about burning them down or blowing them up? Once any form of physical force is justified, how do we define the limits of its use?

Another question is this: If physical force can be justified in fighting abortion, what about using physical force in restraining other evils like idolatry or adultery? Should Christians block the entrances to New Age bookstores or pornography shops? Critics are concerned that the use of physical force would lead to unintended consequences and could be used to justify violent actions by Christians protesting all sorts of evil. Christians are not to fight with "the weapons of the world" (2 Cor 10:4) but instead are to fight social evil with moral persuasion.

BIBLICAL PRINCIPLES FOR CIVIL DISOBEDIENCE

How should Christians engage in civil disobedience? Here are five principles that should guide an individual's decision about civil disobedience. First, the law or injunction being resisted should clearly be unjust and unbiblical. Christians are not allowed to resist laws merely because they disagree with them. Given our sin nature and our natural tendency toward anarchy, it seems appropriate for Christians to make a strong case for civil disobedience before they act. The burden of proof should be on the person advocating civil disobedience. In a sense, we should be talked into disobedience. If the case is not compelling for civil disobedience, then obedience is required by default.

Second, the means of redress should be exhausted. One of the criteria for a just war is that the recourse to war must be the last resort. Civil disobedience should follow the same rigorous criterion. When all recourse to civil obedience has been exhausted, then and only then can discussion of revolution begin. Even then minimum resistance should be used if it can achieve a just result. If peaceful means can be used, then force should be avoided. Only when all legal channels for change have been closed or exhausted should civil disobedience be seriously considered. The only exception may be when the injustice is so grave and immediate that time for lengthy appeals is impossible.

Third, Christians must be willing to accept the penalty for breaking the law. The various biblical examples mentioned provide a model for Christian behavior in the midst of civil disobedience. Christians should submit to authority even when disobeying government. Such an attitude distinguishes civil disobedience from anarchy. By accepting punishment under the law, believers can often provide a powerful testimony to non-believers and awaken their concern for injustice.

Fourth, civil disobedience should be carried out in love and with humility. Disobeying government should not be done with an angry or rebellious spirit. Martin Luther King taught that "whom you would change you must first love."[5] Bringing about social change requires love, patience, and humility, not anger and arrogance.

A fifth and more controversial principle is that civil disobedience should be considered only when there is some possibility for success. Similarly another criterion for a just war is that there be some reasonable hope of success. In the case of civil disobedience, success is not an ultimate criterion, but it should be a concern if true social change is to take place. An individual certainly is free to disobey a law for personal reasons, but any attempt to change a law or social situation should enlist the aid and support of others. Also Christians should prayerfully evaluate whether the social disruption and potential promotion of lawlessness that may ensue is worth the action of civil disobedience. In most cases Christians will be more effective by working within the social and political arenas to affect true social change.

BIBLICAL PRINCIPLES FOR SOCIAL ACTION

How then should Christians be involved in the social and political arena? We should be distinctively Christian in our approach and should learn from the mistakes of other Christians in the past so that we might be effective without falling into compromise or sin.

First, Christians must remember we have a dual citizenship. On the one hand, our citizenship is in heaven and not on earth (Phil. 3:17–21). Christians must remind ourselves that God is sovereign over human affairs even when circumstances look dark and discouraging. On the other hand, the Bible also teaches that Christians are citizens of this earth (Matt. 22:15–22). We are to obey government (Rom.13:1–7) and work within the social and political circumstances to effect change. Christians are to pray for those in authority (1 Tim. 2:1–4) and to obey those in authority.

Jesus compared the kingdom of heaven to yeast hidden in flour (Matt. 13:33). The flour represents the world and the yeast represents the Christian presence in it. We are to exercise our influence within the mass of society, seeking to bring about change that way. Though the Christian presence may seem as insignificant as yeast in flour, nevertheless we are to bring about the same profound change.

Second, Christians must remember that God is sovereign. As the Sovereign over the nations, He bestows power on whom He wishes (Dan. 4:17) and He can turn the heart of a king wherever He wishes (Prov. 21:1). Christians have often been guilty of believing that they alone can make a difference in the political process. Christian leaders frequently claim the future of this country depends on the election of a particular candidate, the passage of a particular bill, or the confirmation of a particular Supreme Court justice. While it is important for Christians to be involved in social and political affairs, we must not forget that God is ultimately in control.

Third, Christians must use their specific gifts within the social and political arenas. Christians have different gifts and ministries (1 Cor. 12:4–6). Some may be called to a higher level of political participation than others (e.g., a candidate for school board or for Congress). All have a responsibility to be involved in society, but some are called to a higher level of social service, such as a social worker or crisis-pregnancy-center worker. Christians must recognize the diversity of gifts and encourage fellow believers to use their individual gifts for the greatest impact.

Fourth, Christians should channel our social and political activity through the church. Christians need to be accountable to each other, especially as we seek to make an impact on society. Wise leadership can prevent zealous evangelical Christians from repeating mistakes made in previous decades by other Christians.

The local church should also provide a context for compassionate social service. In the New Testament, the local church became a training ground for social action (Acts 2:45; 4:34). Meeting the needs of the poor, the infirm, the elderly, and widows is a responsibility of the church. Ministries to these groups can provide a foundation and a catalyst for further outreach and ministry to the community at large.

Christians are to be the salt of the earth and the light of the world (Matt. 5:13–16). In our needy society, we have abundant opportunities to preach the gospel of Jesus Christ and meet significant social needs. By combining these two areas of preaching and ministry, Christians can make a strategic difference in society.

Endnotes

CHAPTER 1—ABORTION

1. National Center for Health Statistics, Atlanta, Ga.
2. *Abortion: Facts at a Glance* (New York: Planned Parenthood of America), 1.
3. Edward Lenoski, *Heartbeat* 3, December 1980, quoted in John Wilke, *Abortion: Questions and Answers* (Cincinnati: Hayes, 1988), 140–41.
4. Abortion Surveillance Report, U.S. Department of Health and Human Services, Center for Disease Control, May 1983.
5. Josephus, *Apion* 2.202.
6. *Didache* 2.2.
7. *Epistle of Barnabas* 19.5.
8. Athenagoras, *A Plea for Christians* 35.6.
9. Clement, *Paedagogus* 2:10.96.1.
10. Tertullian, *Apology* 9.4.
11. Augustine, *On Marriage* 1.17.15.
12. The Greek word *brephos* used in Luke 1:41, 45 to identify the unborn John the Baptist is the same word used for the infant Jesus (2:12, 16) and for babies who received His blessing (18:15–17). Also, the Hebrew word *yeled,* used in the Old Testament to refer to the unborn (Exod. 21:22–25), is the same word used to describe young children.

13. Volman and Pearson, "What the Fetus Feels," *British Medical Journal,* 26 January 1980, 233–34.

14. Francis Crick, "Logic of Biology," *Nature,* 2 November 1968, 429–30.

15. Ashley Montagu, *Sex, Man and Society* (New York: Putnam, 1967).

16. Joseph Fletcher, *Humanhood: Essays in Biomedical Ethics* (Buffalo: Prometheus, 1979).

17. Joseph Fletcher, "Indicators of Humanhood: A Tentative Profile of Man," *Hastings Center Report 2* (November 1972).

CHAPTER 2—EUTHANASIA

1. Plato, *Republic* 3.405.

2. Katrine Ames, "Last Rights," *Newsweek,* 26 August 1991, 41.

3. A further discussion of the care and counseling of dying patients can be found in my book *Life, Death, and Beyond* (Grand Rapids: Zondervan, 1980).

4. Paul Cundiff, quoted in Debbie Decker, "Euthanasia is Not the Answer—A Hospice Physician's View," in *Currents in Science, Technology, and Society* 1 (1991): 20.

5. Rita Marker, "What's All the Fuss about Tube Feeding," *New Covenant,* January 1991, 19.

6. Susan Moran, "Medical Choices: A Will Doesn't Always Mean a Way," *Insight,* 15 February 1993, 12.

7. R. Finigsen, "The Report of the Dutch Committee on Euthanasia," *Issues in Law and Medicine,* July 1991, 339–44.

8. Herbert Hendlin, Chris Rutenfrans, and Zbignlew Zyliez, "Physician-Assisted Suicide and Euthanasia in the Netherlands: Lessons from the Dutch," *Journal of the American Medical Association,* 4 June 1997, 1720–22.

9. Interview with Surgeon General C. Everett Koop, "Focus on the Family" radio broadcast, 1986.

10. "The Hemlock Maneuver," *Physician* (March /April1991): 2.

11. Interview with Koop, "Focus on the Family" radio broadcast.

12. Robin Benhoft, quoted in *Euthanasia: False Light,* published by IAETF, P. O. Box 760, Steubenville, Ohio 43952.

13. Joni Eareckson, *Joni* (Grand Rapids: Zondervan, 1976).

14. Joni Eareckson, *A Step Further* (Grand Rapids: Zondervan, 1978).

CHAPTER 3—GENETIC ENGINEERING

1. "Three Families, Three Decisions," *USA Today*, 18 August 1997, D1.

2. Geoffrey Cowley, "The View from the Womb," *Newsweek*, 8 November 1993, 64.

3. Ethan Singer, quoted in Nicholas Wade, "Gene Splicing: Congress Starts Framing Law for Research," *Science*, April 1977, 39.

4. Michael Crichton, *The Andromeda Strain* (New York: Dell, 1969).

5. "The DNA Furor: Tinkering with Life," *Time*, 18 April 1977, 45.

6. Kenneth Woodward, "Thou Shalt Not Parent!" *Newsweek*, 29 May 1995, 68.

7. Ibid.

8. Testimony by Ethan Singer before the Subcommittee on Health and the Environment, House Committee on Interstate and Foreign Commerce, *Hearings*, 15 March 1977, 79.

9. Julian Huxley, quoted in Joseph Fletcher, *The Ethics of Control* (Garden City, N.Y.: Anchor, 1974), 8.

10. Erwin Chargaff, quoted in George Wald, "The Case against Genetic Engineering," *The Sciences*, May 1976, 10.

11. Nancy McCann, "The DNA Maelstrom: Science and Industry Rewrite the Fifth Day of Creation," *Sojourners*, May 1977, 23–26.

12. Philip Elmer-Dewitt, "The Genetic Revolution," *Time*, 17 January 1994, 49.

13. Skeptics sometimes argue that fighting disease is the same as fighting against God's will. Albert Camus poses this dilemna for Dr. Reux in *The Plague*. Christians should follow the cultural mandate (Gen. 1:28) and use genetic technology to treat and cure genetic diseases.

14. Paul Ramsey, *Fabricated Man* (New Haven, Conn.: Yale University Press, 1970).

15. Sharon Begley, "Little Lamb, Who Made Thee?" *Newsweek*, 10 March 1997, 55.

16. Ibid.

17. James Bonner, quoted in *Los Angeles Times*, 17 May 1971, 1.

18. N. N. Glazer, *Hammer on the Rock: A Short Midrash Reader* (New York: Schocken, 1962), 15.

CHAPTER 4—REPRODUCTIVE TECHNOLOGIES

1. Diane Swanbrow, "Immaculate Conceptions," *Newsweek*, 25 August 1980, 28.
2 Lori Andrews, "Embryo Technology," *Parents*, May 1991, 63–64.
3. Lewis Lord, "Desperately Seeking Baby," *U.S. News and World Report*, 5 October 1987, 58.
4. M. Curie-Cohen, M. Jutrell, and S. Sharpiro, "Current Practice of Artificial Insemination by Donor in the United States," *New England Journal of Medicine*, 1979, 585–90.
5. Many states have enacted legislation to protect the legal rights of the child. Other state courts are affected by case law concerning AID.
6. "Artificial Insemination by Donor: Survey Reveals Surprising Facts," *Journal of the American Medical Association*, 23 March 1979, 1219.
7. Karl Ostrom, "Psychological Considerations in Evaluating AID," *Soundings* (fall 1971): 325–30.
8. Aphrodite Clamar, quoted in Carin Rubenstein, "Little Known Hazards of AID: Disease, Inbreeding, Guilt," *Psychology Today*, May 1980, 23.
9. David Rorvick with Landrum Shettles, *Your Baby's Sex: Now You Can Choose* (New York: Bantam, 1970).
10. Lisa Busch, "Designer Families, Ethical Knots," *U.S. News and World Report*, 31 May 1993, 73.
11. Charles Westoff and Ronald Rindfuss, "Sex Preselection in the United States: Some Implications," *Science*, 10 May 1974, 633–36.
12. "Against the Odds: How the Methods Compare," *Newsweek*, 4 September 1991, 58.
13. Philip Elmer-DeWitt, "Making Babies," *Time*, 40 September 1995, 40.
14. Paula Mergenbagen DeWitt, "In Pursuit of Pregnancy," *American Demographics*, May 1993, 52.
15. Sharon Begley, "The Baby Myth," *Newsweek*, 4 September 1995, 40.

16. Luigi Mastroianni, chairman of obstetrics and gynecology, University of Pennsylvannia, quoted in "Lab Growth of Human Embryo Raises Doubt of Normality," *Washington Post*, 21 March 1971.

17. Otto Friedrich, "The New Orgins of Life," *Time*, 10 September 1984, 46.

18. Stephen Budiansky, "The New Rules of Reproduction," *U.S. News and World Report*, 18 April 1988, 67.

19. Traci Watson, "Sister, Can You Spare an Egg?" *U.S. News and World Report*, 23 June 1997, 44.

20. Andrews, "Embryo Technology," 69.

21. Thomas Giles, "Test-Tube Wars," *Christianity Today*, 9 January 1995, 38.

CHAPTER 5—SEXUAL PROMISCUITY

1. Warren Leary, *New York Times*, 9 February 1989.

2. "American Teens Speak: Sex, Myth, TV and Birth Control," *The Planned Parenthood Poll*, Louis Harris and Associates, September/October 1986, 13.

3. David Van Biema, "What You Don't Know about Teen Sex," *People*, 13 April 1987, 110–21.

4. William Bennett, "Sex and the Education of Our Children," in *School Based Clinics* (Westchester, Ill.: Crossway, 1987), 159.

5. Wendy Cole, "How Should We Teach Our Children about Sex?" *Time*, 24 May 1993, 61.

6. Ibid., 63.

7. Barbara Dafoe Whitehead, "The Failure of Sex Education," *Atlantic Monthly*, October 1994, 55–80.

8. Ibid., 57.

9. Ibid., 69.

10. Lawrence Criner, "Safer Sex Ads Downplay Risks," *Insight*, 9 May 1994, 22.

11. Ibid.

12. Ibid.

13. Ibid.

14. Nicholas Fiumara, "Effectiveness of Condoms in Preventing V.D.," *New England Journal of Medicine*, 21 October 1971, 972.

15. Criner, "Safer Sex Ads Downplay Risks," 22.

16. Asta Kenney, "School-Based Clinics: A National Conference," *Family Planning Perspectives* 18 (January/February 1986): 6.

17. FDA, *Compliance Policy Guidelines*, chapter 24, guide 7124.21, 10 April 1987, 1.

18. Criner, "Safer Sex Ads Downplay Risks," 24.

19. Victor Cline, "Correlating Adolescent and Adult Exposure to Sexually Explicit Material and Sexual Behavior," University of Utah Department of Psychology, National Conference on HIV.

20. Douglas Kirby, *School Based Health Clinics: An Emerging Approach to Improving Adolescent Health and Addressing Teenage Pregnancy*, (n.p., 1985), 14.

21. Michael Schwartz, "Lies, Damned Lies, and Statistics," *American Education Report*, March 1986, 4.

22. Laurie Zabin, "Evaluation of a Pregnancy Prevention Program for Urban Teenagers," *Family Planning Perspectives* 18 (May/June 1986): 124.

23. Joseph Olsen and Stan Weed, "Effects of Family Planning Programs on Adolescent Birth and Pregnancy Rates," *Family Perspective*, July 1986.

24. Douglas Kirby (speech given at the annual meeting of the National Family Planning and Reproductive Health Association, 2 March 1988).

25. Louis Harris poll, "Planned Parenthood Poll" (New York: Louis Harris, 1986).

26. Report of the Select Committee on Children, Youth, and Families, 99th Congress, *Teen Pregnancy: What Is Being Done? A State by State Look* (Washington, D.C.: U.S. Government Printing Office, 1986), 375–78.

27. Deborah Anne Dawson, "The Effects of Sex Education on Adolescent Behavior," *Family Planning Perspectives* 18 (July/August 1986): 166.

28. Reprinted in Josh McDowell, *The Myths of Sex Education* (San Bernardino, Calif.: Here's Life, 1990), 68.

29. Charles Donovan, *An Estimate of Federal Spending on Contraceptive "Safe Sex" Services for Adolescents* (Washington, D.C.: Family Research Council, 1994).

30. Douglas Kirby, "Sexuality Education: A More Realistic View of Its Effects," *Journal of School Health* (December 1985): 422.

31. Tom Smith, *Attitudes toward Sexual Permissiveness: Trends, Correlates, and Behavioral Connections* (Chicago: University of Chicago Press, 1992), 66.

32. Tom McNichol, "Sex Can Wait," *USA Weekend,* 25–27 March 1994, 4–6.

33. Centers for Disease Control, 1992 National Health Survey, *Morbidity and Mortality Weekly Report,* 8 April 1994, 231–33.

34. M. Howard and J. S. McCabe, "Helping Teenagers Postpone Sexual Involvement," *Family Planning Perspectives* 22 (January/February, 1990): 21–26.

35. William Bennett, "Sex and the Education of Our Children," 164.

36. Dinah Richard, *Has Sex Education Failed Our Teenagers?* (Pasadena, Calif.: Focus on the Family, 1990), 59–60.

37. Larry Withan, "As Washington Pushes Safe Sex, Others Preach Abstinence," *Washington Times,* 3 October 1993, A4.

38. Conversation with Audrey Armstrong, sex-education teacher, quoted in *Abstinence Programs Show Promise in Reducing Sexual Activity and Pregnancy among Teens* (Washington, D.C.: Family Research Council, 1994).

39. Project Respect, *Final Report: Office of Adolescent Pregnancy Programs,* Performance Summary Report, #000816, Title XX, 1985–1990.

40. Cole, "How Should We Teach Our Children about Sex?" 65.

41. Andres Tapia, "Abstinence: The Radical Choice for Sex Ed," *Christianity Today,* 8 February 1993, 28.

42. Joe McIlhaney, *Safe Sex* (Grand Rapids: Baker, 1991), 23.

43. *The Common Appeal,* 7 November 1988, A12.

44. Roper Starch Organization, "Teens Talk about Sex: Adolescent Sexuality in the 90s," April 1994, 25.

45. Larry Bumpass, James Sweet, and Andrew Cherlin, "The Role of Cohabitation in Declining Rates of Marriages," *Journal of Marriage and the Family* 53 (1991): 913–27.

46. Edward Laumann, John Gagnon, Robert Michael, and Stuart Michaels, *The Organization of Sexuality: Sexual Practices in the United States* (Chicago: University of Chicago Press, 1994), 363–65.

47. Robert Levin and Amy Levin, "Sexual Pleasure: The Surprising Preferences of 100,000 Women," *Redbook*, September 1975, 51–58.

CHAPTER 6—CRIME AND PUNISHMENT

1. U.S. crime statistics for 1990, United States Justice Department 1990 report.

2. "Cost of Crime: $674 Billion," *U.S. News and World Report,* 17 January 1994, 40–41.

3. Daniel Patrick Moynihan, "Defining Deviancy Down," *American Scholar* (winter 1993): 17–30.

4. William Bennett, *The Index of Leading Cultural Indicators* (Washington, D.C.: Empower America, 1993), 2.

5. U.S. Department of Justice, Bureau of Justice Statistics, "Lifetime Likelihood of Victimization," March 1987.

6. John Dilulio, "Defining Criminality Up," *Wall Street Journal,* 3 July 1996.

7. Eric Press, "A Crime as American as a Colt .45," *Newsweek,* 15 August 1994, 22.

8. "Killer Teens," *U.S. News and World Report,* 17 January 1994, 26.

9. Ibid.

10. Ted Guest and Dorian Friedman, "The New Crime Wave," *U.S. News and World Report,* 29 August 1994, 26.

11. James Wooten, "Lesson of Pop Jordan's Death," *Newsweek,* 13 September 1993, 12.

12. Eugene Methvin, "Mugged by Reality," *Policy Review* (July–August 1997): 33.

13. Brad Edmonson, "Crime Crazy," *American Demographics,* May 1994, 2.

14. John Dilulio, "Getting Prisons Straight," *American Prospect* (fall 1990).

15. Morgan Reynolds, "Why Does Crime Pay?" *National Center for Policy Analysis Backgrounder,* no. 110 (March 1990).

16. Morgan Reynolds, "Crime Pays, but So Does Imprisonment," *National Center for Policy Analysis,* Policy Report no. 149 (March 1990).

17. Ann Willette, "How Crime Is Changing the Look of America," *USA Today,* 18 July 1995, 2A.

18. Ibid.

19. Mortimer Zuckerman, "War on Crime, by the Numbers," *U.S. News and World Report,* 17 January 1994, 67–68.

20. Ben Wattenberg, "Crime Solution—Lock 'Em Up," *Wall Street Journal,* 17 December 1993.

21. *Wall Street Journal,* 21 March 1989.

22. Wooten, "Lessons of Pop Jordan's Death," 12.

23. Bureau of Justice Statistics, National Corrections Reporting Program, 1988.

24. Zuckerman, "War on Crime, by the Numbers."

25. Edmonson, "Crime Crazy," 2.

26. William A. Rusher, "Liberal 'Solutions' Leave America Crime-Ridden," *Human Events,* 14 January 1994, 15.

27. Frank Graham, *Prison Chapels Make Safer Texas* (Dallas: Chapel of Hope Ministries, 1995).

28. Cal Thomas, "Programs of the Past Haven't Reduced Crime," *Los Angeles Times,* 13 January 1994.

CHAPTER 7—CAPITAL PUNISHMENT

1. U. Cassuto, *A Commentary on the Book of Genesis, Part II* (Jerusalem: Magnes, 1964), 127.

2. Hyman Barsham, quoted in "On Deterrence and the Death Penalty," Ernest van den Haag, *Journal of Criminal Law, Criminology and Police Science* 60 (1969).

3. Isaac Erlich, "The Deterrent Effect of Capital Punishment: A Question of Life and Death," *American Economic Review* (June 1975).

4. *Journal of Legal Studies* (January 1977); *Journal of Political Economy* (June 1977); and *American Economic Review* (June 1977).

5. Frank Carrington, *Neither Cruel nor Unusual: The Case for Capital Punishment* (New Rochelle, N.Y.: Arlington, 1978), 118.

6. Further discussion of these points can be found in an essay by Ernest van den Haag, "The Collapse of the Case against Capital Punishment, *National Review,* 31 March 1978, 395–407.

CHAPTER 8—DRUG ABUSE

1. Elizabeth Tener, "You Can Help Kids Resist Drugs and Drinking," *McCall's,* August 1984, 92.
2. "Survey Links Drugs to TV," Associated Press story, 29 June 1995.
3. Ibid.
4. David Lynn, "The Church's Drug of Choice," *Eternity,* November 1988, 20.
5. Russ Pulliam, "Alcoholism: Sin or Sickness?" *Christianity Today,* 18 September 1981, 22–24.
6. James R. Milan and Katherine Ketcham, *Under the Influence* (New York: Bantam, 1982), 34–37.
7. Wayne Roques, *Legalization: An Idea Whose Time Will Never Come,* U. S. Drug Enforcement Administration, Miami Field Division: U.S. Department of Justice, 27 December 1994.
8. L. J. West, D. S. Maxwell, E. P. Noble, and D. H. Solomon, *Annals of Internal Medicine* 100 (1984): 405–16.
9. George Gallup, "Alcoholism's Spreading Blight," *Christianity Today,* 18 September 1981, 27.
10. Charles Leerhsen, "Alcohol and the Family," *Newsweek,* 18 January 1988, 62–68.
11. William Alden, "The Scope of the Drug Problem," *Vital Speeches of the Day* (speech given at the Transportation Security Workshop, American Society of Industrial Security, 24 June 1986).
12. "Monitoring the Future Study: Trends in Prevalence of Various Drugs for 8th Graders, 10th Graders, and High School Seniors," *NIDA Capsules* (November 1994).
13. Quoted in "Marijuana Research Review," *Drug Watch Oregon* 1 (July 1994).
14. Daniel Brookoff et al., "Testing Reckless Drivers for Cocaine and Marijuana," *New England Journal of Medicine,* 25 August 1994, 518–22.

15. "The Facts about Marijuana," National Institute on Drug Abuse, National Institutes of Health, n.d.

16. Leslie Robison, "Maternal Drug Use and Risk of Childhood Nonlymphoblastic Leukemia among Offspring," *Cancer* 63 (1989): 1904–11.

17. "Drug Legalization: Myths and Misconceptions," U.S. Department of Justice, Drug Enforcement Administration, Seattle, 12 May 1994, 43.

18. *Marijuana Research Review*, July 1994.

19. "National Survey Finds Teen Drug Use Up: 13% of 9th-Graders Have Used Marijuana," *St. Louis Post-Dispatch*, 13 December 1994, 1A.

20. Peggy Mann, "Reasons to Oppose Legalizing Illegal Drugs," Drug Awareness Information Newsletter (September 1988).

21. "Battle Strategies," *Time,* 15 September 1986, 71.

22. Kurt Anderson, "Crashing on Cocaine," 11 April 1983, 23.

23. "Users, One and All," *Newsweek,* 11 August 1986, 15.

24. Tom Seigfried, "Pleasure, Pain: Scientists Focus on Cocaine's Highs to Unlock Mysteries of Addiction," *Dallas Morning News*, 11 April 1989, 12A.

25. Anderson, "Crashing on Cocaine," 25.

26. Dan Sperling, "But We Are Not Winning on Addiction," *USA Today,* 1 August 1989, 2A.

27. Ronald Taylor, "America On Drugs," *U.S. News and World Report,* 28 July 1986, 50.

28. The basic outline of this section is adapted from the article "Battle Strategies: Five Fronts in a War of Attrition," *Time,* 15 September 1986, 69–73.

29. Ibid., 71.

30. Ibid., 73.

31. Mark Gold, *The Good News about Drugs and Alcohol* (New York: Villard, 1991), 245.

32. "Drug Legalization: Myths and Misconceptions," 39.

33. Ibid., 43.

34. Richard Clayton and Carl Leukefeld, "The Prevention of Drug Use among Youth: Implications of Legalization," *Journal of Primary Prevention* 22 (spring 1994).

35. "Substance Abuse: The Nation's Number One Health Problem," (Princeton, N.J.: Institute for Health Policy, Brandeis University for the Robert Wood Foundation, October 1993), 16.

36. Peggy Mann, *Reasons to Oppose Legalizing Drugs* (Danvers, Conn.: Committee of Correspondence, September 1988), 3.

37. Wayne Roques, "Decriminalizing Drugs Would Be a Disaster," *Miami Herald*, 20 January 1995.

38. "Poll Says One-Third of Inmates Used Drugs before Committing Crimes," *Dallas Times Herald*, 21 August 1983, A3.

39. J. Fagan et al., "Delinquency and Substance Abuse among Inner-City Students," *Journal of Drug Issues* 20 (no. 3): 351–99.

40. William Bennett, "How Intellectuals Have Failed in the Drug War," *Human Events*, 6 January 1990, 10–11.

41. Don Feder, "Legalizers Plan Harvard Pot Party," *Boston Herald*, 19 May 1994.

42. Bennett, "How Intellectuals Have Failed in the Drug War," 10–11.

43. Merrill Unger, *Demons in the World Today* (Wheaton, Ill.: Tyndale, 1971), 10–13, 75–76.

44. Charles Tart, "Work with Marijuana: II. Sensations," *Psychology Today*, May 1971, 41–44.

45. Alan Watts, *The Joyous Cosmology* (New York: Vintage, 1962), 18–19.

CHAPTER 9—BREAKDOWN OF THE FAMILY

1. Karl Zinsmeister, "Raising Hiroko," *American Enterprise* (March/April 1990.

2. Daniel Yankelovich, "Foreign Policy after the Election," *Foreign Affairs* (fall 1992).

3. U.S. Department of Health and Human Services, Vital Statistics of the United States, 1991 (Washington, D.C.: U.S. Government Printing Office, 1993).

4. Nicholas Eberstadt, "A Revolution in 'Family' That Is Eating Its Children," *Washington Times*, 24 September 1993.

5. Bureau of the Census, Current Population Reports No. 470, "Fertility of American Women: 1992" (Washington, D.C.: U.S. Government Printing Office, 1993).

6. Charles Murray, "The Coming White Underclass," *Wall Street Journal,* 29 October 1993.
7. Michael Novak, "Families: The Best Anti-Poverty Plan," *Washington Times,* 5 February 1993.
8. Vice President Dan Quayle (speech given to the Commonwealth Club of California, San Francisco), 19 May 1992.
9. Barbara Dafoe Whitehead, "Dan Quayle Was Right," *Atlantic Monthly,* April 1993, 47–84.
10. Ibid., 84.
11. *The Adolescent and Young Adult Fact Book* (Washington, D.C.: Children's Defense Fund, 1991).
12. "Parents! What You Must Know about Your Teenager's Sex Life," *Good Housekeeping,* June 1993, 144–45, 196–99.
13. Joseph Shapiro, "Sins of the Fathers," *U.S. News and World Report,* 14 August 1995, 51.
14. Ibid.
15. Ibid., 52.
16. Bureau of the Census, Current Population Reports No. 461, "Marital Status and Living Arrangement" (Washington, D.C.: U.S. Government Printing Office, 1993).
17. Daniel Patrick Moynihan, "Toward a Post-Industrial Social Policy," *Public Interest* (summer 1989).
18. National Center for Health Statistics, *Survey on Child Health,* 1988.
19. Nicholas Zill, Donna Morrison, and Mary Jo Coiro, "Long-Term Effects of Parental Divorce on Parent-Child Relationships, Adjustment, and Achievement in Young Adulthood," *Journal of Family Psychology* (1993).
20. Daniel Patrick Moynihan, quoted in Ralph Reed, "Casting a Wider Net," *Policy Review* (summer 1993), 3.
21. David Popenoe, "The Controversial Truth," *New York Times,* 26 December 1992.
22. Gracie Hsu, "Taking the Pledge," *St. Louis Post-Dispatch,* 9 August 1994, 13B.
23. Shapiro, "Sins of the Fathers," 51.
24. *Illegitimacy's Disastrous Effects* (Washington, D.C.: Family Research Council, 1995).

25. Ibid.
26. Christopher Bacorn, "Dear Dads: Save Your Sons," *Newsweek*, 7 December 1992, 13.
27. *Illegitimacy's Disastrous Effects*.
28. Ibid.
29. *Restoring the Dream* (New York: Times, 1995), 195.
30. *A Few Facts about Illegitimacy* (Washington, D.C.: Family Research Council, 1995).
31. Ibid.
32. Carl Horowitz, "The Human Cost of Illegitimacy," *Investor's Business Daily*, 8 March 1995, 1.
33. States that paid on average $200 or more a month in welfare benefits were roughly 33 percent more likely to have illegitimate white births that did not result in marriage.
34. Patrick Fagan, "U.S. Should Ease, Encourage Adoption," *Dallas Morning News*, 21 August 1995.

CHAPTER 10—DIVORCE

1. Diane Medved, *The Case against Divorce* (New York: Donald I. Fine, 1989), 1–2.
2. "Advance Report of Final Divorce Statistics, 1983," *NCHS [National Center for Health Statistics] Monthly Vital Statistics Report*, 26 December 1985, Table 1.
3. Dennis Ahlburg and Carol DeVita, "New Realities of the American Family," *Population Bulletin* 47, August 1992, 15.
4. Landon Jones, *Great Expectations: America and the Baby Boom Generation* (New York: Ballantine, 1980), 215.
5. David Popenoe, *Disturbing the Nest: Family Change and Decline in Modern Societies* (New York: de Gruyter, 1988), 223.
6. Norval Glenn and Michael Supanic, "The Social and Demographic Correlates of Divorce and Separation in the United States," *Journal of Marriage and the Family* 46 (1984): 566.
7. William Mattox, "Split Personality," *Policy Review* (summer 1995): 51.
8. Pollster Louis Harris first used this phrase in the 1980s to illustrate

his concern over the misuse of the statistic that one out of every two marriages end in divorce.

9. Cheryl Russell, *100 Predictions for the Baby Boom* (New York: Plenum, 1987), 107.

10. Judith Wallerstein and Sandra Blakeslee, *Second Chances: Men Women and Children a Decade after Divorce* (New York: Ticknor and Fields, 1989).

11. Robert H. Coombs, "Marital Status and Personal Well-Being: A Literature Review," *Family Relations* 40 (1991): 97–101.

12. Edward Beal and Gloria Hachman, *Adult Children of Divorce: Breaking the Cycle and Finding Fulfillment in Love, Marriage, and Family* (New York: Delta, 1991), 27–28.

13. Paul Amato and B. Keith, "Parental Divorce and Well-Being of Children: A Meta Analysis," *Psychological Bulletin* 110 (1991): 26–46.

14. Paul Amato and B. Keith, "Parental Divorce and Well-Being: A Literature Review," *Journal of Marriage and the Family 53* (1991): 43–48.

15. Sheila Fitzgerald Klein and Andrea Beller, *American Demographics* (March 1989): 13.

16. Sara McLanaghan and Gary Sandefur, *Growing Up with a Single Parent: What Hurts, What Helps* (Cambridge, Mass.: Harvard University Press, 1994), 103.

17. Bureau of the Census, *Statistical Abstract of the United States, 1992* (Washington, D.C.: U.S. Government Printing Office, 1993), Table 719.

18. William Dunn, " 'I Do,' Is Repeat Refrain for Half of Newlyweds," *USA Today,* February 15, 1991, A1.

19. "Family: Neo-nukes," *Research Alert,* 17 August 1990, 6.

20. "When the Family Will Have a New Definition," *What the Next 50 Years Will Bring,* special edition of *U.S. News and World Report,* 9 May 1983, A3.

21. Arland Thornton and Deborah Freedman, "The Changing American Family," *Population Bulletin* 38 (1983):10.

22. Lynn K. White and Alan Booth, "The Quality and Stability of Remarriages: The Role of Stepchildren," *American Sociological Review* 50 (October 1985): 689–98.

23. John Leland, "Tightening the Knot," *Newsweek,* 19 February 1996, 73.

24. Robert Plunkett, quoted in Elizabeth Schoenfeld, "Drumbeats for Divorce Reforms," *Policy Review* (May–June 1996): 8.

25. Pitrim Sorokin, quoted in Martin King Whyte, *Dating, Mating and Marriage* (New York: de Gruyter, 1990), 1.

26. Maggie Gallagher, *The Abolition of Marriage* (Washington, D.C.: Regenery, 1996), 135.

27. Frank Furstenberg and Andrew Cherlin, *Divided Families: What Happens to Children When Parents Part* (Cambridge, Mass.: Harvard University Press, 1991), 22.

28. G. J. Wenham, "Gospel Definitions of Adultery and Women's Rights," *Expository Times* 95 (1984): 330.

CHAPTER 11—PORNOGRAPHY

1. *Report of the Attorney General's Task Force on Family Violence* (Washington, D.C.: U.S. Department of Justice), 112.

2. "Effect of Pornography on Women and Children," U.S. Senate Judiciary Committee, Subcommittee on Juvenile Justice, 98th Congress, 2d Session, 1984, 227.

3. "The War against Pornography," *Newsweek,* 18 March 1985, 60.

4. Michael McManus, ed., *Final Report of the Attorney General's Commission on Pornography* (Nashville: Rutledge Hill, 1986), 8.

5. Ibid.

6. Edward Donnerstein, "Pornography and Violence against Women," *Annals of the New York Academy of Science* 347 (1980): 277–88.

7. Edward Donnerstein, "Pornography: Its Effects on Violence against Women," in *Pornography and Sexual Aggression,* ed. Neil Malamuth and Edward Donnerstein (New York: Academic, 1984).

8. Neil Malamuth, "Rape Fantasies as a Function of Repeated Exposure of Sexual Violence," *Archives of Sexual Behavior* 10 (1981): 33–47.

9. Daniel Linz, Edward Donnerstein, and Steven Penrod, "The Effects of Multiple Exposures to Filmed Violence against Women," *Journal of Communication* 34 (1984): 130–47.

10. James Check, "The Effects of Violent and Nonviolent Pornography," Department of Justice, Ottawa, Canada, June 1984.

11. Dolf Zillman and Jennings Bryant, "Pornography, Sexual Callousness, and the Trivialization of Rape," *Journal of Communication* 32 (1982): 10–21.

12. Dolf Zillman, Jennings Bryant, and R. H. Carveth, "The Effect of Erotica Featuring Sadomasochism and Beastiality of Motivated Inter-Male Aggression," *Personality and Social Psychology Bulletin* 7 (1981): 153–59.

13. Dolf Zillman, "Effects of Prolonged Consumption of Pornography" (paper presented at the Surgeon General's Workshop on Pornography and Public Health, Arlington, Va., 22–24 June 1986).

14. Zillman and Bryant, "Pornography, Sexual Callousness and the Trivialization of Rape," 15.

15. Larry Baron and Murray Strauss, "Legitimate Violence and Rape: A Test of the Cultural Spillover Theory," *Social Problems* 34 (December 1985).

16. Joseph Scott and Loretta Schwalm, "Rape Rates and the Circulation Rates of Adult Magazines," *Journal of Sex Research* 24 (1988): 240–50.

17. David Alexander Scott, "How Pornography Changes Attitudes," in *Pornography: A Human Tragedy*, ed. Tom Minnery (Wheaton, Ill., Tyndale, 1987).

18. Victor Cline, *Where Do You Draw the Line?* (Provo, Utah: Brigham Young University Press, 1974).

19. Kenneth Kantzer, "The Power of Porn," *Christianity Today,* 7 February 1989, 18.

20. Berl Kutchinsky, "The Effect of Easy Availability of Pornography on the Incidence of Sex Crimes, The Danish Experience," *Journal of Social Issues* 29 (1973): 163–81.

21. Dolf Zillman, "Pornography Research and Public Policy," in *Pornography: Research Advances and Policy Considerations*, ed. Dolf Zillman and Jennings Bryant (New York: Academic, 1989), 387–88.

22. Deborah Baker, "Pornography Isn't Free Speech," *Dallas Morning News*, 17 March 1989.

23. John B. Rabun, deputy director, National Center for Missing and Exploited Children (testimony before the Subcommittee on Juvenile Justice of the Senate Judiciary Committee, 12 September 1984).

24. W. Marshall, "Pornography and Sex Offenders," in *Pornography Research Advances and Policy Considerations.*

25. *The Men Who Murdered,* FBI Law Enforcement Bulletin, August 1985.

26. Cass R. Sunstein, "Pornography and the First Amendment," *Duke Law Journal* (September 1986): 595.

27. *Final Report of the Attorney General's Commission on Pornography,* xvii.

28. Ted Bundy, interview by James Dobson, Starke, Florida, 23 January 1989.

CHAPTER 12—GAMBLING

1. *Final Report of the Commission on the Review of the National Policy toward Gambling,* 1976.

2. "Gambling in America," *Gambling Awareness Action Guide* (Nashville: Christian Life Commission, 1984), 5.

3. Sylvia Porter, "Economic Costs of Compulsive Gambling in U.S. Staggering," *Dallas Morning News,* 4 January 1984, 6C.

4. *Final Report of the Commission on the Review of the National Policy toward Gambling,* 1976, 65.

5. Charles Colson, "The Myth of the Money Tree," *Christianity Today,* 10 July 1987, 64.

6. Gary Becker, "Higher Sin Taxes: A Low Blow to the Poor," *Business Week* (5 June 1989): 23.

7. Brad Edmonson, "Demographics of Gambling," *American Demographics,* July 1986, 40–41.

8. Curt Suplee, "Lotto Baloney," *Harper's,* July 1983, 19.

9. Julian Taber, "Opinion," *USA Today,* 14 August 1989, 4.

10. Borden Cole and Sidney Margolis, *When You Gamble—You Risk More Than Your Money* (New York: Public Affairs Pamphlet, 1964), 12.

11. Joseph Shapiro, "America's Gambling Fever," *U.S. News and World Report,* 15 January 1996, 58.

12. John Warren Kindt (statement before a hearing of the U.S. House of Representatives Committee on Small Business, 21 September 1994).

13. "State Lotteries and Gambling—Results Have Not Equaled Expectations," *USA Today,* April, 1979, 1.

14. *New York Times,* 9 February 1980.

15. Charles Clotfelter and Philip Cook, *Selling Hope: State Lotteries in America* (Cambridge Mass.: Harvard University Press, 1991).

16. Emmett Henderson, *State Lottery: The Absolute Worst Form of Legalized Gambling* (Atlanta: Georgia Council on Moral and Civil Concerns, n.d.), 26.

17. *Final Report of the Commission on the Review of National Policy toward Gambling,* 1976, 71.

18. John Warren Kindt, "The Economic Aspects of Legalized Gambling Activities," *Duke Law Review* 43 (1994): 59.

19. David Neff and Thomas Giles, "Feeding the Monster Called More," *Christianity Today,* 25 November 1991, 20.

20. Quoted by William Petersen, *What You Should Know about Gambling* (New Canaan, Conn.: Keats, 1973), 37.

21. James Mann, "Gambling Rage: Out of Control," *U.S. News and World Report,* 30 May 1983, 30.

CHAPTER 13—HOMOSEXUALITY

1. At recent United Nations Conferences some participants have proposed that five genders be recognized: male heterosexual, female heterosexual, male homosexual, female homosexual (lesbian), and bisexual.

2. Two prominent pro-homosexuality commentators are Sherwin Bailey, *Homosexuality and the Western Christian Tradition* (London: Longmans, Green, 1955; reprint, Hamden, Conn.: Shoestring, 1975), and John Boswell, *Christianity, Social Tolerance and Homosexuality* (Chicago: University of Chicago Press, 1980).

3. Bestiality was not uncommon in the ancient Near East. Canaanites were guilty of both homosexuality and bestiality (Lev. 18:23–29).

4. Ralph Blair, *An Evangelical Look at Homosexuality* (Chicago: Moody, 1963), 3.

5. Letha Scanzoni and Virginia Ramsey Mollenkott, *Is the Homosexual My Neighbor?* (San Francisco: Harper & Row, 1978), 60–61.

6. Sherwood Cole, "Biology, Homosexuality, and Moral Culpability," *Bibliothecra Sacra* 154 (July–September 1997): 355.

7. Simon LeVay, "A Difference in Hypothalamic Structure between Heterosexual and Homosexual Men," *Science* 253 (30 August 1991): 1034–37.

8. David Gelman, "Born or Bred?" *Newsweek,* 24 February 1992, 46.

9. Joe Dallas, *Desires in Conflict* (Eugene, Oreg.: Harvest, 1991), 90.

10. Gelman, "Born or Bred?" 46.

11. Paul Cameron, "Twins Born Gay," *Family Research Report* (January–February 1992): 3.

12. Gelman, "Born or Bred?" 46.

13. Dean Hamer, *Science,* 16 July 1993.

14. "Study Links Homosexuality to Genetics," *Dallas Morning News,* 16 July 1993, IA.

15. Cole, "Biology, Homosexuality, and Moral Culpability," 357.

16. Dallas, *Desires in Conflict,* 96.

17. Ibid.

18. John Money, *Gay, Straight, and In-Between* (Baltimore: Johns Hopkins University Press, 1988), 117.

19. Glenn Wood and John Dietrich, *The AIDS Epidemic: Balancing Compassion and Justice* (Portland, Oreg.: Multnomah, 1990), 238.

20. Ruben Fine, *Psychoanalytic Theory, Male and Female Homosexuality: Psychological Approaches* (New York: New York Center for Psychoanalytic Training, 1987).

21. William Masters and Virginia Johnson, *Homosexuality in Perspective* (Boston: Little, Brown, 1979), 402.

22. Joseph Nicolosi, interview by John Ankerberg, *John Ankerberg Show,* 1993.

CHAPTER 14—TECHNOLOGY

1. E. F. Schumacher, *Small Is Beautiful* (London: Abacus, 1973).

2. Jacques Ellul, *The Technological Society* (New York: Vintage, 1964).

3. C. S. Lewis, *The Abolition of Man* (New York: Macmillan, 1947), 68–69, 71 (italics his).

4. Philip Elmer-DeWitt, "A Birthday Party for ENIAC," *Time,* 24 February 1986, 63.

5. "Machine of the Year," *Time,* 3 January 1983, 13–24.

6. "Harper's Index," *Harper's,* October 1984, 9.

7. Ted Gest, "Who Is Watching You?" *U.S. News and World Report,* 12 July 1982, 35.

8. David Burnham, *The Rise of the Computer State* (New York: Random, 1983).

9. Martha Farnsworth Riche, "The Rising Tide of Privacy Laws," *American Demographics,* March 1990, 24.

10. Richard Lipkin, "Making Machines in Mind's Image," *Insight,* 15 February 1988, 8–12.

11. Robert Mueller and Erik Mueller, "Would an Intelligent Computer Have a 'Right to Life?'" *Creative Computing,* August 1983, 149–61.

12. Danny Hillis, "Can They Feel Your Pain?" *Newsweek,* 5 May 1997, 57.

13. Robert Jastrow, "Toward an Intelligence beyond Man's," *Time,* 20 February 1978, 59.

CHAPTER 15—ECOLOGY AND THE ENVIRONMENT

1. Calvin DeWitt, ed., *The Environment and the Christian* (Grand Rapids: Baker, 1991), 15–22.

2. Stephen Budiansky, "The Doomsday Myths," *U.S. News and World Report,* 13 December 1993, 82.

3. Al Gore, *Earth in the Balance: Ecology and the Human Spirit* (New York: Houghton Mifflin, 1992), 28.

4. DeWitt, *The Environment and the Christian,* 16.

5. James Lovelock, *The Ages of Gaia: A Biography of Our Living Earth* (New York: Norton, 1988), 208–12.

6. Lynn White, "The Historical Roots of Our Ecological Crisis," *Science,* 10 March 1967, 1203–7.

7. Francis Schaeffer, *Pollution and the Death of Man: The Christian View of Ecology* (Wheaton, Ill.: Tyndale, 1970), 83.

8. Ibid., 83–84.

9. Glenn Schicker, "Tending the Garden as God's Stewards," *Eternity,* September 1988, 68.

CHAPTER 16—MEDIA

1. Marshall McLuhan, *Understanding Media* (New York: New American Library, 1964).
2. Neil Postman, *The Disappearance of Childhood* (New York: Vintage, 1994), 72.
3. *National Family Values: A Survey of Adults* (Bethesda, Md.: Voter/ Consumer Research, 1994).
4. Neil Malamuth and Edward Donnerstein, *Pornography and Sexual Aggression* (New York: Academic, 1984).
5. Edward Donnerstein, "What the Experts Say" (forum at the Industry-wide Leadership Conference on Violence in Television Programming, 2 August 1993), in *National Council for Families and Television Report*, 9.
6. Irving Kristol, "Sex, Violence and Videotape," *Wall Street Journal*, 31 May 1944.
7. Jerry Adler, "Kids Growing Up Scared," *Newsweek*, 10 January 1994, 49.
8. Peter Plagen, "Violence in Our Culture," *Newsweek*, 1 April 1991, 48.
9. Ibid., 51.
10. John Johnston, "Kids: Growing Up Scared," *Cincinnati Enquirer*, 20 March 1994, E1.
11. Elizabeth Jensen, "One-Day Study Finds Rise in Violence on TV, but Research Method Is Disputed," *Wall Street Journal*, 5 August 1994.
12. "Warning from Washington," *Time*, 17 May 1982, 77.
13. James Mann, "What Is TV Doing to America?" *U.S. News and World Report*, 2 August 1982, 27.
14. Leo Bogart, "Warning: The Surgeon General Has Determined That TV Violence Is Moderately Dangerous to Your Child's Mental Health," *Public Opinion* (winter 1972–73): 504.
15. Plagen, "Violence in Our Culture," 51.
16. Ibid.
17. Mark Robichaux, "MTV Is Playing a New Riff," *Wall Street Journal*, 9 February 1993.
18. Phil Rosenthal, "MTV Is Playing with Fire," *Los Angeles Times*, 11 October 1993.

19. Stewart Powell, "What Entertainers Are Doing to Your Kids," *U.S. News and World Report,* 28 October 1985.

20. George Gerbner and Larry Gross, "The Scary World of TV's Viewer," *Psychology Today*, April 1976, 41–45, 89.

21. Ibid.

22. S. Robert Lichter and Stanley Rothman, "Media and Business Elites," *Public Opinion* (October–November 1981): 42–46.

23. S. Robert Lichter, Stanley Rothman, and Linda S. Lichter, *The Media Elite* (New York: Adler and Adler, 1986).

24. S. Robert Lichter, "Consistently Liberal: But Does It Matter?" *Media Critic* (summer 1996): 26–39.

25. Linda S. Lichter, S. Robert Lichter, and Stanley Rothman, "Hollywood and America: The Odd Couple," *Public Opinion* (December 1982–January 1983): 54–58.

26. Stanley Rothman and S. Robert Lichter, "What Are Moviemakers Made Of?" *Public Opinion* (December 1983–January 1984): 14–18.

CHAPTER 17—GOVERNMENT AND CIVIL DISOBEDIENCE

1. Francis Schaeffer, *A Christian Manifesto* (Westchester, Ill.: Crossway, 1981), 116.

2. Henry David Thoreau, "On the Duty of Civil Disobedience" (n.p., 1849).

3. Samuel Rutherford, *Lex Rex or The Law and the Prince* (n.p., 1644).

4. Schaeffer, *A Christian Manifesto, 91.*

5. Martin Luther King, quoted in Richard John Neuhaus, *Naked Public Square* (Grand Rapids: Eerdmans, 1984), 237.

Bibliography

Alcorn, Randy. *Pro Life Answers to Pro Choice Arguments.* Portland, Oreg.: Multnomah Press, 1992.

Anderson, J. Kerby, ed. *Living Ethically in the 90s.* Wheaton, Ill.: Victor Books, 1990.

Dallas, Joe. *Desires in Conflict.* Eugene, Oreg.: Harvest House Publishers, 1991.

Davis, John Jefferson. *Evangelical Ethics.* Phillipsburg, N.J.: Presbyterian and Reformed Publishing Co., 1985.

Feinberg, John S., and Paul D. Feinberg, *Ethics for a Brave New World.* Wheaton, Ill.: Crossway Books, 1993.

Geisler, Norman L. *Christian Ethics: Options and Issues.* Grand Rapids: Baker Book House, 1989.

Maddoux, Marlin. *What Worries Parents Most.* Eugene, Oreg.: Harvest House Publishers, 1992.

Myers, Ken. *All God's Children and Blue Suede Shoes: Christians and Popular Culture.* Westchester, Ill.: Crossway Books, 1989.

Neuhaus, Richard John. *The Naked Public Square.* Grand Rapids: Wm. B. Eerdmans Publishing Co., 1984.

Olasky, Marvin. *Prodigal Press: The Anti-Christian Bias of the American News Media.* Westchester, Ill.: Crossway Books, 1988.

Schaeffer, Francis. *A Christian Manifesto.* Westchester, Ill.: Crossway Books, 1981.

_____. *Pollution and the Death of Man: The Christian View of Ecology.* Wheaton, Ill.: Tyndale House Publishers, 1970.

Tada, Joni Eareckson. *When Is It Right to Die?* Grand Rapids: Zondervan Publishing House, 1992.

Young, Curtis. *The Least of These.* Chicago: Moody Press, 1983.

Scripture Index

253

Subject Index

257